P9-CFM-975

ALSO BY ERIC JAFFE

The King's Best Highway

A CURIOUS MADNESS

An American Combat Psychiatrist,
a Japanese War Crimes Suspect,
and an Unsolved Mystery
from World War II

ERIC JAFFE

SCRIBNER

New York London Toronto Sydney New Delhi

Scribner
A Division of Simon & Schuster, Inc.
1230 Avenue of the Americas
New York, NY 10020

Copyright © 2014 by Eric Jaffe

All rights reserved, including the right to reproduce this book or portions thereof
in any form whatsoever. For information address Scribner Subsidiary Rights
Department, 1230 Avenue of the Americas, New York, NY 10020.

First Scribner hardcover edition January 2014

SCRIBNER and design are registered trademarks of The Gale Group, Inc., used
under license by Simon & Schuster, Inc., the publisher of this work.

For information about special discounts for bulk purchases, please contact Simon
& Schuster Special Sales at 1-866-506-1949 or business@simonandschuster.com.

The Simon & Schuster Speakers Bureau can bring authors to your live event. For
more information or to book an event contact the Simon & Schuster Speakers
Bureau at 1-866-248-3049 or visit our website at www.simonspeakers.com.

Jacket design by Marlyn Dantes
Jacket photographs: top © Associated Press; middle courtesy of the Jaffe family;
bottom © Alfred Eisenstaedt/Time & Life Pictures/Getty Images

Manufactured in the United States of America

1   3   5   7   9   10   8   6   4   2

Library of Congress Control Number: 2013040208

ISBN 978-1-4516-1205-9
ISBN 978-1-4516-1212-7 (ebook)

For Harry Jaffe
(1876–1936)

Contents

✦

Author's Note

B ECAUSE THIS BOOK is intended for a general English
readership, I have not applied diacritical marks to Japanese
words. However, I have followed the Japanese custom of placing
surnames before first names. Taking Okawa Shumei as an example: Okawa is the family name, and Shumei the given name. Any
exceptions are noted.

A CURIOUS MADNESS

Chapter 1

+≈+

The Slap Heard Round the World

Class-A war criminal—Adjudged insane—Suspected
insanity was feigned.

> —Personality file on Okawa Shumei, Records of the CIA,
> July 25, 1958

O KAWA SHUMEI ARRIVED at the arraignment looking
every bit the madman. It was May 3, 1946. The bus from
Sugamo Prison dropped off the defendants at half past eight
in the morning. Okawa entered the courtroom wearing traditional Japanese geta, or wooden clogs, and a wrinkled light blue shirt that looked
like a pajama top. He took his place at the center-back of the two-row
prisoner dock that faced the international panel of judges. In front of
him was Tojo Hideki, the former general recognized the world over for
his flat bald head and round spectacles, who wore a bush jacket and the
sober expression of a man resigned to his execution. Of all the defendants, only Okawa lacked the sharp formality the occasion demanded.
The goofy sight of him in that loose pajama top gave the impression of
a sleepwalker having wandered into a funeral, or a clown into a church.

Most people knew the International Military Tribunal for the Far
East as the "Tokyo trial." Some called it "Japan's Nuremberg." By any
name, its purpose was to draw a legal and moral curtain on Imperial

1

Japan the way Nuremberg was, at that very moment, drawing one on Nazi Germany. To that end, the Allies had indicted twenty-eight Japanese considered most responsible for their country's aggression during World War II. Tojo, who'd been prime minister when Japan attacked Pearl Harbor in December of 1941, was the star defendant. Joining him was a collection of leaders that included three more former premiers, a number of generals and admirals and war and navy ministers, an assortment of other cabinet members, a pair of ambassadors, and a chief advisor to the emperor. The indictment for the Tokyo trial referred to this alleged crowd of agitators as a "criminal militaristic clique."

Pajamas aside, Okawa Shumei seemed a bit out of place inside this circle of influence. (His name is pronounced Oh-ka-wa Shoe-meh, with *meh* taking a small verbal step toward *may*.) He was the lone civilian on trial; he'd neither held political office nor been in the military. At the same time, certain members of the Allied prosecution team considered him the stitching that held together the entire pattern of Japanese imperialism they were trying to prove. One attorney for the prosecution described Okawa as "the sparkplug that kept the whole conspiracy alive and going over the whole period covered in the indictment." Shortly before the Tokyo trial began, an intelligence officer who'd been stationed in Japan said he'd rather see Okawa indicted than even Tojo himself. "He was really the heart of it," the officer said. Okawa was viewed as the brain trust of Japanese militarism—the mind that directed the country's might.

The courthouse was in the neighborhood of Ichigaya, a high point overlooking the bombed-out ruins of Tokyo. During the war the three-story building had been a headquarters for the Japanese Army; it even had the slight look of a pillbox. Workers had toiled for months to prepare the venue for the trial. They'd lined the main hall with wood paneling and installed bright lighting. They'd built a booth for interpreters, perched on a balcony, and enclosed it in glass. They'd set down a thousand seats and wired each one into a three-channel translation system so the audience could follow in English, Japanese, or Russian as their ears preferred. At about a quarter past eleven on May 3, 1946, the wooden doors closed and a gentle bell announced the start of the proceedings. Perhaps to nudge the Tokyo trial out of the shadows of Nuremberg and into the klieg lights, Chief Justice William Webb opened by saying there'd been "no more important criminal trial in all history."

The morning session adjourned to await the late arrival of two defendants. At half past two, the court reconvened for a full reading of the indictment. A small unit of police in white helmets were positioned around the courtroom perimeter; their helmetless commander, Colonel Aubrey Kenworthy, stood directly behind the prisoner dock. As the clerk recited every word of the fifty-five charges, Okawa Shumei grew restless. He squirmed in his chair and released occasional chirps of gibberish. He bothered the defendant to his right, Matsui Iwane, commander of the Japanese troops who'd committed grave atrocities in Nanking, and the one to his left, Hiranuma Kiichiro, a former prime minister. He unbuttoned his pajama shirt, exposing his thin chest, and flapped a loose piece of garment that had slipped off his shoulder. He clasped his hands together, as if in prayer, then split them apart.

Around 3:30, as the clerk reached count 22 of the indictment, Okawa rose halfway in his seat. Wearing what some reporters later called a "cunning grin," he extended his long arm forward with an open palm and slapped the top of Tojo Hideki's bald head. The startled general looked up from his copy of the indictment and turned back to see Colonel Kenworthy restraining Okawa by his gangly shoulder. When Justice Webb announced a fifteen-minute recess, a newsreel man approached Tojo for a photograph. Just then Okawa freed himself from Kenworthy's grasp, rose up under the newsreel camera's eye, and slapped the head of Tojo again.

The courtroom erupted in a symphony of murmur. Justice Webb shouted for order. Some people later said they heard Okawa blurt nonsense as the helmeted police dragged him away. Others said they heard him shout a clear message above the clamor—"This is act one of the comedy!"—as if in protest of a trial he considered an elaborately staged farce. Recalling this moment a few years later, he said he'd felt annoyed that the audience had mistaken the show trial for an honorable one, and got the sudden urge to slap Tojo as a way of shattering the court's ridiculous solemnity.

When the court reconvened that day, however, Okawa didn't look the least bit capable of such calculated defiance. He sat barefoot in a chair pulled back from Tojo and the rest of the defendants. A coat had been draped over the pajama shirt that sagged atop his scrawny frame. He sobbed into a handkerchief throughout the rest of the afternoon session. It was such a sorry display that Colonel Kenworthy felt compelled to pat Okawa on the back now and then, *There, there,* in the universal gesture of pity.

The next morning Justice Webb ordered Okawa to undergo a psychiatric examination. Webb then removed him from the dock so the reading of the indictment could proceed without further interruption. In the anteroom Okawa delighted reporters with behavior that seemed alternately deranged and deliberate. He demonstrated his slapping technique on a public relations man from Ohio, then said he'd wanted to kill Tojo for the good of his country. He said (in perfect English) that he didn't like the United States because it was "demo*crazy*," then added that he was good friends with Happy Chandler, the commissioner of Major League Baseball. He said he hadn't eaten in seventy-two days and had discovered a way to get nourishment from the air, then demanded a cigarette.

The newspapers found Okawa irresistibly quotable and devoted considerable space to his antics. Only a few printed the names of the two psychiatrists who would examine him for the Tokyo trial. For the defense, a Japanese man named Dr. Uchimura. For the prosecution, a "Brooklyn Man," as the *New York Sun* called him, named Major Daniel S. Jaffe.

IN MAY OF 1946 my grandfather was not, strictly speaking, a Brooklyn man. Daniel Jaffe had been born a Brooklyn baby in 1914, and raised a Brooklyn boy until he left home for medical school in 1934, but during his commission as a medical officer in the United States Army his official residence made him a man of Washington, D.C. At the time of his enlistment, in October of 1942, he was in the middle of a psychiatric residency at St. Elizabeth's Hospital. He stood just under five foot six with dark, bushy eyebrows, a somewhat pointy nose to balance somewhat pointy ears, and a thin, well-swept mustache that kept him from looking boyish.

My grandfather hadn't seen a great deal of combat action in World War II, but he had covered a great deal of distance. He began his service as a psychiatrist at Stark General Hospital in South Carolina, and a few months later was transferred to perform the same role at Valley Forge General Hospital in Pennsylvania. In late 1943 he joined the medical battalion of the 97th Infantry Division on maneuvers in Louisiana, then took amphibious training in camps up and down the California coast. He'd accepted the fate of a dangerous landing in the Pacific when the heavy losses suffered during the Battle of the Bulge required reinforcements in Europe. So the 97th raced across the country to New York and sailed the Atlantic into a French port. They chased the Germans through the valley of the Ruhr River into Czechoslovakia, and fired the theater's official last shot. After VE Day the division returned immediately to New York, rendezvoused at Fort Bragg in North Carolina, and crossed the country again, this time for Fort Lawton in Washington State, where they embarked for the Pacific island combat they'd been expecting from the very start. When the Japanese surrender became official en route, they went to Tokyo for occupation duty instead. Altogether the 97th was considered the most traveled division in the Army, covering some thirty-five thousand miles of land and sea.

By the time he got home from the war, in 1946, my grandfather didn't want to talk about it. Now, my grandfather wasn't the speaking type. It was his defining characteristic, his not being the speaking type. But even if he *had* been the speaking type, he'd earned the right not to speak of the war again, and for the rest of his days he rarely did.

This restraint was unfortunate because, as I later learned, his role in the military was quite special. He was a division neuropsychiatrist, a position held by fewer than a hundred soldiers in a wartime army that numbered in the millions. At the start of the war, the American military believed it could screen out mental weakness during enlistment. After two years of brutal conflict, with psychiatric casualties remarkably high, officials came to terms with the fact that all men, pushed hard enough in combat, had a psychological breaking point. So in November of 1943, the Army arranged for a single psychiatrist to join each division in action. They were responsible for the mental health of troops over the full course of service—from morale during training camps to treatment on the front lines. The lone protectors of the mind, helmets aside, for every fifteen thousand active soldiers.

During combat the division psychiatrist cared for mental casualties in the medical battalion's clearing company, a makeshift treatment center situated a few miles from the front lines. His primary task was to relieve "combat fatigue," the updated term for what during World War I had been called "shell shock"—that moment, by any name, when the sound of artillery and the sight of shrapnel and the taste of smoke and the smell of blood and the memory of all that matters formed a sensory signal that scrambled a young man's nerves. When ignored, combat fatigue was extremely debilitating and often required evacuation to a general hospital back in the United States. But when treated quickly near the battlefield, with a heavy dose of sedatives and reassurance, recovery rates were high in World War II, and many soldiers returned to action within days.

In March of 1946 the Army dissolved the 97th Infantry. While many of its members drifted back across the Pacific toward home, my grandfather stayed on at the 361st Station Hospital in occupied Tokyo to serve as chief of neuropsychiatry. He remained there through the spring with little to do but treat the rampant venereal disease one might expect from young men with lots of free time half a world from home. When his repeated efforts to obtain a discharge failed, he struggled with bouts of desperation and developed an unhealthy resentment toward the Army for keeping him away from his young family and his future. He'd begun to have nightmares of being stranded in Japan forever when the order arrived to determine whether Okawa Shumei was capable of standing trial.

OKAWA SHUMEI'S CURIOUS outburst at the Tokyo trial made head-lines around the world. An Associated Press account of the incident that "startled the court" ran in major papers across the United States. *Time* magazine wrote that the trial had opened with "the flavor of Gilbert & Sullivan." One correspondent wondered if years from now people would recall anything about the opening of the historic trial *other* than the slapping of Tojo Hideki. The *Washington Post* ran four newsreel shots in sequence under the title "Shumei Okawa's Big Moment."* In the first image Okawa raises his hand in Tojo's direction. In the second he completes the slap just as Colonel Kenworthy grabs his collar. In the third Tojo turns toward Okawa and manages a weak grin. In the fourth Okawa sits with his shoulders subdued by Kenworthy, staring blankly into the distance.

At the time of the trial Okawa was half a year shy of age sixty. He was taller than most Japanese, standing roughly six feet, and pencil thin and frail. He once likened his own lanky figure to "a jerry-built shack." He normally had an aristocratic taste for clothing and presented his awkward frame with a professorial dignity. At the same time, his teeth were crooked and his ears big and his face narrow and gaunt, and it's easy to see why an American once described him as "decidedly unattractive." His facial features in particular struck his own countrymen as something vaguely other than Japanese. His dark eyes, covered by thick lenses set in perfectly circular frames, could just as soon seem wild as wise.

Whatever Okawa lacked in looks he more than recovered in neurons. From an early age he'd written heady books at a prolific pace on a stunning breadth of topics. He completed an exhaustive analysis of Western colonialism, a survey of twenty-six hundred years of Japanese history, and a translation of the Koran. He once wrote a six-hundred-page autobiography and, feeling satisfied with the personal insights he'd drawn, promptly destroyed the whole thing. He was as conversant in Kant and Plato as in Confucius and Mencius, and he had at

---

*While the Japanese place family names before given names, American publications often reverse this order to reflect Western custom.

least eight languages, from English to Sanskrit. When he wasn't writing books he was lecturing as a professor. When he wasn't doing either of those things he was working as an economic research analyst at one of Japan's most important think tanks. When he wasn't doing *any* of those things he was organizing radical activist groups to see that his ideas achieved some tangible impact on Japanese society.

For years and years they did. In the mid- to late 1920s Okawa's books and speeches urged Japan to unite East Asia and challenge Western global hegemony, an effort that prepared the Japanese people "psychologically" for war in the eyes of his Tokyo trial accusers. In the early 1930s he funded an uprising that resulted in the assassination of a prime minister and, according to some historians, signified the moment when Japan's aspiring democracy effectively ceded control to the military. In late 1941, days after Pearl Harbor, he broadcast a popular series of radio lectures that outlined the history of Western political aggression and reminded listeners of a prophecy he'd once made: that Japan and the United States would meet in a "life-and-death struggle" for world order, and that Japan would win.

His exceptional intelligence came fused with a quick temper—a sort of enlightened explosiveness that inspired descriptions of him as an "intellectual malcontent" or "brilliant madman." One contemporary said Okawa had too much education to be a patriot but was too hot-blooded to be a scholar. He was imprisoned twice. He coveted close ties with the military and closer ties with geisha; he even married one. He's been called the "Goebbels of Japan" for his ideological convictions and an "Oriental Don Quixote" for his peculiar antics. "His character is by nature fastidious and methodical, nervous and passionate," a psychiatrist once wrote. Alcohol turned his passions against his methods: he became rude, talkative, irritable—a very bad drunk. The proprietor of his favorite geisha house once said he almost became a different person when intoxicated, like a Japanese Jekyll and Hyde, and that in this state it wasn't unusual for him to hit another man on the head.

A few days after Okawa's latest, far more infamous head slap, my grandfather examined him at the 361st Station Hospital in Tokyo. By that point Okawa's great mind seemed a shadow of its former strength.

My grandfather recommended that Okawa be removed from the Tokyo trial on the grounds that he was "unable to distinguish right from wrong, and incapable of testifying in his own defense." Dr. Uchimura independently concurred, and Okawa was transferred from Sugamo Prison to Tokyo University Hospital and later to Matsuzawa Hospital for the Insane. The Allies hoped he'd recover his faculties there, and when the trial lingered into 1947, Justice Webb ordered a new examination. Once again Dr. Uchimura found Okawa incompetent, but this time a new pair of American psychiatrists—my grandfather had since been sent home—believed he could reasonably stand trial.

By this point everyone was tired of the Tokyo trial and longed for it to end. Justice Webb responded to the conflicting reports by dismissing Okawa from the proceedings, though he left the door open for a future indictment on the same charges. That legal purgatory ended in late 1948, just after the trial's drawn-out conclusion, when Okawa's case was dismissed. The decision confused some Japanese, who told American reporters that Okawa was an "ideological instigator" and thus among "the biggest criminals of all."

On December 23, 1948, Tojo and six other defendants were hanged on the gallows outside Sugamo Prison. The rest, with the exception of two who hadn't survived the lengthy legal process, began prison sentences that ranged from seven years to life. A week later Okawa left the hospital for his peaceful home just southwest of Tokyo, having completely recovered his senses. An Associated Press report from the time called him "the only one of the top twenty-eight Japanese war trial defendants to go free."

If Okawa had remained on trial, there is little doubt he would have received a harsh sentence. His perceived counterpart at Nuremberg, the ideologue Alfred Rosenberg, was hanged. During the Tokyo trial some of the Western correspondents kept an informal scorecard of the proceedings in the pressroom. They thought the evidence supporting the early phase of Japan's alleged conspiracy weighed most heavily on ten of the accused. Of these, ultimately five were put to death and four received life in prison.

The tenth was Okawa Shumei.

MY GRANDFATHER'S SILENCE on the subject of his military service took no one who knew him by surprise. He was nothing if not quiet by nature. As a young boy he spoke so seldom that a casual remark made once before dinner caused his mother to stop everything she was doing in the kitchen and exclaim, "Well, what do you know, the boy's got a tongue!" He entered an Eagle Scout honor society after refraining from speech for twenty-four hours; it was the type of test designed to strain the willpower of the adolescent male, but for my grandfather it was like being asked to tie a shoe. As an adult he cultivated the wordless hobbies: fishing and photographs (he built his own darkroom), landscaping and nature watching (he kept a field guide to birds in the kitchen), chess and classical music and martinis (the latter taken every night at 6:00 p.m. sharp). After movies he offered a strict three-word review (*The Manchurian Candidate:* "country versus individualism").

He was so good at not talking he made a career of it, which is to say he became a psychoanalyst. He was like some emotional jazz virtuoso: you had to listen to the things he *didn't* say to get the full meaning of the things he did. In his later years his favorite saying, borrowed from Twain, was that it's better to keep your mouth shut and be thought a fool than to open it and remove all doubt.

In exchange for reserving his powers of speech, nature endowed him with an enormously retentive mind. He memorized an elaborate mnemonic for the American presidents that began, "When a jealous man makes apple jam," for Washington (*when*) through Jackson (*jam*). So if you found yourself in his company and curious about the country's fifteenth leader, he would recite the jealous man's tale until he reached the part about the French pie *baker,* then deliver the name of James Buchanan. If during a delicious dessert he heard you call the dish something dreams are made of, you received a full recitation of Prospero's speech toward the end of *The Tempest.* He once corrected my grandmother, during a story about a gift given fifty years earlier, to say that it hadn't just been *any* old recording of Tchaikovsky, but the composer's *Manfred Symphony.* He could identify a tree upon seeing its leaf and a bird upon hearing its song, and if he saw the bird before he heard it, he would whistle its call. If he were alive today he'd be an iPhone app.

Whatever people mean when they talk about a photographic memory, he had something like it. A cousin of mine once recalled the time he was in our grandfather's library and took a book at random off the shelf. Grandpa Dan issued the book some general praise without so much as a glance up from *Masterpiece Theatre.* My cousin was always something of a benevolent rascal, though. As if challenging the statement, he announced an arbitrary page number. A beat later Grandpa Dan was reciting a sentence as if he were holding the book himself. He punctuated this display with a smug grin and returned to his program. "I wish I could have seen my face," my cousin said. Even if the story is semi-apocryphal—my cousin remains a rascal—the fact that no one would doubt it speaks to the larger truth about my grandfather. He had a mind that worked overtime and a mouth that was underemployed. It was a mental system built for storage: he took a lot in and, except for the occasional slip of insight or wit, let very little out.

If anything, his natural reticence seems to have intensified after he returned from Japan in 1946. "It's not that he was noisy before," his little sister, my great-aunt, told me once. "But after the war he became very quiet." He wrote my grandmother every day while in the service. It was a collection of letters she once called her "complete accounting of the war." For forty years she kept them stored in the attic. Then one day, as they prepared to leave the house they'd lived in most of their married lives, he discovered the letters and demanded their destruction. He'd evidently seen some serious things in war and felt no need to shine a light on the darkest corners of a vault he kept shut even for the nonserious nonwar things. Despite my grandmother's protests, that was that.

We'll never know just what was in those letters, but toward the end of his life my grandfather finally broke the silence about his wartime experiences in the form of a manuscript he called "Memoirs of a Combat Psychiatrist." The work reflects the strength of his remote memory, which remained largely intact even as the Alzheimer's overwhelmed his final few years. Once, shortly before he died, my aunt asked him what he had eaten for lunch that day. He couldn't answer her, but the question reminded him of an anecdote from decades earlier, which he proceeded to tell with great clarity.

"Dad, how come you can remember something from fifty years ago but not what you had for lunch today?" my aunt asked.

"If you really want to know what I had for lunch today," he replied, "then ask me in fifty years."

While the objective facts in his manuscript are reliable, the memoir as a whole is light on personal revelations. Whatever psychological security guard told my grandfather to destroy those wartime letters was moonlighting as copy editor of "Memoirs of a Combat Psychiatrist." Like many veterans I've met, my grandfather just didn't consider anything he'd done during the war worthy of elaboration. He'd constructed a flat version of events that occurred outside the emotional context of the people who performed them. It's an approach that might as well be styled on trench warfare: the mind momentarily exposes itself to the fight while the heart stays protected below.

The exception to this rule was the forceful medical argument he offered in support of his conclusion about the insanity of Okawa Shumei. In that part of his memoirs, more than any other, he seemed willing to exchange detachment for passion. The reason for this rare effusiveness was that not everyone who'd followed the Tokyo trial agreed with his evaluation. At some point in the late 1990s, as he was preparing his memoirs, my grandfather came across a two-volume, 1,600-page tome on imperial Japan written by a former *Time* magazine reporter named David Bergamini. The book attracted international attention for its unconventional claim that Emperor Hirohito deserved the bulk of the blame for Japan's actions. (It even had a gushing introduction from Justice Webb of the Tokyo trial.) My grandfather didn't read the book for its contrarian position. He cared more for the doubt it cast on his psychiatric assessment of Okawa Shumei. The author believed Okawa had orchestrated both his courtroom outburst and the bizarre behavior that followed it—that his insanity, in a word, had been a hoax.

My grandfather had fulfilled his own Twainian mantra in a way he'd never intended: for years he'd kept his mouth shut about his military service, and now he was being thought a fool.

I NEVER ASKED my grandfather about his examination of Okawa Shumei—a bit too afraid to offend his wisdom, a bit too certain there would always be another chance—but shortly after he died, propelled perhaps by guilt, I took a borderline unhealthy interest in it. In the course of some regular research trips to the National Archives, I blocked out pieces of time to look through the research guides of the records on World War II. Eventually I located some intelligence files on Okawa that had been opened to unrestricted review. Whatever American documents remained classified in the years following the Tokyo trial were released to researchers in 2000 by the Japanese Imperial Government Disclosure Act. So on a warm spring day, back in 2009, I set out to discover that vulnerable part of my grandfather's history available to anyone in the general public.

The main repository of World War II records is the campus of the National Archives located near College Park, Maryland, just off the Washington beltway. It's known as Archives II in deference to the original repository in the city. Archives II is a clean, bright, modern place—not the dark, dusty catacombs one often associates with historical research. As inviting as the facility itself may be, accessing its records is a labyrinthine affair that feels designed to test the very limits of human patience. The first thing you must do when you arrive is announce your business to a security guard standing outside the parking deck. A sign commands you to remain a certain distance back from the driver who's currently announcing his business until it's your turn to approach and announce your business. If you creep past the sign while the car ahead is still announcing itself, the security guard flashes an irritated palm and a threatening face. If you stay too far back of the sign and the car ahead of you finishes announcing, then you get a rapid wave to indicate you're holding up the line.

Once inside Archives II, visitors must run their items through a security belt and present their researcher's card. Those without a card must complete a computerized research etiquette primer then pose for a photograph. Electronic equipment—document scanners, digital cameras, computers, and the like—must conform to accepted standards and be registered by serial number with the front desk. Items forbidden in the research room, from coats to pens to personal notebooks, must be stored in the locker room in the basement. If you don't have a quarter for the locker you first have to stop at the change desk; if you don't have bills to make change you first have to stop at the ATM. At this point, to reach the actual research room, you must pass through a second security line. Here a guard swipes your researcher's card and asks you to recite the serial numbers of your equipment while confirming them against the paper registration you received at the front desk. If you have a laptop you must flip it open to show you aren't concealing loose sheets of paper between the monitor and the keyboard. Loose sheets of paper must be precertified with a red stamp signed by an archives official and carried unconcealed.

At the back of the main research area is a small room filled with rows and rows of binders that might be easy to navigate, provided you have an advanced degree in library studies. These are the finding aids for Archives II. They offer brief descriptions of the types of documents held in various collections and provide the proper calling numbers to locate the boxes that hold these documents. The numbers must be recorded onto a quadruplicate official request form in pencil pressed hard enough to conquer all four levels. That's presuming you know which numbers go where, which you don't, which means you must ask the assistance of one of the few archivists on duty that day, which means you must find one who isn't assisting another researcher, which you cannot. (This is no fault of their own; the archivists are extremely capable but severely understaffed.) The only way to undercut the tiresome procedure is to pray that an electronic finding aid on your preferred topic has been compiled by a professional archivist, then go online far ahead of your visit and see if your prayers have been answered, then download this guide and set aside several days and possibly hire an intern to wade through it. The Japanese War Crimes guide is more than seventeen hundred pages long.

All this for what's often a single slim folder of material. The whole process can feel like reading an encyclopedia to prepare for reading a Post-it note.

Still, sometimes the note is worth the effort. I found the one I was looking for in the declassified records on Okawa Shumei kept by the CIA. It was a summary page from 1958, prepared shortly after Okawa's death, that offered a sort of official last word by the intelligence agency on the subject who'd been tracked since the end of the war. It read: "Class-A war criminal—Adjudged insane—Suspected insanity was feigned."

WHEN I VISIT my parents in Washington, D.C., I prefer to work out of my father's den. On the wall behind the desk hangs a picture of my grandfather in his later years, sporting a sharp suit and his trademark thin mustache, white with age. Beside this picture is one of my grandfather sitting on a ledge of the Grand Canyon with his youngest son, my father. They are facing the chasm with their backs to the camera and wearing Western hats and perhaps contemplating grandness. Beside *this* picture is one taken decades later of my father sitting with his own youngest child, my little brother, choreographed to echo its predecessor down to the backs and the hats and the contemplation. My grandfather's old classical albums collect dust on the bottom two shelves of one of the den's floor-to-ceiling bookcases. His old psychiatry books drop dust from two high shelves of another: Fenichel's *The Psychoanalytic Theory of Neurosis,* Reik's *Listening with the Third Ear,* Lidz's *The Origin and Treatment of Schizophrenic Disorders,* and on and on. Above the wet bar that splits the bookcases is the samurai sword he brought back from the occupation of Japan. Ceiling light outlines the blade as it sits above the scabbard on a two-tiered sword stand. Near the sword, enclosed in a brass frame, is a picture of my grandfather from World War II. He is wearing his medical officer's uniform and smiling beneath his mustache, still thin then, but dark with youth.

The den is a shrine.

I was raised to deny the possibility of my grandfather's fallibility. But

while the author David Bergamini might be a conspiracy-monger—
and academic historians do scoff at his methods and conclusions—the
CIA note served as an official state denial of my grandfather's examination of Okawa Shumei. I came across other doubters over time: a
wire story, dated a day after the slapping, reporting that some people
in the court felt Okawa "was staging an act"; a reference to one defense
attorney from the Tokyo trial who believed Okawa did what he did "to
escape from this dangerous playhouse"; a reference to another lawyer
who found the timing of Okawa's breakdown too fortuitous to believe;
a reliable book quoting the Dutch justice at the trial, B.V.A. Röling, as
saying he believed Okawa had "deceived" both the court and the psychiatrists; and finally an interview with Okawa himself, given in 1952,
after he'd recovered from his insanity to live a quiet and productive life.
He told a reporter from a Tokyo newspaper that "there was no serious
trouble with my mind."

So I made it a mission to vindicate my grandfather's analysis. Anything less might threaten the sanctity of his legacy. "I spent my whole
life with people asking if I realized how brilliant my dad was," my uncle
once told me, with a thinly veiled tone of contempt, when I described
the CIA note. "No patient would fool him." One day, while looking
through a filing cabinet in the den that is a shrine, I found a letter my
grandfather had sent to the editor of the *New England Journal of Medicine*. It detailed a thorough scientific explanation for Okawa's insanity
and subsequent recovery. He'd prepared it in 1996, shortly after he'd
finished the memoirs. I had the sudden realization that he'd missed the
chance to tell his side, and that he'd died knowing it.

The main problem with writing about my grandfather was I didn't
know anything about him. He shared so little throughout his life and
left only scraps to posterity. My only option was to start at the shell and
scrape inward—to analyze the psychoanalyst. I plucked names from his
memoir and transformed them, through the great filter of Google, into
some locatable form. I traveled the country to meet surviving veterans
from his medical battalion. I returned to Archives II, and I also dug up
records on the old "Brooklyn Man" in some old Brooklyn archives.
After fortuitous hits I entertained fantastical notions. Like maybe

he'd burned the war letters he kept in the attic, and maybe the oxygen released from the fire had been floating around the place when I'd visited as a boy, if oxygen floats, and maybe I'd inhaled some of it, maybe it had entered my nerves and was guiding my instincts. I thought I could give the family that revered him what his silence had denied them: the spirit, if not the contents, of the memories he'd withheld.

Of course, to give Okawa a fair shake I had to learn something about him as well. I read everything available in English, beginning with the thousands of pages of documents compiled by the Tokyo trial prosecution. I watched (and re-watched) the newsreel footage of the Tojo slap that someone—bless the Internet's collective heart—bothered to turn into an animated GIF. I learned all about the social, political, and historical mind-set that led a tiny Asian nation to attack the United States, and wondered why, despite far too many years of school, I'd never really learned that side of the story. I spent six weeks in Japan. I met the small group of fans who gather each year to celebrate Okawa's life at the commemorative monument in his hometown. I met the scholars who've devoted their lives to understanding his ideology. I even met the granddaughter of Tojo, who found the slap funny. Some of the people I met remained pretty convinced Okawa faked the whole thing. All of them wondered.

And I returned now and then to the den that is a shrine and paced the floor, occasionally looking up at the samurai sword above the bar and watching the streak of white ceiling light glide back and forth along the blade, a little like a restless ghost.

Chapter 2

+≡≡+

A Young Philosopher-Patriot

What is life?

—Okawa Shumei, diary entry, January 12, 1904

O KAWA SHUMEI NEVER wanted his father's life, but it took him many years to discover what he wanted instead. He was born on December 6, 1886, known in Japan as the nineteenth year of the reign of the Meiji emperor. The family lived in a port town called Sakata, on the Sea of Japan, toward the northern end of the main island of Honshu. The Okawa men had been doctors for generations. In feudal times they'd served the local lords; in more recent ones they'd served the townspeople. Fortunes had fallen a bit by the time Shumei came along: the family status was no longer so great, the estate no longer so considerable. Still, from the very start, Shumei was expected to perpetuate the lineage of Okawa physicians, even as he felt destined for something other than what his heritage prescribed.

His father, Okawa Shuken, was famous around Sakata for making his medical rounds on an Arabian horse. Shuken was an ophthalmologist by training but served the largely rural area as a general practitioner out of necessity. He kept a respectable practice and showed a compassionate side, often accepting whatever trade the poor villagers could muster as payment, but he also liked to drink and flashed an occasional nasty streak. Sometimes he pretended to be out of the office; other times he flatly refused patients he didn't want to treat. That volatility stood in contrast to the quiet presence of his wife, Tayome. Shumei once equated his mother with a Buddhist deity of compassion, a sacred figure who could filter the tumult of existence into moments of tranquility. In tough times throughout his life Shumei turned to her for strength.

The young Shumei often behaved as if these conflicting genetic strands were locked in a constant struggle. He could be stubborn and emotional and restless and rowdy. This caprice led him to plunge from a tree in his youth, an accident that caused lasting damage to his vision and gave rise to the thick glasses that became, along with his unusual height, Shumei's most recognizable feature. He was also remarkably studious. He was drawn to Chinese classics and foreign languages and philosophical texts and religious doctrine the way most boys are drawn to comics. Visitors to the Okawa home alternately found Shumei lost in a book or scampering through the house in a game of war with his two younger brothers. He showed this curious blend of high and low character throughout his life—a sort of passionate patience.

The Okawa boys didn't get much attention from their father. The generous interpretation is that Okawa Shuken wanted his sons to make their own decisions; the less generous, that he didn't much care. In either case, while reflecting on his life in prison some years later, Shumei recalled no instance when his father offered intellectual guidance or moral advice. Instead, as a young man, Shumei found a role model in the great samurai hero Saigo Takamori. Modern Americans may know Saigo's tale from the Tom Cruise film *The Last Samurai*. Young Japanese in late-nineteenth-century Sakata studied him in school as a paragon of warrior virtue. At junior high, Shumei absorbed one of Saigo's teachings above the rest: *Revere heaven, love man*. He would never forget it—would teach it to students of his own four decades later.

Saigo represented the mixture of toughness and thoughtfulness that Shumei might have recognized in himself. Here was someone whose devotion to spirituality existed in perfect harmony with his instinct for action. Here was a philosopher-patriot.

Despite his father's personal distance, Shumei grew up knowing he was supposed to follow in the family's professional footsteps. Japan had long been a place where traditional duties outranked selfish desires. For centuries a person's position had been fixed at birth. The children of samurai became warriors, those of *nomin* became peasant farmers, those of lowly *chonin* became lowly merchants. Those of Okawa became doctors. But the more Shumei considered his own fate, the more he questioned it. He could hardly follow his father into ophthalmology while being half blind. He'd also developed an appreciation for Christianity and liked the idea of helping the mind as well as the body. Before he could pursue a new path, however, he'd need his father's blessing to break from the old one.

Sometime around his seventeenth birthday Shumei settled on becoming an educator. He formalized this request in a ten-page letter to Shuken that comes off as remarkably thoughtful and thorough. There was a physical component to the choice (his poor eyesight), a moral rationale (education improves individual conduct, and thus elevates all of society), and a sound plan to achieve it (he'd prepare in Tokyo then crown his studies at an American college). Shuken brushed aside these arguments like so many patients he'd snubbed, and proposed an ultimatum in reply: either Shumei would accept the family profession, or he would no longer be part of the family. The exchange left Shumei wounded to the core.

"What is life?" he wrote in his diary on January 12, 1904. "Unless I can resolve the questions that plague my heart, I won't feel comfortable. Sadness, pain, agony—they all overwhelm me."

In a sense, late-nineteenth-century Japan suffered the same crisis of character that plagued young Okawa Shumei. Up to that time, since 1603, Japan had been a feudal society ruled by the Tokugawa shogunate, and had existed in willful seclusion from the rest of the world. Then, in July of 1853, Commodore Matthew Perry led a squadron of American ships into Edo Bay—Edo being the old name for Tokyo—with a directive to open the country to foreign trade. A treaty was eventually completed, but the ordeal split Japan into competing factions that soon clashed in a civil war. In the end, rebels led by Saigo Takamori ousted the shogunate and restored Emperor Meiji to power. As the Meiji era began, in 1868, Japan's new leaders turned their attention toward the country's uncertain future, asking themselves in so many words, *What is life?*

Their answer was to form a civilization sculpted almost entirely from a Western mold. First, Japan replaced its feudal domains with statelike prefectures serving a central authority. Then, piece by piece, the country's new leadership constructed a new social infrastructure. Soon the Japanese people kept time on the Gregorian calendar instead of a lunar one. They communicated through telegraph and postal and railroad networks, and gave their children a well-rounded education based on the liberal arts and sciences. They embraced taxation and banking and industry and other elements of a robust economy. They lived in Western architecture and dressed in Western fashion. They ate beef and drank beer and cut their hair. One Japanese official said in 1874 that "there is nothing which we are not today taking from the West."

Such was life following the Meiji Restoration. This swift and thorough overhaul of national identity culminated in a new constitution that braided Japanese heritage with Western ideals. On the one hand, it named the emperor "sacred and inviolable"; on the other, it echoed strongly a parliamentary system. The emperor may have been the sun of this new government, but a prime minister, a cabinet, and a two-tiered legislature comprising an upper House of Peers (appointed) and a lower House of Representatives (elected) were his orbit. On February 11, 1889, when Emperor Meiji received the new constitution, this cultural marriage was displayed in full force. The date was the anniversary of the founding of Japan in 660 BCE, but the emperor accepted the document at a European-style reception while wearing Western clothing.

Japan's rapid redevelopment impressed the world, but it also angered many of its own countrymen. Samurai culture all but vanished with the feudal clans. Without lords to serve, the warriors soon lost their sustenance (the traditional rice stipend was too costly for the new government), their role as fighters (a conscription army was considered superior), and finally their image (they were forbidden from wearing a sword). Many became *ronin,* or samurai vagabonds. Labor problems surfaced as the country's farm-based economy transformed into one that relied heavily on manufacturing, and moral conflicts emerged with the new emphasis on material goods. As the slouching *ronin* dissolved into a landscape increasingly dominated by smokestacks and train tracks, Japanese history dissolved into Western modernity.

Japan's leading minds watched with mixed emotions as the country sacrificed centuries of established culture for a future of global relevance. In 1887 the writer Nakae Chomin published a philosophical parable of the Meiji era called *A Discourse by Three Drunkards on Government.* As the title suggests, the story describes three Japanese who argue about the country's path over a few too many cups of brandy. One drunkard is certain that Japan must embrace Western ideals at full speed. Another prefers traditional samurai values and a strong national identity. Their host moderates the discussion toward a middle course. The three men drink the last drop without reaching a consensus.

The young Okawa Shumei was just so torn. He was the first Okawa male to come of age in the warm cultural promise of the Meiji era. He aspired to a life worthy of Saigo Takamori even as he recognized the merits of Christianity and a Western education. He respected his family tradition enough to ask permission to abandon it. He was much like the Japan in which he came of age: stunningly capable and charmingly eager but still a bit confused by his own ambition.

In time, Okawa Shuken relented to Shumei's desires. Maybe it was the triumph of Shuken's compassionate side over his fiery one. Maybe it was the strength of Shumei's persuasiveness. Whatever the case, Shumei wasted no time with his newfound freedom. He prepared for the high school entrance exam in Tokyo, during the summer of 1904, then made the long move to Kumamoto prefecture, about a thousand miles from home, once he was accepted into High School Number 5.

At that time, high school was viewed as an elite grooming ground for Japan's future leaders. The minister of education had been quoted, just a few years earlier, as saying that high school graduates should become "men worthy of directing the thoughts of the masses."

Whether or not Okawa Shumei knew about this national mission, he spent most of his three years at High School Number 5 nurturing his instincts for it. He joined the debate team and honed an oratorical blend of logic and outrage that gave equal weight to both. In one telling instance he criticized a fellow debater for stating a position in a "non-inflammatory" manner, as if to equate an exclusively measured argument with a losing one.

He entertained a brief but spirited interest in socialism and used his position as editor of the high school journal to amplify his activist voice. His essays from that time championed two core beliefs: first, that materialism was at odds with the pursuit of an ethical life; and second, that the pursuit of an ethical life required the basic earthly comforts that only economic equality provided. He tickled emotions with titles like "Is Money a Filthy Thing?" but anchored his ideas in the teachings of contemporary economist Richard T. Ely and Karl Marx and Jesus. He mastered the rhetorical flourish: "Only by working together," he wrote, "all of us, simultaneously giving it a single blow right at the root, a revolution—this is how we can change the system."

The passionate patience maturing within young Shumei was finding outward forms of expression. He was learning when to rouse and when to ruminate, when to inspire and when to instruct. His words demonstrated a burning inclination to lead. All he needed now was a reason to do so.

He got it in late August of 1906. A rumor was floating around school that the son of Kurino Shinichiro, a high-powered Japanese ambassador, had been granted permission to transfer. Since transfers were universally denied in those days, the decision was an obvious result of family influence. Shumei recognized the chance to act, and acted quickly. He and some classmates wrote a letter to school authorities blasting this display of favoritism as a "flagrant abuse" of wealth and power, and imploring them to reverse the decision. Then, at an all-student assembly, Shumei delivered a furious speech that challenged each young heart to elevate principles into action. "Everyone!" he yelled. "Won't you stand up with me?" The enraged student body closed down the school for two days and, in the end, forced the resignation of the principal and the head teacher. The students themselves received no punishment at all for their part in the uprising. For years to come the hallways of High School Number 5 filled with reverent chatter about the so-called Kurino Incident, lifting the name of Okawa Shumei into a thing of local legend.

At nineteen Okawa had shown himself worthy to direct the thoughts of the masses. That he'd done so not just through informing their minds but also boosting their spirits was a testament to his peculiar code of philosophical patriotism. He knew his unique character could conquer authority—it had done so twice now at a young age, if you counted his father's submission—but he could not have known that many more such "incidents" would dot the course of his life, and even less, that they would alter the course of Japanese history.

OKAWA SHUMEI MATRICULATED at Tokyo University in the fall of 1907—a tall and lean twenty-year-old his classmates nicknamed "The Giraffe." He chewed on philosophy books as a giraffe chews the high branches, consuming them with such great hunger that by year's end his faculties had frayed. In quick succession he suffered a nervous breakdown and contracted pulmonary tuberculosis. For a bad stretch it seemed he might not make it.

He survived, and after a year of recuperation he returned to university a changed young man. The heart that had "burned for the poor manual laborers" in high school now felt an "urgent interior need to save myself," Okawa told a classmate. He enrolled in the university's new department of religion, immersing himself in Oriental thinkers and German ethicists alike, and eventually focused on ancient Indian texts. (His thesis was about a Buddhist philosopher named Nagarjuna, who's sometimes compared to Saint Augustine.) Outside the classroom he joined a new student group called Doukai—a sort of theological salad that grabbed ideas from Confucianism and Buddhism and Christianity. Doukai encouraged its members to pursue an "ever-evolving search" for truth rather than adhere to "one unchanging path." Shumei couldn't have adopted a better mission statement for his life to that point if he'd written it himself.

After his graduation from Tokyo University in 1911, Shumei spent much of his time at the library reading whatever caught his intellect. Some days it was Vedic literature, some days classic Indian philosophy, some days Islamic texts. For a brief time he taught English at a middle school, but he seems to have lost his youthful desire to become an educator. At one point he even refused an offer from Doshisha University to become a professor of religion. Instead, he supported himself by translating German documents part-time for the Japanese Army. Each day, once those duties were done, he headed for the library once more, drifting further into his own mind with each new flick of the page.

He was stuck in this intensely spiritual stage on July 30, 1912, the day Emperor Meiji breathed his last. Even within the rarefied realm of Japanese emperors, few if any were as beloved as the great Meiji. The public grieved openly for the loss. Newspapers ran special editions that recounted Japan's achievements during his remarkable reign. Writers memorialized *Meiji no hokori,* the "Pride of Meiji." Cannons thundered through the Tokyo sky as the imperial hearse passed through the palace gates. At that very moment, in their home not far away, the war hero Nogi Maresuke and his wife sat down in front of a portrait of Meiji and committed *junshi*—a ritual suicide performed by samurai in the days of Old Japan as a sign of fidelity to a fallen lord.

Together these two great deaths snapped Shumei awake from his existential slumber. Meiji's passing reaffirmed for him the emperor's essential role in the lives of the Japanese people. Nogi's sword reminded him of the warrior tradition he'd glorified as a young boy. In this rush of devotion to country he experienced a surge of what he'd later call his *Japanese-ness.* "I began to realize the grandeur of the spirit of Japan," he later said. "I came to have the idea that this nation should be made to prosper by this race." He felt as if his soul had gone on a long journey and finally returned.

———————

SHUMEI'S METAPHORICAL HOMECOMING forced him to face the burning cultural question of his day: What had Japanese society sacrificed during its reformation into a modern country? He arrived at an answer through the writings of Okakura Tenshin, the celebrated scholar of Oriental art and critic of Japanese culture. Few writers at the time spoke about Japan's place in the world with as much authority as Okakura. He'd traveled extensively throughout the West during his life, speaking perfect English even while wearing traditional *haori* and *hakama* wardrobe. He spent a decade in charge of the Japanese collection at the Museum of Fine Arts in Boston. He wrote *The Book of Tea,* a long essay on the Oriental lifestyle that remains a ubiquitous item in American New Age stores. Along the way he reframed Japan's national debate in international terms. "A great battle is raging among us . . . a contest for supremacy between Eastern and Western ideals," he once said.

Okakura's most famous book, *The Ideals of the East,* called on Asian nations to unite in defense of their common Eastern "spirit" against the onslaught of Western "matter." (The book, published in 1903, was written in English.) As a general rule, Okakura saw material goods and military power as the pillars of Anglo-American civilization, and spiritualism and morality as the foundation of Asian life. He expressed his hope for a unified East in the book's famous opening line—"Asia is one"—and echoed it at the end by calling on Asian nations to protect and restore Eastern culture. If an Eastern coalition did emerge to oppose Western ideals, Japan would be its logical leader, since it had stayed "true to the Asiatic soul" even as it reached "the rank of a modern power." In his closing pages Okakura spelled out the task facing his country: "Not only to return to our own past ideals, but also to feel and revivify the dormant life of the old Asiatic unity, becomes our mission."

In early 1913 Shumei attended a series of lectures given by Okakura at Tokyo University. He was flush with his rediscovery of Japanese heritage at the time and felt a powerful kinship with the speaker. Much of Okakura's philosophy served to vindicate Shumei's own path through life: a middle route at the fork of tradition and rebellion. Okakura Tenshin would die that September, but by then Shumei was already preparing to become his ideological heir. He was so taken with Okakura's work that after the three-month lecture series he pitched a complete Japanese translation of *The Ideals of the East* to a magazine editor. He may even have provided the transcripts of these lectures that were printed later that year. The contrasting values of East and West were certainly flowing through Okawa's rangy frame during an evening stroll, in the summer of 1913, when his youthful search for meaning finally ended.

THE WALK TOOK place in the Tokyo ward of Kanda. Shumei was passing by a secondhand bookshop when the title *New India* caught his eye from the window. He went inside and opened the book right then. He expected to read a description of India that matched the vision conjured by years of spiritual readings: a serene paradise where one attains great religious wisdom, a place worthy to be home of the Buddha. Instead, the book introduced readers to a country suffering from miserable oppression at the hands of its British colonial rulers. Its author, Sir Henry Cotton, had served in the British Indian embassy for decades. During this time he'd sensed a simmering patriotism ready to boil over into a "new" India controlled by the country's native people.

Cotton wanted Britain to guide India's transition toward independence rather than suppress this urge, but he feared the English sense of superiority would never permit such an approach. "The waves of the ocean of Indian progress," he wrote, "are dashing against the breakwater of English prejudice." Okawa admired Cotton's sincere and straightforward style, but the contents of *New India* left him "surprised, saddened, and angered," he later recalled. Surprised at the true conditions of India. Saddened at the oppression of its British rulers. Angered that none of its Asian neighbors—in particular Japan—had done anything to help.

After finishing the book Okawa returned to the library and read every work he could find on contemporary India. "As I read, I realized that, not only India, but every place on the vast continent of Asia had been trampled underfoot by the white man, and every race had been enslaved by the white man," he later wrote. Okawa described this understanding as if it came to him in a flash. Most likely the change was gradual—personality rarely shifts in bursts—but it's true that from this point forward he no longer led his life as a hermetic scholar. "My heart could no more bear keeping aloof from worldly affairs and losing itself in meditation," he later wrote. The wisps of theory assembled in his mind like a storm cloud then: the beauty of Japanese history, the clash of East and West, the hope of Asian advance. He'd long had the personality of the philosopher-patriot, that unusual marriage of action and introspection, and now, at twenty-seven, he'd found the purpose of one, too.

His father died on May 3, 1914, the third year of the reign of the Taisho emperor. Okawa Shuken had contracted typhus from a patient; to prevent the disease from spreading, a cremation took place immediately on a hilltop facing Mount Chokai. Shumei sat in mourning with his mother for three weeks without taking any visitors. Okawa Shuken left his eldest son the remainder of the family estate; true to his word, Shuken had permitted Shumei to follow his own course. Shumei was touched. He pledged to support his younger brothers through school, as his father had supported him, and wrote a commemoration comparing Shuken's death in the line of duty to a soldier's death on the battlefield. He saw his father as a samurai in spirit—not unlike the Saigo Takamoris and the Nogi Maresukes of the world—placing personal virtues above all else. From about that time on, Shumei would regard himself the same way: as "a warrior," he later wrote, "who dedicated his life to the revival of Asia."

I WENT TO the town of Sakata in the company of my translator—a mild-mannered woman named Chiaki—to learn about the Okawa family history. My guide was Okawa Kenmei; he was Shumei's great-nephew, but since Shumei never had any children of his own, Kenmei was also the closest thing I had in this story to a Japanese doppelganger. We met over green tea in the lobby of the traditional inn where I was staying. Within minutes I'd presented Kenmei with a copy of my grandfather's evaluation of Shumei. He thanked me for it but offered no opinion on its conclusions. I decided not to press him just yet. Once the topic was broached, I wasn't sure whether or not I'd still be welcome.

I must confess to entertaining the vague possibility of something scandalous awaiting me in Sakata. Understand that I'd been reading a lot about the wild days of Okawa Shumei—sake bottles, geisha scents, military whispers, what have you—and that most documents I'd found from the Tokyo trial portrayed him as a war crimes suspect. Visions of a yakuza knocking at my chamber door in Sakata, warning me to cease asking about the sanity of his ideological master, then slicing off the tip of his pinky to show he meant it—something like that did cross my simple American mind. All right, so that precise scenario seemed unlikely. Still, I could see how the people closest to Okawa might not appreciate some Westerner riding into town on a bullet train waving psychiatric reports.

In hindsight, the only thing I had to fear was excessive generosity. Kenmei proved a gracious family man who went out of his way to quench my curiosity. He took off work to meet me. He came in wearing a surgical mask over his mouth to protect against hay fever. He was pushing fifty but could have passed for thirty-five, with a face that resembled photos of Shumei—except Kenmei kept his hair long instead of short, and wore rectangular glasses instead of round ones. He told me he'd started to receive a lot more requests for information about Shumei from Japanese writers in recent years, and that he felt a responsibility to get them accurate information. I was his first American.

"Sixty years after World War II, people started taking an interest in him," he said. "All of the sudden we get frequent visitors."

The next morning we visited the Okawa Shumei memorial stone. It stood just inside the entrance to the Hie Shrine—marked by a tall red gate whose sign was apparently drawn by Saigo Takamori himself. The stone was a giant oblong oval, maybe ten feet wide and half as tall, cut from nearby Mount Chokai. There was a poem engraved in classical Chinese on its flat face that praised Okawa Shumei for fighting to restore Asia to glory. The poem said he never gave up speaking his mind even when his thoughts landed him in prison. It compared his ideas to a fresh breeze sweeping over society. The Sea of Japan had whipped up a fresh breeze of its own that day, and limbs of trees and patches of grass leaned toward the stone in the wind, as if bowing in agreement.

Later we went to Kenmei's house for lunch. We ate sushi with his family around a Western-style table; they knew that Americans can't sit on their knees for long periods of time, like the Japanese typically do. A framed print of the poem from the memorial stone hung just above a little samurai doll in the adjacent room. The stone and the poem had been arranged by a national group called the Okawa Shumei Kenshokai. When I asked what *kenshokai* meant, the response was laughter; the closest translation might be "fan club," but there's also a hint of "cult following," with a dash of "limited liability corporation." Each October they all gathered in Sakata to pray at the stone then go drinking and swap stories about the man himself.

We were joined that day by a Kenshokai member named Kato Kenshiro—a short boulder of a man, and probably the only ninety-year-old on the planet to wear his facial hair in a chinstrap. Kato was one of Okawa's students, back in the late 1930s, at an Asianist academy called Okawa Juku. He still referred to his old teacher with the honorific suffix *sensei* and his name cards still mentioned Okawa Juku, as if he'd graduated yesterday.

"Okawa-sensei told students you have to be honest and benevolent," Kato said at lunch. Those lessons, he said, originally came from Saigo Takamori. "Be honest, meaning: with yourself, with others, and with heaven. Benevolence means: sincerity and kindness."

Kenmei said he'd never met his famous uncle, but his father had always told him that Shumei "was a great person." Kenmei's name was formed from the ending characters of Shu*ken* and Shu*mei*. He took his role as family steward seriously.

"Since I was a small child like him, I've seen Kenshokai people visiting our house," he said, patting his adorable eight-year-old son, who was playing a video game and narrating his own thoughts aloud. "Before, people only associated Okawa Shumei with this rather comical slapping scene at the Tokyo tribunal," he said. "People have started to take a different perspective of him."

I asked if Shumei's reputation ever caused Kenmei problems growing up. He told me about a time in fifth grade when his teacher announced to the class that his relative had promoted Japanese aggression. (Kenmei's mother, who hadn't said a word the entire lunch, chimed in that she still remembered that teacher's name.) "I shared this story with my father, and he said, 'I think that teacher's wrong,'" Kenmei said.

We worked our way around to the Tokyo trial and, a few minutes later, I saw another chance to ask what Kenmei thought of the idea that Okawa had faked his insanity.

"People still talk about that—it's because of the timing of him slapping Tojo, the coincidence," said Kenmei. "But he went through the scientific examination like your grandfather conducted, so I don't think there's any doubt."

Kato agreed. "We all think, the local people, that Okawa Shumei wanted to attend the tribunal, in order to explain logically why Japan got involved in the war," he said. "I don't think he was the kind of person who pretended to be insane to escape from the court."

At dusk Kenmei drove us to the family grave site on a hill overlooking the mountains. Some of Shumei's ashes were buried there, alongside those of his father, Shuken. Kenmei put flowers in the little vases, and lit incense, and poured water over the stone in the Buddhist tradition. We took a short ride down the hill to another shrine. It was dark now, and still windy, and quite cold, and even colder once we removed our shoes and stood inside the shrine on the bare floorboards. Kenmei pointed to a sign hanging above us with the name of the shrine in big Japanese characters. He said Shumei had drawn the sign himself. I realized how important it was to him that I see all these things—that I see the spiritual side of Shumei, the side that Allied documents didn't care to capture. Kato and Kenmei had surprised me a little by agreeing that Shumei had lost it at the Tokyo trial. I would have thought that anyone on Shumei's side would be against my grandfather's psychiatric assessment. But standing in a cold shrine near Shumei's grave, it made sense. You would only try to avoid a court if you've done something wrong, and as far as Kato and Kenmei were concerned, Shumei was a moral soul. I'd been so curious about whether Okawa had faked insanity to hide his guilt that I hadn't stopped to consider the possibility that he saw himself as innocent. We stood there in the dark for a few minutes more as the wind rattled the wooden boards. They had ghosts in the shrines of their ancestors, too.

OKAWA KENMEI CAME to the inn the next evening to say good-bye, but Chiaki made sure he'd left before Sato Shoichi arrived. Evidently the two didn't get along. This despite the fact that Sato was on the executive board of the Okawa Shumei Kenshokai and, technically speaking, ran the group's Sakata office. You would think two people living in the same town and following, if not quite worshipping, the same deceased historical figure would be quite close. Apparently not. Something had happened, and it would be another day before I found out what.

Sato was more what I'd expected a member of the Kenshokai to look like: that is to say, vaguely outcast. He entered the inn wearing dirty pants and a strange baseball cap that said "The Bird of the Fighter," twisted sideways. His top teeth stuck out five in a straight row. He was seventy-one at the time and, unlike most Japanese I've met, could have passed for his age. He came in soaking wet from the rain, without an umbrella, dripping everywhere. Judging by her face, the proprietor of the inn probably wouldn't have let him past the front desk if he hadn't been there to see me.

"Twenty-five years ago, in Sakata, if you visited the Okawa family, the local police put you on the watch list," he said. "It's still true that I'm often visited by the police because I belong to the Kenshokai, but I don't have any dangerous thoughts."

Sato pulled out from under his windbreaker several of his favorite books and papers related to Okawa Shumei. He'd wrapped them in plastic to keep them dry—unlike himself.

"What we're doing is just to commemorate Okawa Shumei," he said. "We're not planning any coups."

I invited Sato for dinner and the three of us walked down the hall to the inn's restaurant. The hostess made a face I recognized from the proprietor a few minutes earlier, and seated us at the back. Sato kept his hat on at the table. After we ordered Sato said he got along well with the Okawa family in former times but doesn't anymore.

"Kenmei is an ordinary person with common sense," he said, "but not so with other Okawas, like his father or grandfather. I knew them." He paused for a moment. "Kenmei probably thinks I'm not ordinary."

"What were they like?" I asked.

"Kenmei's father was a person who turned left when he was told to turn right," he said. "He was like Okawa Shumei."

Then he adjusted his Bird of the Fighter hat a bit, to make it a little more sideways.

The next morning Sato led us on a walking tour of the city. He was still wearing the Bird of the Fighter hat, backward now. Sakata had once been a bustling port, but it felt like a place whose better days were behind it; we passed a storefront sign that read "Sorry we are open," in English. That about said it. Sato had moved there with his mother shortly after World War II. He said his father was killed on a naval ship just a month before the surrender. He knows Sakata as well as any-one—in fact, he's the city historian—but he doesn't care much for it. When I asked why he became historian of a town he dislikes, he said, "To kill time."

Around midday, Sato took us to a private home where the Ken-shokai kept a little statue of Amida Buddha once owned by Okawa Shumei. He said it was the only thing in town he could show us that

Kenmei could not. A nice-looking young couple let us inside a room covered with tatami mats and served us tea around a low table. (They said I didn't have to sit on my knees; word of the American kneeling problem gets around.) The statue was about a foot tall, standing on a platform in a case against the wall, behind a little glass cover.

When Sato approached the statue, he took off his hat.

Sato said Okawa Shumei had received the statue as compensation for one of his bestselling books; Okawa had told the publisher he didn't need any more royalties, so the publisher sent him the statue instead. I wondered once more if I hadn't acquired something of a distorted view of Okawa from the Tokyo trial documents. The villains I know from Western life don't pass up money on the strength of their convictions. We sat there admiring the statue, listening to Sato discuss it with affection. How he'd taken it to the Tokyo National Museum to be appraised. How he'd refused to let it out of his sight—even carried it to the bathroom with him. How the statue had been in Okawa Kenmei's home for a while, until one day Sato went in and took it back.

"The Okawa family really wants this statue, but I want the Kenshokai to own it," he said. "That's one reason we don't get along."

Outside, walking back to the inn, Sato said that sometimes people studying Okawa Shumei only contact Kenmei, instead of himself, when they come to Sakata. I could see why the Okawa family would want it that way. Kenmei kept a very clean image of his great-uncle; Sato was rough around the edges. In some ways, Sato seemed in touch with the duality of Shumei that the Okawa family might not have wanted an outsider to see: spiritual and reverent enough to honor a statue, but capricious and mischievous enough to steal it on principle. Traveling the streets of Sakata, Sato told me he often gets requests from young right-wing nuts to join the Kenshokai, but that he turns them down because they don't understand Okawa Shumei's complete character.

"They only take actions, without thinking much," he said.

Back at the inn, I asked Sato what he thought about the rumors that Okawa had faked his insanity at the Tokyo trial. He said he never doubted that Okawa went insane. He also said that some people thought Okawa had been mimicking samurai who feigned insanity during the old days of Japan to escape from a region they served. What makes it so hard to judge, explained Sato, was that Okawa himself often changed what he said about the situation. Often turned left, you might say, when many expected him to turn right.

"People often ask me about that," Sato said. "When we were trying to raise money to build the memorial stone, that sort of story got in the way." He paused for a moment so Chiaki could catch up with the translation, or maybe just to think. "A genius of religion, or a writer, is often just one step away from insanity."

Chapter 3

The House on Lyme Avenue

We were clearing away the supper dishes when I became aware that she was humming very softly, almost inaudibly. I asked about it, and she said that she had always sort of hummed to herself when occupied or troubled. It had never clearly registered for me, or only subliminally.

—Daniel Jaffe, in *Psychoanalytic Quarterly,* v. 52, no. 4, 1983, describing a visit with his mother

FROM EVERYTHING MY grandfather knew about his mother's life, it could come as no surprise she had a nervous mind. She was born Esther Zuckerman in the small town of Minsk in 1884. Today Minsk is part of Belarus. In the late nineteenth century it was part of the Pale of Settlement—that narrow western rim of the Russian Empire, where 94 percent of its Jewish population was stuffed into 5 percent of its territory. Jews in the Pale suffered frequent waves of violence called pogroms. A woman named Pauline Wengeroff, who lived in Minsk around this time, later wrote that the "air was charged" with fear. That was no way to raise a family, and when Esther was still a girl the Zuckerman clan left the cold doom of Minsk for the warm shores of America.

They'd been in Brooklyn a short time when her mother died in childbirth. With five or six children to tend—whether the baby survived, no one knows—Esther's father had no choice but to remarry. He chose a horrible shrewish woman still known in my family as the "wicked stepmother." She yanked little Esther from grade school and put her to work constructing artificial flowers. Paper flowers were a great cottage industry at the time: wives loved their durability enough to ignore reports that young, unpaid laborers did most of the production. Each afternoon, staring out the window, Esther saw other children returning home from school, her tired fingers sticky from the chemical treatment that made the leaf texture feel authentic. Her unfinished education haunted the rest of her days: into her eighties she still attended night school at P.S. 100, returning home to do her assignments with the nub of a pencil.

Her father died and she moved in with a great-aunt known simply as "Auntie," a savvy businesswoman but a bitter spirit. Several of her siblings died, too—impossibly horrible deaths. One fell beneath a pile of coats at a house party and probably smothered. Another raced to catch a ferry pulling away from a harbor and made a poor jump. Another reached from his hospital bed for a glass of water and grabbed carbolic acid. Esther spent her early twenties working in Auntie's candy store, listening over and over to the story of how Auntie had lost her one true love. (Auntie had wanted to wait for him, but everyone said she was *crazy* to do that, and lo! He came back for her—after she'd already married.) Esther had endured many lifetimes of sadness by this young age, but she probably seemed normal to the customers who just came in for a newspaper, like Harry Jaffe.

Esther and Harry were married on August 25, 1906, by the powers invested in Brooklyn. The match was not perfect. Esther was an Orthodox Jew and Harry had abandoned his faith. But he was a man of great personal conviction and she admired his sincerity. As a young woman Esther framed her round pretty face with dark wavy hair cut just below the ears. She was terrifically short, standing inches under five feet, and always content in a cotton housedress. Despite her hardships she kept a cheerful demeanor; everyone who knew her called her uncommonly sweet. She had enormous gray eyes, as if perpetually in need of a little extra light.

The new couple had their first child the following year, a girl named Beatrice, and Esther had just given birth to the second, a boy named Arthur, when she felt herself slipping. It was early summer of 1910. She and Harry had just taken an apartment in the Bushwick part of Brooklyn, but it wasn't ready yet so in the meantime they were living with Auntie. Arthur had been injured at birth and brought to his mother unconscious. Seeing the baby in this condition had a traumatic effect: Esther could no longer breast-feed and felt herself "trembling on the verge of a mental overthrow," she later said. Auntie and Harry sent her to a physician who patted her on the shoulder and said everything would be all right. "I did not think so," she would recall, "but I could not dispute what he said."

The young couple took a brief trip to Rockaway Beach so Esther could rest and recover. When they returned she was like her old self again. Harry and Auntie agreed the worst had likely passed.

Early one morning that September, while she was heating milk on the stove in Auntie's kitchen, Esther felt the trembling return. In an instant it hardened into a force that tugged at her muscles as if working strings: first scooping baby Arthur in her arms, then releasing him out the open third-story window. Auntie screamed from across the kitchen and raced down to the yard. A neighbor heard the cries and called for help, but it was too late to save the baby. When Officer Trumpfeller of the 154th precinct arrived, Esther was pacing the kitchen and pulling her hair. A doctor from Bushwick Hospital questioned her in the ambulance and quickly declared her deranged.

There were news reports and an indictment, of course. Her lawyer urged the court to drop the charges and transfer Esther to the Kings Park sanitarium as soon as possible. He told the district attorney that his own mind had been "very much disturbed" over the case. Another doctor who examined Esther before the hearing said she was suffering from a psychotic episode characterized by melancholia and delusions. Her big eyes shifted "rhythmically and in unison," he wrote, and she had a rapid heartbeat. She didn't respond much to questions except to say that she believed she was being punished for her sins by some "power," which, when pressed to be specific, she called God. She also said she'd seen the dead baby Arthur in the courtroom. He'd been wearing a little red sweater and hadn't recognized her.

On October 4, 1910, the court found her not guilty of murder in the second degree by reason of insanity.

With time the family recovered the scraps of their old life and started a new one. Harry nursed young Beatrice as Esther recovered in the hospital. The sincerity he'd shown as a suitor stayed strong despite his grief as a husband. He waited for his wife, even if some people told him he was crazy to do that, and lo! She came back to him. They resumed making a family. They had Eli in 1913; then Daniel, my grandfather, in 1914; then Sylvia in 1919. There's no telling just when or how my grandfather learned about his mother's condition and the tragedy it wrought, but he knew. They all knew. Maybe from Auntie, who'd been witness to it all and was never one to sugarcoat. Maybe from their birth certificates, which showed a "number of previous children" that didn't quite add up. It wasn't a topic for open discussion: my grandfather never mentioned the incident, and, if he can read this wherever he is, may never forgive me for doing so now. His mother's madness was there, though, following the family like some long psychic shadow they hoped would always stay behind them.

MY GRANDFATHER MOVED around a lot during his first sixteen years. He'd been born on a street filled with Russian immigrants in what's now the Bedford-Stuyvesant neighborhood of Brooklyn. The family made one short move there then left a few years later for Atlantic City, New Jersey, as Harry Jaffe looked for steady work. They soon returned to Brooklyn, this time to Coney Island, after he bought a 50 percent share in a linen business. Two more moves on Coney found them at Lyme Avenue. By the springtime of 1930, they'd been there three years and seemed to be settling down. Esther had a hysterectomy; the family would expand no further. (It had even contracted a bit when Beatrice married the year before.) For the first time in a long time they'd found somewhere to call home.

Coney Island is that skinny landmass clinging to the south of

Brooklyn that's known for its hot dogs and on maps kind of looks like one. The Jaffe family occupied the top apartment of a two-story house in Sea Gate, a small community tucked into the island's western pocket. One side of the development was enclosed by a perimeter of beaches that sloped toward Gravesend Bay (on the north) and the Atlantic Ocean (on the south). The other side was guarded by a secure entrance at Surf Avenue. That design kept Sea Gate residents isolated from the rowdy masses who swarmed to the beaches, the Luna and Steeplechase entertainment parks, and the famous Coney Island boardwalk, all summer long.

My grandfather spent his weekdays at Abraham Lincoln High in Brighton Beach, toward the other end of Coney. With a school day done, a spring afternoon might have tempted him in several directions. He often played ball with his older brother, Eli, on the sandlots. The two got along well enough but were stark contrasts in personality: Eli gregarious and athletic, my grandfather introspective and brainy. Eli was his mother's "sonny boy." (He once wrote that he could drop a "two-pound bag of shit" at her feet and she'd clap with pride.) My grandfather never felt the same adoration from his mother. This disparity of affection was clear to both boys, whether or not they connected it with their mother's first breakdown and the fact that Eli had been the next to arrive after the child she'd lost.

Then again the library on Stillwell Avenue might have tempted him instead. He was drawn most to works of science and nature. One of the books that left the greatest impression on his youth was *Microbe Hunters* by Paul de Kruif. *Microbe Hunters* read like a detective novel— with hospital infections and anthrax and malaria the villains, and Ignaz Semmelweis and Robert Koch and Ronald Ross the heroes—in part because de Kruif traced each discovery to the personal history of its discoverer. My grandfather later recalled the chapter on Louis Pasteur as one of his favorites. Because a young Pasteur had seen a mad wolf bite a farmer, he understood rabies "a hundred times more vividly than an ordinary boy would," in de Kruif's eyes.

Suppertime was six o'clock sharp, so whatever my grandfather had done that day he was sure to reach Lyme Avenue by late afternoon.

Like much of Brooklyn at that time, the street seemed uprooted from the shtetls of the Russian Empire. Dress cutter Abraham Edelstein; butcher Lewis Katz; pharmacist Alexander Scolnik; carpenter Morris Finks with his seven sons and his (poor) wife, Gussie; editor of a Jewish newspaper Benjamin Miller; Hyman and Molly Seidman right next door. All in modest two-story homes, all middle-aged Yiddish-speaking immigrants from Eastern Europe, all hoping for futures much brighter than the pasts they'd endured.

Sea Gate attracted its share of the wealthy along with the working class. Across from the Jaffes stood a twenty-thousand-square-foot plot of land with a three-story, twelve-room house and a brick garage, according to advertisements of the day. The son of Governor Alfred Smith lived in the neighborhood, and sometimes Smith himself would visit—sunbathing on the porch and playing with his infant grandson as news reporters watched. For this proximity to ethnic kin and political elite the Jaffes paid $85 a month.

The Alfred Smiths they were not. Still, Harry Jaffe earned a healthy living as half owner and general manager of Victory Barber Towel Supply. Victory supplied towels for barbers, as its name suggests, but also furnished patient gowns for doctors and tablecloths for restaurateurs and various other linen supplies for various others who needed them. The income was sufficient to buoy the family through the hard times that followed the great stock market crash of the previous October.

The house where the Jaffes lived on Lyme Avenue had a sunroom and a living room and a dining room. Their apartment had only one bathroom, but it was a large bathroom, and with Beatrice gone it probably felt a bit larger. A thin rail protected the second-story balcony and a brick portico surrounded the entrance. There was a flower bed out front that Harry Jaffe tended with affection in the spring. My grandfather would have passed it on his way inside the day he returned home, in the springtime of 1930, to find his mother gone.

She'd broken down that morning, just after Eli and Danny left for school. Little Sylvia was in the kitchen with her coat on, waiting to go off as well, when Esther started to sing at the top of her lungs. She was in bed, recuperating from the hysterectomy. In the ebbs of the song

Sylvia heard her father consoling her mother in a tender voice, trying to pull her back into his world, but she was too far gone. Some men came and took her away to the first of many sanitariums that would become her new home.

My grandfather had not seen it as vividly as his kid sister, but he knew. The people of Sea Gate knew, too. The people talked. One day, a neighbor asked little Sylvia if her mother was still in the "loony bin." Probably my grandfather and the others were getting some of the same, for the family was soon on the move again—away from something just a little too persistent, and toward something just a little too elusive.

No one knew quite why American immigrants had a higher prevalence of insanity than the native population in the early twentieth century. Still, no one disputed that they did. In 1903, despite forming just 13.5 percent of the country's population, immigrants made up 31 percent of its mental patients. Nowhere in the country was the problem worse than in New York, where immigrants made up a quarter of the state population but half the hospitalized insane population circa 1906. And nowhere in the state of New York was the problem worse than in New York City.

One of the first professionals to investigate the connection was a physician named Thomas W. Salmon. In his role as head of psychiatric services for Ellis Island, Salmon spent a year collecting data on immigration and mental health. In 1907 he reported that mentally ill immigrants tended to have some type of dementia praecox, a condition literally meaning "premature dementia." Today it's called schizophrenia.

Salmon used his findings to form broad cultural judgments about America's new arrivals. He believed nature had endowed many of them—namely Russians, Eastern Europeans, Jews, and Italians—with inferior mental constitutions. They reached America primed for mental breakdowns, then they broke down. Jews in particular, wrote Salmon, demonstrated a "remarkable susceptibility to mental and nervous disease."

The proposed link between insanity and race amplified a shrill cry for eugenics being heard across the country at the time. Many people believed that if mental illness was all hereditary, as physicians like Salmon suggested, then the children of insane immigrants would contaminate the mental fabric of American society. In 1912 New York's commissioner of immigration feared that mentally ill entrants "may leave feeble-minded descendants and so start vicious strains leading to misery and loss in future generations." Some states passed forced-sterilization laws to prevent that grave day from arriving. Salmon himself thought, in certain cases, that "the right of the individual to bear children must be disregarded in the interests of ordinary humanity as well as the interests of the race."

Not everyone in the psychiatric community agreed. These dissenting voices did not refute the high prevalence of insanity among immigrants, nor did they doubt some hereditary role in mental illness. They did, however, think any thorough discussion of insanity must include both biological and social factors. This crowd argued that immigrant life was a series of personal struggles and cultural adjustments that placed abnormal strain on one's mental state. As newcomers adapted, their rates of insanity would regress toward the mean—especially in later generations. Familiarity would inoculate these kids from the stressors of a world their parents had found so terrifying and strange.

The chief proponent of this contrary position was a psychiatrist at Kings Park State Hospital on Long Island named Aaron Rosanoff. A strong believer in the heritability of madness, Rosanoff nonetheless recognized that one's environment played a role, too. In 1915 he published a witty refutation to Salmon showing that New Yorkers who moved to California had a much higher admission rate to mental hospitals than did the state's natives. You could believe New Yorkers were more prone to mental illness than Californians—just as Salmon believed some immigrants were more prone to it than Americans—or you could admit that major changes to one's social setting often upset the healthy mind. Rosanoff concluded that the "much-feared menace" of immigrant insanity infecting American health was "not real but imaginary."

The conversation had turned this way by the time my grandfather took an intellectual interest in mental illness to go with his emotional one. He was almost sixteen when *The Human Mind* by Karl Menninger was published in early 1930, a book he later called "an inspiration for me in my youth." Menninger ran a psychiatric clinic in Topeka, Kansas, known for treating mental patients instead of hiding them away from society, as most asylums did in that day. *The Human Mind* was a collection of case studies meant, in part, to disabuse simplistic eugenicist notions of madness. Menninger thought the "accidents of life" could strain a personality beyond its natural powers of adaptation. He felt schizophrenics, for instance, often maintained a fine front until they broke—either in a moment of intense change or at the end of a gradual slipping. Afterward the odds of their recovery were slim, though some did improve.

What most readers took away from the book was that there was a thin line between so-called mental illness and so-called mental health. What a reader like my grandfather might also have seen is that sometimes a person could cross back over this line to the good side.

AFTER HIS MOTHER was institutionalized, my grandfather moved with the rest of the family to the Flatbush neighborhood of southern Brooklyn. In the early twentieth century, Brooklyn was a land full of immigrants and industry. Distinct little cultural pockets, stitched by shipyards and sugar refineries and factory whistles, together formed one of the country's leading manufacturing centers. Brooklyn was no longer its own city—most Americans saw it as one of those four New York boroughs that weren't Manhattan—but it maintained a fiercely independent spirit. (If nothing else it still had the Dodgers.) A reminder of where you'd come from was never far away, but neither was the promise of where you might go.

My grandfather finished high school and in the fall of 1931 enrolled at Brooklyn College while living at home. His father would have needed the extra hands. Harry Jaffe had two kids in college now (with Eli at Brooklyn as well) and another in grade school. He also had his wife's costly medical care and a business to run. He drove to the Victory linen shop in Williamsburg six days a week to make ends meet, and on Sundays he cooked food and brought it to Esther, who always complained about the food at whatever hospital was her home at the time. He never thought of leaving her or finding another companion.

As a young father Harry Jaffe had short dark hair combed neatly back from the crown. He wore spectacles slightly down on his nose, in front of an intense pair of hooded blue eyes. He was short, no taller than five foot seven, with a build described on his World War I draft card as "stout." (Forty-two when he registered, he never served.) He always dressed well: each May he famously exchanged his winter wardrobe and Knox felt hat for a Palm Beach suit and a straw boater. He spoke five languages, if you count Yiddish.

Even among his own children, Harry Jaffe's integrity was a thing of legend. He never spoke to them about the Old World—refused even to tell them his birthday was April 26, 1876—but they collected scraps of backstory here and there. That he'd grown up the son of an intense Jewish scholar in a small Lithuanian town called Panevezys. That he'd longed to be a doctor but was forbidden to read any books except the Torah and the Talmud. That he'd considered a life without intellectual freedom a life not worth living. That he'd fled Panevezys as a young man (family lore says sixteen; naturalization records say twenty-two). That he'd sailed for New York alone.

Somewhere along the way he'd acquired a natural moral compass. He once entered a business venture with a relative named Charlie Maslow, only to break off the arrangement when he suspected Maslow of corruption. Decades later the federal government indicted Maslow and five partners for conspiring to monopolize the $50 million laundry industry. The feds let Maslow off with a wrist-slap fine, but the event only elevated the legend of Harry Jaffe's ethical instinct. My grandfather always ended that story by saying, "We would have been rich," with only a tenth of regret to every nine parts pride. Harry Jaffe's honorable conduct, both in business and in marital devotion, left indelible marks on his children. My grandfather once called him "the finest man I've ever known."

By the time he entered college, my grandfather had developed such a thorough respect for his father that he'd begun to act just like him. He'd taken an interest in his father's interests: the classical music of Beethoven, the chess of world champion José Capablanca. He'd thrived in the atmosphere of self-discipline offered by the Boy Scouts, staying on for Eagle Scouts and recalling his lessons years later. He'd adopted an intensely reserved manner of his own and decided "to fulfill my father's ambition," he once wrote, by which he meant he'd become the doctor his father never could. If my grandfather had to share in his father's great sadness, he would share his great dream as well.

MY GRANDFATHER ONLY recorded one substantial recollection of his mother that I've ever found. It was buried at the end of an essay published in a professional journal called the *Psychoanalytic Quarterly* in 1986. He was writing about a dream he had while training to become a psychoanalyst after the war. Before psychoanalysts complete their training they must be analyzed themselves, a process they unsurprisingly call "training analysis." Toward the end of his training analysis, my grandfather was having trouble making some sort of emotional breakthrough. He wouldn't say what the trouble was—even in a personal essay that he'd *volunteered to write*—but apparently it existed.

In the dream he's undergoing open-heart surgery for a "heart valve defect that had been responsible for a crippling state of debility." He's watching the surgeon perform the surgery. He calls the surgeon's technique "skillful." He is evaluating medical competence in his dreams, my grandfather. Skillful or not, the surgeon is flummoxed. He can't fix the ailing heart. He can't tell what's broken.

So my grandfather, in the dream, reaches into his own chest and releases the *chordae tendineae*. (He also dreamed in Latin subtitles, my grandfather.) Those are the stringy tendons that bind the heart valves to the muscle itself. Sometimes they're even called heartstrings. My grandfather reaches in and pulls the *chordae,* if you will, and immediately feels a "marvelous restoration of healthy, vigorous function."

He closes the essay with two more brief anecdotes. The first is about one of his own patients—a "very difficult obsessional patient." My grandfather couldn't fix whatever was wrong with this patient until one morning when he woke up humming "Zing! Went the Strings of My Heart." The old Judy Garland song. Or maybe he was humming the Sinatra version. In any event, something about the melody reminded my grandfather about the dream in which he pulled his own heartstrings to resolve his own very difficult obsessions, and suddenly he helped his patient get better. He doesn't explain how, just that he did.

The other anecdote is the one about his mother. He was visiting his mother in her later years and walked into the kitchen and heard her humming. "I asked about it, and she said that she had always sort of hummed to herself when occupied or troubled," he writes. "It had never clearly registered for me, or only subliminally." That's all he wrote.

I tried many times to make a connection between these brief stories, and came up empty. Maybe it's because I'm not a doctor. Or maybe it's a Judy Garland thing. I once asked one of my grandfather's psychoanalytic protégés to explain it to me. He said the essay's significance was that my grandfather, as a classical analyst writing in a conservative journal, was suggesting a rather progressive therapeutic technique: understanding his patient's problem by identifying it with his own. I pretended that made everything clear and thanked him. The only thing I take away from the essay is that one time, in a dream somehow related to his mother, my grandfather fixed his own heart.

My grandfather never explicitly said that he became a psychiatrist to figure out why his mother behaved the way she did. In fact he went out of his way at times not to draw this link. In his memoir, in a section called "How I Came to Be a Doctor," he mentions his father's unfulfilled wish to go into medicine, and the books *Microbe Hunters* and *The Human Mind,* and that's it. Nothing about his mother. Still, we in his family all kind of assume that's the real reason. There was so much he never stated explicitly that must have been there. Sometimes I feel like the surgeon in that dream: standing over the open cavity of his life, searching in vain for the wound.

Once I called my uncle to ask what he thought. He told me about the time Esther came to live with the family for a while in Washington, D.C. This was in the late fifties or early sixties. My uncle was a young man by then—my grandfather's oldest son—and at one point Esther had a breakdown and they took her to George Washington University Hospital. He saw the episode: saw Esther emerge in a bathrobe, her hair all wild, her big eyes all wide, her cheerful demeanor retreating into silence. My grandfather had tried to pass it off with some humor. "Oh, Mom, you always snap out of it sooner or later. Why don't you snap out of it sooner." But he knew right away they'd have to take her to the hospital. He knew the look.

"I remember going to visit her," my uncle said. "It made quite an impression on me. It was a heartbreak for Grandpa. You could see how painful it was for him that his mom was so sick."

MY GRANDFATHER FINISHED college in three years and enrolled in medical school for the fall semester of 1934. He'd lived at home his whole life—even stayed there after transferring from Brooklyn College to New York University, in Manhattan. Now he'd chosen George Washington for his medical studies and would have to move south. It's nice to think that sometime that summer Harry Jaffe sat down with my grandfather and expressed how happy it made him to see his ambitions survive in his son. They were both such quiet men, neither quick on a sentimental trigger, but if there'd ever been a time to let down their guards that was it. Only the streets of Flatbush know for sure.

In January of 1935, while my grandfather was away at medical school, Esther was transferred from Kings Park State Hospital to a private sanitarium called Louden-Knickerbocker Hall with a diagnosis of "dementia praecox-catatonic type." At Louden her delusions intensified, according to records of her stay. She was "restless, agitated, discontented" upon admission. Her facial expressions were "worrisome, anxious, and at times perplexed." Frequently she interrupted the hospital staff with a plea to go home. Occasionally someone would find her screaming or weeping without any apparent cause—other than, perhaps, the acute frustration of her unrequited wish. She spent a great deal of time pacing back and forth in front of the exit. She knew the day of the week but was off by two on the year, as if she understood that some part of her life had kept going even as another part had come to a stop.

Louden Hall was just outside the town of Amityville, near the southern coast of Long Island, roughly thirty miles east of Flatbush. The entrance was tucked away on a leafy street. The campus itself was carpeted with wide flat green lawns. The original John Louden had established the place in the late nineteenth century as a compassionate alternative to the straitjackets and medical torment he'd seen too often during his career as an inspector of state asylums. The institution's primary psychiatrist was Dr. James Vavasour, who frequently served as an expert witness on psychotic behavior for the Westchester County district attorney. (In early 1935 he was in the process of telling the state supreme court that the "Brooklyn Vampire," Albert Fish, an infamous child murderer who'd pleaded insanity, was in fact "legally sane.")

Harry Jaffe tried to bring his wife back home a few times. These occasions never went well. In preparation for one homecoming he hired a tall, burly Scottish nurse. Though small of stature, Esther showed remarkable strength during an episode—became a different person physically, too. One day, she dashed into the streets of Flatbush and the big nurse needed every ounce of strength to carry her back inside. She wanted nothing more than to return to the house on Lyme Avenue, where life had felt stable for at least a moment, and where the future had promised to outrun the past.

The final attempt to bring her home came in the summer of 1935. My grandfather would have been home on vacation at the time. The family was living on East 17th Street in Brooklyn, near Kings Highway. She lasted six weeks, into early August, before they took her back to Louden. The records show she wept for hours following her readmission. There's nothing to show what Harry Jaffe did when he returned home, once more, alone.

Through it all he tried to endure the emotional burden himself. He rarely spoke to his kids about their mother. Occasionally he'd run off to spend a few hours with her relatives, and only then they'd know she was on his mind. He provided well for them. (The balance sheets for 1935 showed the assets of Victory linen exceeding $43,000, a figure that amounts to $700,000 today.) His existence had been lonesome—leaving his family in Lithuania forever, losing his wife, too, but for one day a week—but he saw brighter days for his children. He never took them to the linen shop for fear they might grow fond of the work. What he really wanted was for his boys to become medical siblings like the Menninger brothers. That would never happen, with Eli the rebellious type, but every now and then, pushing the shop carts with the dirty linens, wiping the sweat from his brow on a break, Harry Jaffe maybe thought about my grandfather's chosen course, and let his steady face slip into a smile.

One day, around Christmas of 1935, one of the carts got away from him. As he ran after it he fell to the ground. It just seemed like a tumble at the time, but pretty soon he turned jaundiced and the family worried it was something more. The doctors were puzzled. He'd never been sick a day in his life, and now he was sallow and bedridden. He passed the time with no outward signs of pain or suffering. He read Hugo's *Les Misérables.*

After a month the family brought him to Beth Moses Hospital for an exploratory surgery and they found the cancer in his pancreas. By then it had spread to other parts and could hardly be stopped. My grandfather got the call at medical school telling him to come quick if he wanted to see his father alive. He took a prop plane, the first time he'd ever flown, and arrived on January 26, 1936, to find his father in a coma. He died that day.

The months that followed Harry Jaffe's death were filled with a frenzy of legal matters. The Brooklyn surrogate court had to determine guardianship for Sylvia, who was still a minor, and now essentially a parentless one at that. Harry's share of stock in Victory linen had to be sold and the estate assets distributed. In a karmic twist, Charlie Maslow, the relative whose sinister business practices had led Harry Jaffe to break off their own partnership, bargained up the sale price to more than twice Victory's appraised value. The children received a considerable sum: roughly $100,000 each in today's currency. Still, they had loads of expenses—the remainder of medical school tuition, in my grandfather's case—and had to establish a separate fund for the continued institutional care of their widowed mother.

Since her return to Louden Hall, Esther Jaffe had been harboring an intense resentment toward her husband. She'd convinced herself he was out to get her. Convinced herself *he* was the reason why she was denied her simple request of returning home to Lyme Avenue. Dr. Vavasour later called this mind-set a "paranoid delusional system." At times simply hearing her husband's name made Esther "extremely excited" and resistant to medical attention. Dr. Vavasour advised the courts to keep her out of all legal matters for her own health.

There was one thing they couldn't avoid: Esther had to renounce administrative rights to the family estate. The papers reached her at Louden in late February of 1936, and she signed them in a shaky hand. She knew then that her husband had died—if she hadn't suspected something when he stopped showing up every seventh day with food. The children would inherit his role in her care along with the estate. My grandfather was just twenty-two when he returned to medical school that semester, still in mourning. The specter of his mother's sickness had followed him since birth, and now he saw it in front of him, too.

Chapter 4

Heavenly Mission

> Our swords must be double-edged. That sword shall be relentless towards injustice pervading Asia, and at the same time shall be still more relentless towards evils nestling in Japan. So the warriors for the revival of Asia must inevitably be warriors for the reform of Japan.
>
> —Okawa Shumei, *Various Problems of Asia in Revival,* 1922

FOLLOWING THE DEATH of his father, Okawa Shumei wasted little time upholding his pledge to become a warrior for Asia. When Japan joined the Great War on the side of the British, in August of 1914, Okawa openly opposed the alliance as a betrayal of Asian brotherhood. He took little pleasure in the fact that Japanese forces routed German territories in China and the Pacific. Instead, he felt that fighting beside Britain was equivalent to endorsing its harsh colonial rule in India. As Okawa saw things, Japan was supporting a white race intent on subjugating the "yellow" one—a term he used to describe all Asians, regardless of actual skin color. He wrote essays urging Japan to abandon its alliance with the West and form a new one with the East. He called this concept *Ajiashugi,* or Asianism.

A small community of Indian revolutionaries living in Japan took notice of their vocal new advocate. One of them was Heramba Lal Gupta, who was part of an Indian liberation movement known as the

Ghadar Party. On a clear afternoon in the early autumn of 1915, Gupta intercepted Okawa outside the Tokyo University library, where he was known to spend so much of his free time. They forged a swift bond—the two men discussed Asian affairs all day and into the evening—and soon Gupta introduced Okawa to other believers in the cause. Among this crowd was a rebel named Rash Behari Bose, who'd been forced into hiding after organizing a failed assassination attempt on the British viceroy of India. The three men became fast friends.

That November, the trio threw a joint Indian-Japanese party at a hotel in Tokyo to celebrate the recent coronation of the Taisho emperor. The festivities quickly escalated into a parade of Asianist pride. Partygoers strung together a series of anti-British speeches. They flew the Indian and Japanese flags but not the Union Jack. At one point a member of the Japanese parliament even called on his country to support India's quest for independence. There was a police officer among the two hundred people in attendance, and word soon got back to the British ambassador, who demanded that Japanese authorities round up Gupta and Bose and deport them back to British territory. The request essentially amounted to a death sentence. Within hours the two Indians went on the lam.

For the next six weeks the Tokyo police kept a close eye on Okawa Shumei lest his new friends try to contact him. Such a move would have been foolish: Okawa's home, in the Harajuku section of Tokyo, was right across the street from a police station. Weeks turned into months, 1915 gave way to 1916, and tensions died down. Then, on a cold gray afternoon in February, Okawa got an unexpected knock at his door. The man outside was dressed just like a Japanese farmer who'd come into the city to sell his wares. He was holding a basket of fruit and wearing a short kimono. He'd pulled his soft brown hat over his eyes. As Okawa looked more closely at the man's face, he realized this was no Japanese farmer at all. It was Heramba Lal Gupta.

Okawa hustled his friend inside. Gupta was starving, so Okawa ordered some food. The two men sat in his drawing room eating *oyakodon,* a bowl of rice topped with chicken and egg, while considering their options. Okawa had come to see the Asianist movement as something of a heavenly mandate—a mission that warriors like himself must accept for the good of humanity. "The reason why we call for 'Asia for Asians' is because there can be no true Asia as long as Asia is under Western control," he'd recently written in an essay. He might have felt the righteous thrill that would define his character; in any case, he realized that accepting this great mission meant undertaking actions like harboring Gupta. Besides, the idea was just crazy enough to work. The police would hardly expect to find Gupta hiding just across the street from one of their stations.

Years later Okawa would recall thinking at this time: "it is dark underneath the lamp."

For the next few months Gupta and Okawa engaged in an intense philosophical exchange about the hardships of India in particular and the nature of Asia in general. Gupta spoke of colonial life with a vividness Okawa could never have found in books. He revealed incriminating details of Indian nationalist efforts that only true rebels would know. Occasionally they interrupted the talks to wrestle so Gupta could get some physical exercise without chancing it outdoors.

In late spring, when the Japanese government relaxed its deportation order after a diplomatic tiff with Britain, Gupta hopped a ship to the United States. Afterward Okawa continued his education on India with Bose, who'd remained in Japan to marry the daughter of the man who'd sheltered him. That fall Okawa published his maiden book, *The Nationalist Movement in India*. It was immediately banned by both the Japanese and British governments.

Despite this censorship, or perhaps because of it, *The Nationalist Movement in India* gained a strong cult following. Okawa had produced a landmark study of the Indian independence movement, a true philosopher-patriot work that blended fresh journalism with weighty scholarship. The book awakened readers to the troubles of life in Greater Asia and exposed them to what Okawa saw as extreme British hypocrisy. (Great Britain championed democracy in the fight against Germany, he wrote, even as it smothered liberties in India.) Okawa encouraged Japan to discard its allegiance to the West and embrace the

Asianist cause of uniting the East—to accept "our Empire's great mission in the world."

As 1916 drew to a close, many more Indian dissidents in Japan came looking for Okawa Shumei hoping to join his growing movement. He had no reason to suspect that one particular Indian man who appeared around this time had been planted by British intelligence to find out what this whole Asianist thing was really about. Part of him might even have appreciated how dark the spy thought things would be underneath the lamp.

IT DIDN'T TAKE Agent P long to report back to British intelligence that Okawa Shumei was a "leading spirit" of Asianism in Japan. By the end of 1916, the operative had insinuated himself into Okawa's life—evidently without incident. They went to dinners and parties together. They scanned books on Indian nationalism in Okawa's voluminous library. Sometimes Agent P loaned money for the cause or paid for an Asianist function, just to stay in the loop. From this privileged position he watched as Okawa formed the Asiatic Association of Japan in early 1917. Okawa established a headquarters in Aoyama, recruited members, collected donations, drafted publications, organized events, and generally worked, in the words of the group's mission statement, "to make the dream of Asian unity a reality."

At just age thirty, Okawa had become the orbital figure in this blooming Japanese underworld. He arranged his life so Asianism came before everything else. He'd broken off an engagement, preferring to fraternize in the teahouses of Tokyo and find comfort in the arms of geisha. His home in Harajuku was within walking distance of the Asiatic Association's headquarters in Aoyama. A vision of Okawa during that time emerges: standing taller than most, looking slightly un-Japanese, wearing a kimono some days and a sharp Western-style suit others, adjusting his trademark glasses and smoking a cigarette—running the show.

The Asianist movement in Japan at that time represented a loose collection of personalities and partner groups. It was a colorful cast filled with Japanese natives and foreign sympathizers alike. One key player was Taraknath Das, an Indian with an outstanding arrest warrant in San Francisco, on the run from both American and British authorities. Das wrote two inflammatory books promoting Asian unity that Okawa translated into Japanese and distributed on the sly. (Despite being officially banned, one Das work wound up in the library of the Japanese naval department.) Another influential figure was the French expatriate Paul Richard. He wrote a poetic ode to Asianism that Okawa translated and distributed through the Asiatic Association. In it Richard called Japan "the liberator of Asia"; Okawa thought Richard knew the Japanese better than they knew themselves.

The Asianist movement also drew support from Toyama Mitsuru, the paternal figure of the Japanese anti-establishment. A wise old samurai scion who'd once fought beside the great Saigo Takamori, Toyama led the Genyosha, sometimes called the Dark Ocean Society, a network of nationalists that wielded heavy behind-the-scenes political power. He'd arranged asylum for Gupta and Bose back in 1915, and secured the Tokyo headquarters for Okawa's association. His disciple, Uchida Ryohei, was head of a sister group called Kokuryukai, known in the West as the Black Dragon Society. Uchida promoted Asianist messages through the society's publication, *Ajia Jiron,* and helped in other ways to advance the great mission.

The Asiatic Association of Japan held functions all over the city. Members gathered at the Matsumotoro restaurant in Hibiya Park and at the Seiyoken Hotel in Ueno. Editors of respected publishing houses, professors at major universities, even active members of the Japanese parliament made frequent appearances. Okuma Shigenobu, the two-time prime minister who wrote about Japan's "great mission" to unify Eastern and Western cultures in 1915, delivered occasional talks. Officers from the Army General Staff encouraged the movement, and sometimes came to parties themselves. Agent P watched it all unfold with Okawa in the center.

In September of 1918, British intelligence circulated an exhaustive dossier, based largely on Agent P's espionage, called "The Pan-Asiatic Movement." The memo, compiled by an official named David Petrie, offered unique insight into Western fears of Japan's rising power at the time. Petrie and others believed a strong Asianist movement threatened Japan's warm relations with the West. In the short term that threat could translate into Japanese support for an Indian uprising. In the long term, wrote Petrie, the "real danger" of Asianism was its potential to remove Western influence in the Far East and establish Japanese supremacy in its place. If Japan united Eastern nations under the banner of Asianism, the "prospects of the wealth and power so accruing to Japan are as limitless in extent as they are dazzling in their brilliancy," he wrote.

Petrie likened Asianism to social movements that had occurred in Germany before the Great War. Japan, like Germany before it, had a growing sense of global importance. The Japanese, like the Germans, also believed in what Petrie called "the reality of their 'mission.'" He concluded his dossier by wondering whether the "outcome" in both countries would be the same. The question might have seemed absurd to Westerners, especially with the Allies on the verge of winning the Great War, but what really mattered was whether or not it seemed absurd to the Japanese.

Petrie wasn't so sure. Some of his intelligence suggested that Japan had already considered expanding its power into Central Asia. In the course of his spy work, Agent P had discovered an enormous map belonging to the General Staff of the Japanese Army—twelve separate pieces, 108 square feet in all. The map outlined a route into India through Tibet and Afghanistan. Agent P had discovered it one day in the home of Okawa Shumei.

ASIANIST IDEOLOGY HAD evolved quite a bit by the time Okawa Shumei took the reins. Its initial purpose was merely to suggest that Eastern nations might better defend themselves against Western advance by forming a broad conglomerate. Throughout the nineteenth century the West had its way with the East time and again. Winning the Opium Wars in China, annexing territories in the Pacific, muscling Japan from global isolation, harvesting natural resources across the region. Early Asianist societies spoke of *koa*—"raising Asia"—or cooperating on the premise that Asians shared a culture and a race. The hope was that Eastern people, all working together, wouldn't be so vulnerable to Western encroachments.

East–West tensions rose after Japan's military victory over China in 1895. Uncomfortable with a new Asian power, a three-way faction of Russia, Germany, and France forced Japan to forfeit its territorial gains from that war—an episode known, with disdain, as the Triple Intervention. Kaiser Wilhelm of Germany commissioned a painting that depicted a group of personified Western nations gazing at a Buddha figure floating toward them on an angry cloud. A hysterical fear of an Asian invasion emerged. Westerners called it the "Yellow Peril."

Japanese foreign officials did their best to discredit the concern. The diplomat Kurino Shinichiro told a Berlin audience in 1904 that the idea of an Asian uprising was a "ridiculous fantasy." But when Japan scored another military victory in 1905, this time over Russia, fantasy seemed very much in line with reality. (The fighting had started over the Liaotung Peninsula in northern China, which Japan had conceded in the Triple Intervention only to watch Russia advance there.) The shocking outcome of the Russo–Japanese War signified a cultural sea change: for the first time in living memory an Eastern nation had defeated a Western one in battle.

Asianism started to change at this time, too, with Japan taking a strong leadership role. Some Japanese saw their country as the natural protectorate for the entire region. In the initial aftermath of the Russian war, many other Asians agreed. Japanese leaders called for an Asian Monroe Doctrine, suggesting a zero-tolerance policy toward outside infringement in the East, based on the U.S. equivalent in North and South America. In 1910, Japan annexed Korea under the guise of creating "permanent peace in the Far East." Soon it became difficult to determine where Japan's sense of regional partnership ended and where its sense of regional superiority began.

Japan now presented the world with conflicting messages. On the one hand, it remained friendly toward the United States and Great Britain, and clearly embraced the Western model of modernity. On the other hand, it viewed itself as the leader of Asian opposition against Western advance in the East. Westerners couldn't help but notice the aggressive undertones running below this new current of Asianism. In 1913 the editors of the *Times* of London wrote that Japan "must make up her mind whether she wishes to present herself as aloof from other Asiatic races or as the avowed champion of Pan-Asiatic ideals."

As the Great War unfolded, more and more Japanese favored the Asian course over the Western one. Europe looked like a civilization in decline; the East, meanwhile, was experiencing nationalist movements and a cultural revival. Japan emerged from this period as a great power. Wartime production boosted wealth, the quick campaign against Germany enhanced military prestige, and a one-sided peace treaty with China (known with infamy as the Twenty-One Demands) improved Japan's position on the mainland. Japanese officials took a new interest in Asianist ideas. A member of parliament named Kodera Kenkichi even released a massive treatise calling for a "glorious new Asian civilization." Cultural figures joined the push, too. In 1916 the famed Indian writer Rabindranath Tagore told a Japanese crowd that their country "has the mission of the East to fulfill."

So by the time Okawa Shumei devoted his life to Asianism, the peaceful idea of nations cooperating to save the East had transformed into a forceful rationale for Japan to lead a charge against the West. For his part, Okawa brought new energy to the movement. He broadened the concept of Asia beyond China and India to include the Middle East. He ignored the obvious cultural differences and emphasized the one commonality: that these various peoples were not part of "the West." He recognized that a growing number of Japanese believed in this mission—even considered it just that, a "mission"—and rallied them behind it. He was not quite a famous ideologue by 1918, but he'd started on the path toward becoming one.

OKAWA SHUMEI LIVED most of his adult life in Tokyo, but he never severed ties to his roots in the villages of Sakata. He returned sometimes to visit his mother and brothers. He joined a horse-riding club in Harajuku. He loved tales of samurai roaming the agrarian regions of Old Japan. He no longer embraced socialism as an ideology, but much of his skill as a writer had been refined arguing its merit back in high school. Even though Okawa made his home in the city, his love for the countryside returned to the fore in the summer of 1918, when Japan experienced the largest social upheaval in its modern history.

The Rice Riots, as they were known, began in July. Japan's economic success during the Great War hadn't quite trickled down to the factory workers or the rural peasants. Already frustrated by the rising cost of commercial goods, the lower classes rose up in protest against the soaring price of rice. For the next several weeks mobs spread to hundreds of towns and villages across the country. Angry citizens marched against profiteering and scrapped in the streets with local police. The situation went from bad to worse when soldiers called in to keep the peace fired on the people. By the end of September, thirty civilians were dead and thousands more had been tossed into prison.

Okawa watched these events with considerable angst and even a little shock. He thought the riots were a sign of hidden national defects. He saw the uprising as a sign that Japan could not become the leader of Asia without first addressing its problems at home.

He wasn't alone in these thoughts. That fall, at the invitation of the Indian rebel Rash Behari Bose, Okawa joined an informal social group that met to discuss Japan's deteriorating social conditions. The group was led by a journalist named Mitsukawa Kametaro, whom Okawa quickly recognized as a kindred spirit. Both men had followed socialism as youths. Both held a great deal of resentment toward the West. (Mitsukawa was so deeply scarred by the Triple Intervention that he referenced it in the title of his autobiography.) Both considered American culture to be crass and vulgar. Both believed only Japan could liberate Asia from the grasp of Western imperialism. Beliefs aside, Mitsukawa enjoyed Okawa's quirky nature, admiring his double life as a sometimes excitable philosopher and a sometimes contemplative patriot.

In the summer of 1919 the new friends broke from Mitsukawa's discussion group to form their own. They wanted to do more than talk about social reform—they wanted to go out and achieve it. They called their group Yuzonsha, a name that translates, more or less, as the Society of Those Who Yet Remain. It came from a line in an ancient Chinese poem: "Though all the paths are ruined, there yet remained the pine trees and the chrysanthemums." Okawa and Mitsukawa saw themselves as the pine trees and chrysanthemums. When their reform of Japan was complete, and the paths of the old country left in ruin, Yuzonsha would be all that remained.

No sooner had Okawa and Mitsukawa formed Yuzonsha than they recognized a critical hole in their plan: neither one of them had ever tried to spark a real reform movement themselves. For all their activist instincts and friendships with Indian dissidents, Okawa and Mitsukawa were virgin rebels. As a first point of business they decided to solicit the skills of a veteran radical. They settled on an activist named Kita Ikki, who had written a provocative critique of the Japanese state some years earlier. The work had been so shocking that after its publication some people called Kita a genius and others called him mad.

And no sooner had Okawa and Mitsukawa recognized this first hole than they encountered a second one: Kita Ikki was living in China, not Japan. Okawa agreed to make the recruiting trip himself. He left on August 8, 1919—an auspicious date, Mitsukawa decided, because it was the eighth day of the eighth month of the eighth year of the reign of the Taisho emperor. Okawa traveled from Tokyo to Japan's southern island of Kyushu and slipped onto a freighter called *Tenko* bound for mainland Asia. Eventually he'd need to reach Shanghai Harbor in China. It could not have escaped his highly analytical mind, especially during several lonely weeks at sea, that he'd been guided on this first phase of his heavenly mission on a ship whose name meant "Heavenly Light."

KITA IKKI WAS about the same age as Okawa Shumei and rather handsome, with a mustache like a poor drawing of a seagull and a right eye that appears, at least in pictures, slightly lazy. Okawa and Kita lacked the natural compatibility of Okawa and Mitsukawa. Okawa dressed with class and wrote with logic. Kita Ikki owned all of two suits and had a clear flair for the extreme. He followed an intense sect of Buddhism called Nichiren and earlier that year had fasted for forty straight days. Despite their differences, Kita was still the sort of person who could appreciate being approached by a tall stranger who'd traveled weeks in the hopes of discussing a national uprising. They went to an inn and became so absorbed with the subject that next thing they knew it was morning.

Kita had spent his life in the service of social reform. Years earlier, as a young man living in Japan, he'd joined the Black Dragon Society run by Asianist sympathizer Uchida Ryohei. After the Chinese revolution began, in 1911, he'd moved to Shanghai as one of the society's representatives. When Okawa arrived with hopes of reinventing his homeland, Kita leapt at the chance. He was already in the process of drafting a new book—every bit as shocking as his first—outlining a thorough plan for Japanese reformation. He agreed to return to Japan and join Yuzonsha. Before they parted ways, as a gesture of appreciation, Kita gave Okawa a walking stick with a hidden blade at one end.

Publishing Kita Ikki's reform plan became Yuzonsha's top priority. *The Outline of a Plan for the Reconstruction of Japan,* as Kita called the work, was certain to attract attention. The book urged a complete overhaul of the Japanese political system, and a rough one at that. Kita wanted the emperor to suspend the constitution and dismiss the parliament under orders of martial law—a sort of authorized coup d'état.

A revolutionary council then would appoint new leadership with a mandate to implement a highly controlled economic state. Strict limitations on private assets would eliminate wealth disparity (even the Imperial Family would get only an allowance). Industrial capitalists, and the corrupt politicians they bankrolled, would no longer benefit at the expense of poor farmers in the countryside.

The plan would undo every step Japan had taken toward becoming a democratic society in the Western mold. It was also just the first phase of a much greater uprising. Down the road, the new-and-improved Japan would assume its rightful place as a leader of the East. Only then, wrote Kita, could Japan emancipate the Asian people.

Kita Ikki's manifesto eventually found a place in the canon of Japanese extremist literature. One scholar later compared it with *Mein Kampf.* That is an overstatement—Kita was no Hitler, despite referring to Japan as "the Germany of the East"—but the book still did plenty of social damage. Blood was shed in its name as early as 1921, when a zealot inspired by Kita's ideas killed a big business leader then took his own life. Subsequently the book achieved a reputation as the bible of the radical Japanese nationalist movement.

In a more immediate sense, the reform plan established Yuzonsha's place on the map of Japanese activism. The group mimeographed Kita's book and circulated at least a hundred copies to various high officials and other selected recipients. The book itself was banned, of course, but not before a few Japanese leaders developed sympathy for its message. Even as the home ministry fined Kita ¥30 for publishing the work, the home minister sent him ¥300 as a nod of personal approval.

Yuzonsha followed this early success by producing a society bulletin called *Otakebi,* which in translation means *War Cry.* The lead editorial in the inaugural issue of July 1920, cowritten by Okawa and Mitsukawa, declared the need for national reformation in the larger scheme of the divine Asianist mission. "The Japanese people must become the vortex of a whirlwind which will liberate mankind," they wrote. "We must be content to begin with the reform of our nation, because we have faith in the Japanese mission to free the universe."

Okawa gave Kita the nickname Mao-o, which meant "Devil King," because Kita "felt at home with Buddha and the Devil at the same time." In exchange, Kita called Okawa Susano-o, after the Shinto god of storms, because when he made up his mind to act he never thought twice. The stormy Okawa had gathered two dark ideological clouds by age thirty-three—one to unite Asia against the West, another to prepare Japan to lead this unification—and he was emerging as the vortex in the whirlwind of them both.

THE WESTERNIZATION THAT Okawa Shumei opposed was all around him in Tokyo during the early 1920s. An emerging urban middle class could be found in every passing banker or teacher or doctor or corporate manager. Women formed a growing part of the workforce. Major corporations built downtown headquarters and large office complexes and modern department stores. Mass media appeared, culminating in 1925 with the birth of Japanese radio. Mass transit appeared, too, with electric trolleys running atop city streets and a subway system emerging below. Public parks brought families into town. A new adventurous youth trotted to the cabarets and jazz clubs and theaters of Ginza. Political parties gained influence and championed liberal virtues: universal (male) suffrage, military disarmament, diplomatic foreign policy. Tokyo Station, with its European-style grandeur, stood at the center of it all.

For everyone who welcomed this democratic lifestyle there were those like Okawa who saw it as a pernicious intrusion on traditional values. This crowd believed capitalism and party politics had corrupted the selfless society of Old Japan. They saw statesmen elevating their own interests above those of the people. They saw financial powers bribing and manipulating the statesmen. They saw farmers, laborers, and country folk stuck at the bottom of a new social hierarchy, unjustly based on money and power, every bit as rigid as the feudal class system it had replaced. Violent rebellion often seemed like the only outlet. In late 1921 Prime Minister Hara Takashi was stabbed to death at Tokyo Station by an extremist railroad worker. Hara had been the first commoner to reach the premiership—the embodiment of Japan's progressive rise.

Okawa fanned the flames of this general frustration in several books and countless articles during the early 1920s. His signature work, *Various Problems of Asia in Revival,* appeared in 1922. (Prosecutors at the Tokyo trial later called it the "standard Pan-Asiatic handbook of the Japanese nationalists.") Okawa argued that the world had become a showcase for Western ideals: politics followed imperial interests, economics followed industrial capitalism, races followed white rule. At the same time, he believed things were beginning to change. The "tide of resistance against white domination is rising" throughout Asia, he wrote. The waves of national and spiritual independence—a so-called

Asian revival—were gaining strength from Turkey and Persia to India and China. It was Japan's duty as the leading Eastern nation to guide this global transition toward a "divine New Asia."

"Our swords must be double-edged," Okawa vowed in the book's introduction. "That sword shall be relentless towards injustice pervading Asia, and at the same time shall be still more relentless towards evils nestling in Japan. So the warriors for the revival of Asia must inevitably be warriors for the reform of Japan."

He acted the part of that warrior through Yuzonsha. In partnership with the Dark Ocean and Black Dragon societies, Okawa's group tried to impose its will on the country's highest leaders. In 1921 a chief advisor to the emperor objected to the bride chosen for Crown Prince Hirohito because color blindness, seen as a potential hereditary flaw, had been found in her family line. Yuzonsha considered this objection an insult to the emperor and spread rumors of assassination until the advisor relented. That same year Yuzonsha tried to prevent young Hirohito from taking a long overseas tour on the grounds that it was too Eurocentric. The prince went on the trip anyway, but Yuzonsha had made its presence felt.

All the while, Okawa developed a taste for the rebellious life. He drank often, and on occasion smoked opium. He frequented the brothels of the Kakurazaka neighborhood of Tokyo and developed a small rotation of favored geisha. One of these regulars moved in with him, but another became so jealous that, in 1923, she forced him to end things with the others. He ignored the consequences of these bad decisions. When he contracted syphilis around this time, for instance, he failed to treat it.

EVEN AS OKAWA Shumei worked to reform mainstream Japanese society, he kept one foot inside it. Since 1919 he'd been employed as an editorial director of a research institute run by the South Manchurian Railway company. The institute analyzed global economic data with a focus on East Asia. Okawa split his time between the think tank's main Tokyo bureau, housed in a redbrick building outside the Imperial Palace, and sites he visited in Manchuria several times a year. The railway company was partly owned by the Japanese government, which put the institute partly under national authority, which meant that Okawa was essentially employed by the very system he was trying to overthrow on his days off.

His links to Japanese officials didn't end there. In the spring of 1922 Okawa became a lecturer for a private academy in Tokyo called the Social Education Research Institute. Each year the academy recruited twenty promising young teachers from the countryside to receive a free term of intensive mid-career training. Later these teachers would return to their local communities and impart the lessons they'd learned to their own students. This program was also financed by the government—it was located in an old meteorology building on the grounds of the Imperial Palace. By selecting Okawa Shumei for the Social Education Research Institute, the country's leaders were endorsing him as an intellectual shepherd of Japanese youth.

A shake-up at the academy in late 1923 left Okawa in a position of greater authority. In the year that followed he molded the school to meet his views on Japanese reformation. He renamed it Daigakuryo, commonly translated as the "College Dorm," and installed a new curriculum that covered subjects like Old Japan, economic and social problems, and national defense. The reorganized Daigakuryo encouraged the broader development of Japanese patriots. Mitsukawa Kametaro, who lectured on current events at the College Dorm, believed these students would ultimately fulfill the great goal of building a new Japan. Okawa's own seminars were known as "Studies in the Japanese Spirit." His basic message, summarized when these lectures were later compiled into a book, was that "Japan is the best country."

As Okawa's conventional influence grew, his relationship with extremists like Kita Ikki suffered. Kita's erratic morality confined Yuzonsha to the unfavorable realm of Japan's fringe subversives; he'd become a notorious political blackmailer, aided by a small gang of tough-guy extortionists, and Okawa disapproved of this thuggish conduct. For the time being, Okawa thought it wiser to pursue a less abrasive route toward reform. Maybe it was a career move; maybe it was a function of entering his midthirties. In any event, sometime in 1923 he and Kita abandoned their revolutionary partnership and dissolved Yuzonsha. If Okawa wanted to have a legitimate impact on the future direction of his homeland, he would need to keep more reputable company.

Free from his unsavory ties, Okawa curried favor with a powerful subset of political and military elite into the middle 1920s. He buddied up to Makino Nobuaki, minister of the imperial household from 1921 to 1925, who sometimes spoke at the patriot academy and considered Okawa a young man of "rare" earnestness. The household's vice minister, Sekiya Teizaburo, also approved of Okawa's pedagogical direction. Army generals Araki Sadao and Watanabe Jotaro were among the high-ranking military officers who met with College Dorm students on occasion. These distinguished friendships went beyond the classroom. When Okawa married a favorite geisha in February of 1925, Admiral Yoshiro Rokuro of the Japanese Navy mediated at the wedding. (Her name was Kaneko. She'd been the jealous one.)

The College Dorm ended abruptly in 1925 when the Imperial Palace decided to renovate the old meteorology station. Okawa let the program drop without a fuss. He didn't need the money—his job at the quasi-government think tank paid him comfortably—and he was already in the process of forming a new activist group more to his taste. His reputation as a philosopher-patriot had enough momentum to stand on its own.

ON FEBRUARY 11, 1925, the national anniversary of the founding of Japan, Okawa announced the creation of a group called Kochisha. He found a headquarters in Tokyo and opened branch offices around the country. He courted an audience with the same crowd of rising military officers who'd enjoyed his lessons at the College Dorm. There was a natural partnership there: most Japanese soldiers hailed from the struggling countryside and favored reform as a result. Meanwhile, Okawa saw these young men as the embodiment of the old samurai spirit he wanted to revive. He spent "an inordinate amount of energy and attention" satisfying this base and trying to expand it, his personal secretary later admitted. He started a monthly magazine called *Nippon*, or *Japan*, and seasoned its message to a military taste. Readership soon climbed to several thousand.

Okawa based Kochisha on seven lofty principles he hoped to anchor in the hearts of the Japanese people—hence its name, the Society of Heaven on Earth. To appreciate the sort of world Okawa envisioned, it's necessary to follow him up his theoretical stairway to heaven for a moment. Tenet Number 1 called for national reformation, as Okawa had been doing for years now. From there it was a short hop to Tenet Number 2: the establishment of a national ideal. To Okawa, achieving this ideal meant transforming each Japanese citizen into an ethical person. This ideal person should show reverence to God (by honoring their parents or ancestry, for instance), to man (by having compassion toward others), and to nature (by demonstrating self-discipline toward instinctual desires like food, money, and sex). Gather a bunch of ethical people into a distinct geographical space and you had the makings of a national ideal.

Even a country built around a national ideal had to follow a code of ethics itself. That's where the next three Kochisha tenets came into play. Tenet Number 3 called for "spiritual liberty" through a national education system that endowed each person with a basic level of thoughtfulness. Tenet Number 4 sought "political equality" with minimal laws and equal rights for all. Tenet Number 5 pursued "economic fraternity" by redistributing wealth so no one had to worry about anything except maintaining their own ethical lives. (This obviously wasn't capitalism, but Okawa argued it wasn't socialism, either, since those systems both cherished material goods more than his ideal society would.) When Okawa Shumei closed his eyes and dreamed of a "revolutionalized Japan," this is what he saw.

Kochisha Tenet Number 6 brought the process of national reformation around to his broader goal of Asian unity. All these aims culminated with Tenet Number 7—the "moral unification" of the entire world, and the endgame of Japan's heavenly mission.

In October of 1925, Okawa published a provocative little book that gave his followers a glimpse of this promised land. The work—called *Asia, Europe, and Japan*—prophesied another world war as a means of achieving this moral unification of East and West. In *Asia, Europe, and Japan,* Okawa intended to show that the whole of human history was a perpetual cycle of "antagonism, struggle and unification" between Eastern and Western civilizations. This recurring contest was not just certain but healthy; its upshot, Okawa believed, was a global harmony founded on the ideals of the winner. In a sense this clash of cultures was a brief necessary evil on the path toward a long great peace.

As Okawa saw things in 1925, this historical cycle of war was coming back around again. Tension between East and West had increased during the past century of imperialism. The West had gotten the better of the East until the Great War, but the ensuing Asian revival signified a simmering retaliation against Western domination. Soon the world would erupt in another great struggle. Only when the fighting ended would the long-awaited moral unification emerge. Okawa concluded:

> Now, East and West have respectively attained their ultimate goals. Indeed, they could no longer go any further if each pursues its own way. World history clearly shows that they have to unite in the end. This, however, can never be attained by peaceful means. In the shadow of the cold steel lieth Bliss Elysian. As history fully proves, in creating a new world, life-and-death struggle between the champion of the East and that of the West is inevitable.

Okawa believed the strongest representatives of East and West—Japan and the United States—would meet in this contest for global supremacy. With a colorful flourish he pointed out that the American flag emphasized stars while the Japanese flag centered on the rising sun. "Accordingly, it will be a war between Day and Night," Okawa wrote. "Japan's brilliant victory in the coming Japanese-American war means a bright dawn of a new world dispelling the dark mists of night." Since no one quite knew when this fight would occur, Okawa urged the Japanese people to get ready at once.

"It is entirely in the hands of Heaven to call you to that holy mission," he wrote. "Prepare yourselves every moment for that heavenly call."

OKAWA SHUMEI WAS hardly the only public figure suggesting that the United States and Japan might go to war in the early twentieth century. Talk of a military showdown went back to the Yellow Peril and the American nativist movement that lobbied hard against certain types of immigrants. Anxiety toward Asians was greatest in California, the place of settlement for most arrivals from the East. In 1906 the San Francisco board of education moved to segregate Asian schoolchildren under the pretense of "relieving the congestion" in public classrooms. The situation escalated into a diplomatic crisis. "The infernal fools in California and especially in San Francisco insult the Japanese recklessly," wrote President Theodore Roosevelt, "and in the event of war, it will be the Nation as a whole which will pay the consequences." The two countries reached an accord on immigration reform, but in 1907 Roosevelt sent the powerful Navy (dubbed the Great White Fleet) on a world tour to demonstrate America's military might.

New tensions arose after the Great War. Japan joined the peace talks at Paris as one of the world's five major powers. One of the demands it brought to the treaty table was a provision declaring racial equality in the charter for the newly proposed League of Nations. Tokyo leadership viewed the racial equality clause as essential to the "future interests of the Empire." Makino Nobuaki, the de facto head of the Japanese treaty delegation, tried to secure the clause without success. Several countries objected to it on the grounds that such a clause might be viewed as an open invitation for Japanese immigration. In the end the racial equality clause failed to receive the required unanimous approval. Emperor Hirohito later called this event a critical turning point on the path toward the Second World War.

To many Japanese this decision reflected a deep-seated racial prejudice toward Asians in general and the Japanese in particular. It seemed not only antithetical to the very purpose of the League of Nations but disrespectful toward Japan's rising position in the world. In February of 1919, as the racial equality clause was being debated in Paris, the Dark Ocean Society organized a conference of its supporters in Japan. Okawa Shumei joined the event as head of the Asiatic Association of Japan. Much of his subsequent disillusionment with the West can be traced to the proposal's failure. In *Asia, Europe, and Japan* he wrote that the League of Nations existed solely "to enable the Anglo-Saxons to be the permanent dominators of the world." (In an ironic twist, the United States never joined the League anyway.)

Cracks in the diplomatic bond between the United States and Japan spread quickly from there. The last straw for many Japanese came in 1924, when Congress drafted an immigration bill that excluded all Japanese aliens from entry into the country. Proponents wanted zero new arrivals; they refused even to issue the same quota that was in place for European immigrants, which would have allowed only 146 Japanese newcomers each year. The Japanese ambassador protested the bill, saying it would stigmatize his people and fearing the measure would have "grave consequences" for both countries. Senator Henry Cabot Lodge, a strong supporter of restricted immigration, interpreted the term "grave consequences" as a "veiled threat" of war—and pushed even harder for the bill to be passed. In April it was.

Protests erupted across Japan before President Calvin Coolidge even had a chance to sign the bill into law. Newspaper editorials considered the act a disgrace and declared a great race war imminent. Activist groups held public rallies full of incendiary speeches. Asianist sympathy rose. In May a Japanese man committed hara-kiri outside the old U.S. embassy in Tokyo, carving his abdomen crosswise then lengthwise with a six-inch dagger. A letter found near the body urged Japan "to avenge the insult embodied in the action of America." A few days later, at a rally of some thirty thousand protestors held by the Dark Ocean Society, the mob declared the indignity unforgivable, and called on Japan to initiate hostilities.

Reaction in the United States was mixed. Ten California newspapers explicitly supported Japanese exclusion, and the *Washington Post* also "applauded" the law. Other publications saw the act as a foreboding sign of things to come. The editors of *Life* magazine sent certificates to members of Congress "with best wishes for a Happy War."

These events formed the backdrop of Okawa Shumei's prophecy, in 1925, that the United States and Japan would one day meet in battle. The prediction marked the end of Okawa's ideological maturation and the beginning of his widespread influence. He'd reached the precipice of becoming what Allied prosecutors at the Tokyo trial later called the "foremost revolutionary intellectual in Japan from 1925 to 1945." That others were also entertaining the possibility of a great East–West war did nothing to reduce the significance of Okawa's heavenly mission. If anything it showed that he was not just spouting an extreme desire but articulating, more eloquently than most, a common despair.

THE POSSIBILITY THAT Okawa Shumei was not some great ideological villain, as the Tokyo trial suggested, but in fact a great ideological hero, as the Kenshokai seemed to believe, had been weighing on my mind for weeks by the time I took a bullet train south from Tokyo toward Fukuoka. The Tokyo trial view of history, championed by the West, considered Okawa's Asianism a mere pretext for the aggressive expansion that Japan pursued until its surrender in 1945. The sympathetic view, still endorsed by a (mostly) conservative subset of Japanese, held that Japan really did fight to unite and free Asia. Of course, there was room for a middle ground—Japan might have had legitimate gripes toward the West yet pushed its claim over Asia too far—but Okawa Shumei seemed planted at the poles of both good and evil. I wanted to know where he really stood.

I came to Fukuoka because if anyone could reconcile my problems with Asianism it was Christopher Szpilman. Few if any scholars are as knowledgeable about Asianism as Szpilman, who's a professor at Kyushu Sangyo University, and none have done more to introduce it to the English language. He's written biographical profiles of Okawa, Kita Ikki, and Mitsukawa Kametaro, and recently coedited a two-volume collection of primary Asianist documents. When I told Szpilman how helpful I'd found his work, he invited me to stay at his seaside apartment, where he lives with his Japanese wife, to discuss it further.

Part of the reason Szpilman has emerged as a leading mind on Asianism despite being a Westerner is that few Japanese have been willing to touch the subject since World War II. There's a general fear among mainstream intellectuals in Japan that if they study the doctrine they'll be aligned with its nasty wartime reputation. In Szpilman's case that's not a problem. No one could possibly mistake him for an advocate of Asianism. He considers the ideology to be basically "fraudulent," and says he studies it precisely to expose the error of its ways.

"To understand the past of Japan—ideological changes that shaped it and perhaps influenced in some way Japan's fate—it's important to get a full picture," he told me. "You cannot get a full picture if you avoid studying Okawa and others of that ilk who were influential at the time intellectually. In a way they contributed to the vision the Japanese had of themselves and of the world. That mission, let's say. Divine mission."

When we met, Szpilman was sixty-one and, in the last rays of daylight, looked a good bit like Ben Kingsley—an image assisted by his deep voice and British accent. He had a charming negativity and a sense of humor so dry it was sometimes hard to know when he was joking. (When I asked how he'd happened to study Japanese history, he replied that "it was obviously some sort of insane moment.") He mentioned Hitler a lot, no doubt a result of his father being Wladyslaw Szpilman, the Holocaust survivor whose memoirs were immortalized in the Roman Polanski film *The Pianist*. I kept waiting for him to bring up that connection, but he didn't.

Instead, we discussed the ideological standing of Okawa Shumei for several hours over hors d'oeuvres and dinner and wine. Szpilman thought Okawa might have held some genuine feelings toward Asian unity, but he found too many "idiotic inconsistencies" to take Okawa completely at his word. Take the time Okawa went to Hong Kong in 1921. The self-described warrior for Asia and enemy of Western materialism expressed no moral outrage at life in the British colony; on the contrary, he noted in his journal that he'd love to stay there for a few weeks "with plenty of money and have some fun." Then there was the section of his 1922 book *Various Problems of Asia in Revival* that considered Zionism part of the Asianism movement. When the book was reprinted in the late 1930s, with Japan and Germany then allies, Okawa conveniently took this section out—a sign that his great "mission" also had great flexibility. Then there were his friendships with the Indian rebels. Notice how Okawa didn't extend the same Asianist generosity to the people in Japan's immediate sphere of influence, such as China, Korea, or Manchuria. In those places it was very hard to discern attempts at Asian unity from efforts to secure Japan's own interests. India was farther away and therefore much less vulnerable to conquest.

If you gave Okawa Shumei enough credit for brains, which even his detractors did, then you had to imagine he was aware of the flaws in his ideology and chose to ignore them.

"So what was he, then?" I asked at one point.

"He's a talented writer who thought he knew which side his bread was buttered on," Szpilman said. "Having said that, I think there's a core of ideas he believes. He does believe in the deep cultural superiority of the Japanese."

This intense nationalism explained why Okawa, unlike some thinkers before him, tied the great Asianist mission so tightly to the rise of Japan. He had a sense that Japan was the perfect state because it was the only one that had been ruled by the same family—a divine family, so the legend held—since the beginning of time. If other countries only realized how great this virtue was, they would accept Japanese leadership in their own best interests; they would exchange Western imperialism for a kinder, more brotherly Asian guide. Szpilman told me some Asianists in Okawa's day even used the word *emperorization*. After expanding the great empire to all Asia, the divine mission would then turn its gaze on the whole world.

"Anyway, I really don't know what to say," Szpilman said, finally coming back to my question. "I think it's safe to say he wasn't a very consistent thinker, and there's a degree of opportunism. There's a core of ideas that he believed, nevertheless, and they were based in anti-Westernism."

By then it was the other side of midnight and I soon retired to my guest mattress in the living room. Before going to bed I looked around for a few minutes. There were two old maps of Szpilman's native Poland hanging on a wall, and a number of his father's classical piano compositions occupied the top shelf of a music cabinet. Szpilman hadn't mentioned his famous father all night. I suspect he could have made a big name for himself as a Nazi scholar, but he chose to study prewar Asianists because he thought they'd been ignored too long. ("It's not a particularly interesting motive," he admitted.) He certainly had the moral ground to portray someone like Okawa as an opportunist. That description went a long way toward explaining how Okawa could seem like a scoundrel to some people and a patriot to others. It also left me wondering, faceup in the darkness, whether Okawa had seen an opportunity to embarrass the West during the Tokyo trial and taken that one, too.

Chapter 5

╬═══╬

Loose Ends

Even during my years at medical school, the challenge of finding answers to the questions of how and why the body and the mind function, and especially how and why they malfunction, became a central interest for me.

—Daniel Jaffe, "Memoirs of a Combat Psychiatrist," ca. 1996

L IFE AFTER THE death of Harry Jaffe felt very unsettled to my grandfather. In early 1936 the family left Brooklyn for an apartment in the South Bronx. The place was so close to Yankee Stadium it was reasonable to joke about whether Lou Gehrig, who led the league in home runs that year, could hit a ball up to the front porch. The surviving children took turns driving out to Long Island to visit their mother at Louden Hall, where she was still being treated for schizophrenia. In this regard, as the family's own fledgling physician, my grandfather felt a unique responsibility. He was the only child in a position to offer an informed endorsement of her treatment course—or, if necessary, an informed dissent. It was a weighty obligation for someone still finding his own way through the world. He later described himself during this period as being at "loose ends."

In the fall of 1936 he returned to Washington for his third year of medical school. The facilities at George Washington University weren't much to write home about at the time. James Watts, a neurologist who joined the medical school faculty a year earlier, after working at the great New England medical institutions, formed a dim first impression of his new affiliation. As far as Watts was concerned, the X-ray machine at George Washington University Hospital was a better fit at the Smithsonian. If there was one department on the rise, however, it was that of mental health. The school employed one of the most popular neurologists in the country, and by far the most provocative: Dr. Walter J. Freeman.

Freeman was forty years old at the time and a touch over six feet tall, with a goatee and eyeglasses covered in scratches from a few too many close encounters with a microscope. On September 14, 1936, he and Watts performed the first lobotomy in the United States. The patient's name was Alice Hammatt. She was suffering from "typical agitated depression." Freeman and Watts made a pair of incisions in Hammatt's scalp, then drilled holes in her skull above the frontal lobes, then fed a wire through the white matter six times on each side using an instrument called a leucotome. The concept of the surgery was to sever the connection between the frontal lobe of the brain and other regions producing intense psychoses and neuroses. When Freeman and Watts stitched up Hammatt, an hour later, they'd not only altered one life but the entire course of mental health care in the United States.

My grandfather's initial encounter with Walter Freeman came just days after that historic operation. On September 26, 1936, he entered the medical school around noon and found a seat in lecture hall A. He took out a piece of three-hole notebook paper and a black pen and wrote "Neurology" at the top, underlined it twice, and boxed the name "Dr. Freeman" to the side. Like most students at the time, he supplemented his third-year, first-semester core neurology course with a voluntary weekend clinic led by Freeman and a colleague named H. D. Shapiro. September 26 was a sunny Saturday, with temperatures in the 70s, but my grandfather was happy to forfeit it for the pleasure of Freeman's lecture. Freeman was known to put on such a dazzling performance that many students brought dates.

Indeed, Freeman prided himself on being something of a pedagogical Barnum. His most beloved classroom feat was the ambidextrous chalkboard drawing: Freeman diagrammed the brain sections associated with neurological disorders, from the basal ganglia to the relevant lesions, using both hands at once. Guided by the philosophy that a teacher had to be interesting above all, Freeman left the textbook regurgitations to Shapiro and often conducted his part of the seminar by evaluating live patients. In one memorable case, he demonstrated a cisternal puncture—typically done with great care, since the cisterna magna is extremely close to the brain stem—by plunging a needle into a patient's spine without taking any measurements. "Awfully simple if it goes right—but simply awful if it doesn't," he said. Some people might have seen Walter Freeman as reckless, but to my grandfather he was fearless.

TODAY LOBOTOMY HAS a sinister reputation that, in many respects, it deserves. The person who rose from the operating table was not the same one who lay down on it before the procedure. "[E]very patient probably loses something by this operation, some spontaneity, some sparkle, some flavor of the personality, if it may be so described," Freeman and Watts once wrote. When measured against the suffering, however, many patients and their families considered it an acceptable—if admittedly desperate—risk. These were patients who'd spent years in the care of seasoned psychiatrists and exhausted all treatment options. They were doomed to live in an institution or to remain burdens on their families. Freeman and Watts called lobotomy an operation of "last resort" for people who would otherwise "have only pain and death to look forward to."

After her lobotomy, Alice Hammatt lost her fixations and lived outside of mental hospitals for five years before dying of pneumonia. Her husband later told Freeman that those had been the happiest years of her life.

The 1930s marked a bold new era of psychiatric treatment that exchanged the bleak passivity of the asylum for the hopeful action of alternative interventions. Lobotomy was seen as a potential savior for all kinds of patients enduring severe mental anguish. Freeman believed it might prove effective against agitated depression, acute anxiety, debilitating fixations, even schizophrenia. The latter disorder, in particular, had eluded clinical treatment for years. Schizophrenic patients typically presented with delusions and disordered thoughts. At the time, physicians fought the condition with a feckless arsenal of treatments: occupational therapy, lectures, irradiated milk, ovarian transplants, a strange procedure that replaced spinal fluid with horse serum, or simple vitamin C. Lacking better options, patients diagnosed with schizophrenia commonly made up 60 percent of mental hospital populations.

Freeman's Saturday clinic ran straight through the fall of 1936. My grandfather's diligent notes don't mention lobotomy, but everyone in America knew about the procedure come November. At a meeting of the Southern Medical Association in Baltimore that earned wide media coverage, Freeman described the novel surgery to the amazement of his colleagues. The announcement stirred a frenzy of debate. "Psychiatrists and brain surgeons stormed at each other concerning the good sense of Drs. Freeman & Watts's work," reported *Time* magazine. One doctor declared the surgery a historic example of "therapeutic courage." Adolf Meyer, the country's leading psychiatrist, called the work "very interesting" but advised caution. Many other attendees weren't so kind or noncommittal. Freeman defended his procedure in the strongest terms short of the word *cure*.

"I think we have drawn the string, as it were, of the psychoses or neuroses," he told the crowd.

Looking back at his medical school years, my grandfather wrote that his "central interest" at this time was "the challenge of finding answers to the questions of how and why the body and the mind function, and especially how and why they malfunction." In 1936 that interest matured into something closer to a passion. His notes from the Saturday clinic are among the few documents of his to survive—a fact that suggests the degree of Walter Freeman's influence on his professional development. An analytical mind like his own couldn't have helped but relate what he learned to his own life. It stands to reason that around this time he began to see his mother's illness not so much as a loose end but a knotted string, as it were, that might one day be drawn.

ONE DISEASE OF the nervous system received far more space on the pages of my grandfather's three-hole notebook than the rest: syphilis of the brain. Neurosyphilis is the advanced stage of the venereal disease by the same name. Today it's a medical footnote, largely eradicated thanks to antibiotics like penicillin, which enable physicians to treat syphilis before it reaches the brain. In the early twentieth century, however, neurosyphilis was a bold, all-caps, underlined medical heading. In his 1933 textbook on neuropathology, Walter Freeman called it "one of the outstanding problems in modern neurology." The statistics backed that assessment. Neurosyphilitic patients constituted a considerable share of all admissions to state hospitals; my grandfather's lecture notes from early 1937 put the figure at 10 to 12 percent.

Of all the disease variants, "general paralysis of the insane"—often simplified to "general paresis"—received the most attention. During onset, bacterial spirochetes pummeled the brain into a psychotic submission. Paretic patients suffered delusions and a general mental deterioration marked by confusion and incoherence. Many were bedridden and incontinent. (Walter Freeman, familiar with the disease from his time at St. Elizabeth's Hospital, once described those suffering from neurosyphilis as "emaciated patients bent like pretzels, covered with sores and stinking to high heaven.") General paralysis has drawn comparisons with modern AIDS: both have carried the stigma of sexual disease, both proved resistant to treatment for years, both were fatal. At the height of its impact neurosyphilis carried a swift terminal prognosis. If you had it, you had two years to live, at best.

By the time my grandfather went to medical school, however, neurosyphilis had earned a relatively promising outlook. A clear treatment of choice had emerged, called malaria fever therapy. Generally forgotten today, malaria therapy for general paresis was one of the great medical breakthroughs of the early twentieth century. Using a benign strain of malaria, doctors induced up to a dozen bouts of fever in paretic patients. The fever killed off the spirochetes, then the doctors killed off the fever with quinine. The method was far from perfect: it required early detection to work best and it could also only arrest the brain damage, not reverse it. Still, at its peak efficacy, malaria therapy pardoned half of all paretic patients from their two-year death sentence. Many were granted a complete return to normal life.

This revolution began with an Austrian psychiatrist named Julius Wagner-Jauregg. "By all accounts, he was not a friendly person, rather aloof, reserved, even austere," Walter Freeman once wrote of Wagner-Jauregg, whose clinic he visited in 1924. What nature withheld from Wagner-Jauregg in geniality, it granted him in perception. During his decades as a clinician, Wagner-Jauregg had noticed that psychotic patients occasionally improved after enduring a severe fever. His big break came while working at a psychiatric clinic in Vienna during the Great War. In June of 1917, Wagner-Jauregg took blood from a soldier admitted with malaria fever and immediately inoculated a paretic patient with it. By the end of the summer, he'd performed the same procedure on nine others. Six improved considerably, with two patients entering complete remission and resuming their daily lives as if nothing had happened.

Within a few years Wagner-Jauregg was finding significant recovery rates. Before long, the therapy had spread to most developed countries around the world. (The first hospital in the United States to use malaria therapy on general paresis was St. Elizabeth's, at least in the memory of Walter Freeman. In his unpublished autobiography, Freeman wrote that the very first malarial mosquito arrived at the hospital all by itself in a "ten ton truck.") Eventually the therapy settled at a success rate of roughly 50 percent, with 30 percent experiencing a full remission and 20 percent a partial one. In 1927 Wagner-Jauregg became the first psychiatrist to receive the Nobel Prize for Medicine.

The astonishing success of Wagner-Jauregg's work gave rise, in large part, to the entire family of aggressive mental health treatments. By exposing the vulnerability of neurosyphilis, malaria therapy inspired a sweeping "magic bullet" approach to neurology and psychiatry. Not that it was universally accepted. Some of the aspersions later cast on lobotomy were recycled criticisms of fever therapy, and

Wagner-Jauregg's Nobel was delayed for years because one judge considered it criminal to give malaria to someone already suffering from a disease. But in general the treatment inspired broad hope that psychotic illnesses could be arrested, and sometimes even eliminated, by procedures just waiting to be discovered.

My grandfather returned to New York in the summer of 1937 and filed away his notes on general paresis somewhere in the apartment that stood in the shadows of Yankee Stadium. The old scraps didn't betray his thoughts on either the illness or its relatively miraculous treatment. As an emerging clinician he might have taken the advance as a sign of encouragement. As the son of an institutionalized mother he might have seen it as a harsh reminder that there were plenty of afflictions out there eluding medicine's grasp. In any event, he'd snapped the knowledge into his mousetrap of a mind—capable of summoning it, for the rest of his days, whenever some patient presented the need.

ESTHER JAFFE HAD been discharged from Louden Hall just once since her husband's death. In January of 1937 her son Eli had taken her to an alternative healer described by her doctor at Louden, James Vavasour, as a "Christian Science practitioner." She was readmitted to Louden two months later without any signs of improvement. She looked "pale and undernourished" to boot.

Her condition must have been on my grandfather's mind during the summer of 1937. He spent part of his inheritance on a ten-week tour of his parents' native Russia. One day during this tour, he struck up a memorable conversation with another traveler only to realize this was George B. Hassin—the University of Illinois neurologist who'd written the other major neuropathology textbook in English of the time. It might have been nice to find a trip companion with similar interests. Then again, it might have occurred to my grandfather that he couldn't escape the subject of mental illness even when he traveled to the farthest corners of the world.

The tour ships were lined with chessboards. It was a trip to Russia, after all. Harry Jaffe had loved chess. He'd also loved his wife.

When he'd been alive, he'd never been willing to approve the use of any experimental treatment on her behalf. Maybe he figured he'd lost enough of her already and couldn't bear to risk losing it all.

My grandfather returned to New York Harbor aboard the SS *Batory* on September 3, 1937. Later that month he returned to Washington for a final year of medical school that included advanced courses in neurology and psychiatry. The great textbooks and lecture halls insisted the treatment of severe mental illness was less helpless than it once had been. Perhaps it was time to find out just how much less.

Over the summer the mental health community in Washington had acquired a new therapeutic crush. Insulin therapy, sometimes called "shock" treatment, was doing great things for a particularly difficult group of patients: schizophrenics. Doctors had treated these cases with everything from fever therapy to lobotomy without much success. ("Our chief failures were in the schizophrenics," James Watts later recalled.) In late summer Walter Freeman became the first physician in the Washington area to use shock therapy, and by mid-August hospital officials at St. Elizabeth's announced they would do the same.

The Jaffe children reached a consensus as well sometime that fall. In early November, Dr. Vavasour began insulin treatment for Esther Jaffe.

THE PIONEER OF insulin treatment was an Austrian Jew named Manfred Sakel, later called by some the "forgotten Pasteur of psychiatry." Insulin is a hormone that regulates the amount of glucose in a person's bloodstream; too much of it can cause a person to enter a hypoglycemic coma that doctors often called a "shock." Sakel grew familiar with insulin from his work with morphine addicts at a German sanitarium. In the course of giving insulin to patients, as a means of alleviating morphine withdrawal, Sakel at times mistakenly administered a bit too much and sent them into shock. The error was quickly corrected by delivering sugar to the system; to Sakel it was also educational. Patients that had been "restless" before the shock became rather "tranquil" after it, he wrote in 1933. By carefully controlling these shocks, Sakel believed, insulin might serve as a potential therapy for severe forms of psychosis, like schizophrenia, that caused great agitation.

Sakel made his first shock trial in October of 1933 at a Vienna clinic once headed by Julius Wagner-Jauregg. Before long, he was publishing encouraging results. In 1936 he immigrated to New York at the invitation of the state's commissioner of mental hygiene. He trained psychiatrists at Harlem Valley State Hospital and, in January of 1937, presented some of his results at a medical meeting in Manhattan. Those who'd witnessed the treatment recognized its "promise in bringing back to normality, at least in part, a considerable number of those for whom previously no such hope could be held out," reported the *New York Times*. Other papers ran headlines like "New Treatment Restores Sanity." People began to ask if insulin shock therapy could "cure" schizophrenia.

The typical treatment course of shock therapy in the late 1930s lasted anywhere from four to ten weeks. The first phase prepared the body for the jolt to come. Doctors injected the patient with a steadily increasing dose of insulin until they noticed the first signs of hypoglycemia. Once this shock level was established, the patient received a daily dose of insulin high enough to induce a coma. Each time the shock was achieved, doctors terminated the coma a few hours later by feeding the patient 400 cc of sugar solution through the nose. After the shock phase came a rest phase followed by a terminal phase, when very low doses of insulin were delivered. The procedure was staff intensive and costly: nurses had to maintain a vigilance over shock patients, and doctors had to prepare for potential overdoses that might require a swift termination.

When the therapy worked, it really worked. No one could say exactly why. Sakel himself acknowledged that he had found a treatment for schizophrenia before finding a cause; he called it the "wrong end of the right path." But the success stories didn't lie and neither did the improvement rates. "The mental changes that occur in a psychotic subject in the course of treatment are usually so surprising and dramatic that it is difficult to describe them accurately," Sakel declared in early 1937. Patients with schizophrenia often emerged from treatment with great insight into their illness, saying things like: "I know I had a lot of silly ideas, but they're all gone now." In one large survey of 1,039 schizophrenia patients in New York who received insulin shock treatment around this time, two-thirds showed some degree of improvement or recovered completely. For many patients, Sakel once said, the transformation after insulin shock therapy was "as though a cadaver were to awake."

Esther Jaffe's own awakening was not so sudden. The family quadrupled its weekly hospital payments to $100 throughout the course of her shock therapy but got few immediate results for the money. Dr. Vavasour terminated the shock treatment in late January of 1938 after about ten weeks. Esther's physical condition had improved—she gained fifteen pounds and looked healthier—but her mental state had not. A month later hospital staff caught her trying to strangle herself with a bedsheet. The records don't show whether the act was compelled by her delusions or by some small remaining part of her rational self that had been through enough.

That spring, while finishing up his medical education, my grandfather petitioned the Kings County Supreme Court in Brooklyn to adjudge his mother incompetent. Doing so would enable him to become her legal "committee," a role that would effectively put him in control of her personal affairs. He was resigned to believe, as he told the judge on May 3, 1938, that his mother's condition "will in all probability be permanent."

My GRANDFATHER GRADUATED from medical school in June of 1938 and got an internship at Queens General Hospital in New York. The family had moved again. The new place was just a block farther north of Yankee Stadium, but by this time the bat of Lou Gehrig had become too weak to pose a threat to the porch, even in jest. Whatever inadequacy my grandfather might have felt among the other interns from top-tier New York City medical schools didn't last long. On his very first day at Queens General—as he recalled, his very first *patient*— he made a diagnosis of amyotrophic lateral sclerosis. His peers were duly impressed. The illness was pretty obscure at the time, and would remain so until about a year later, when every baseball fan in the country learned about Lou Gehrig's disease (ALS).

The new graduate spent nearly the last of his inheritance on a Plymouth coupe and named it "Betsy" for a girl he liked. In early June he drove Betsy out to Louden Hall, on Long Island, and served his mother with notice of her competency hearing. Despite the nature of the visit, there's reason to believe it was a pleasant one. Following her attempted suicide, Esther Jaffe's health had taken a brighter turn in response to the insulin therapy. In a sworn statement to the court, Dr. Vavasour said his patient remained delusional at times but was far more cooperative and tidy than she'd been in the past. She even joined the others for meals in the dining room. She still wasn't quite fit for life outside an institution, but her mental state had shown some clear improvements.

Others also noticed the changes. A court-appointed guardian who interviewed Esther around this time reported that she responded to questions with "fairly rational" answers. "She also exhibited a well developed sense of humor and considerable astuteness," the guardian said in a sworn deposition. The guardian didn't believe Esther was schizophrenic—though it's unclear what basis he had to issue such an opinion—and was relieved to find that Dr. Vavasour had changed her diagnosis from catatonic dementia praecox to "a chronic delusional form of psychosis." Esther still wanted to go home, and still lacked much insight into her own problem, but she at least recognized that Louden was a hospital for the sick. These were all steps in the right direction.

On June 20, 1938, the family made their way out to Brooklyn for the hearing at the Kings County Supreme Court. There a jury heard my grandfather's petition for committee status, information gathered from interviews with the other children, and Dr. Vavasour's sworn statement. At three in the afternoon the jury returned a decision that Esther was unfit to manage her own affairs. A week later the Honorable George E. Brower appointed my grandfather as his mother's official committee. He'd finished medical school but was still just twenty-four.

His first actions were to ensure his mother's long-term financial security. He opened bank accounts and managed her finances. He kept track of every single transaction, and occasionally proved it to the court with a signed inventory. At the end of July he drove Betsy-the-car out to Amityville again to visit his mother. We don't know if she was aware of the court decision by then—or whether she would have cared. We don't know what they discussed, either. We do know that he brought her food like his father used to do. Except instead of real food he brought ice cream.

It may well have been his final trip to Louden. By August his mother was functioning at a nearly normal level. She was taking good care of herself, keeping her things tidy, eating on her own, staying in shape. "During the last three months of this patient's residence she held the improvement noted previously following her insulin therapy," wrote the chief of the sanitarium, John Louden. "She ceased her talk which was of a paranoid nature and was not so impetuous in regard to going home."

No sooner had Esther stopped begging to go home than her persistent wish was granted. On August 23, 1938, she was discharged to live at the family apartment in the Bronx. Her eldest daughter, Bea, would take care of her. (My grandfather had his internship; little Sylvia was away at Cornell; Eli—her favorite child—had run off to the Dust Bowl in the service of civil rights.) My grandfather issued Bea a court-approved allowance of $65 a month from Esther's account to support the new arrangement. With that, his mother came home again, more than eight years after the day he'd returned from school to find her gone, this time with the promise of staying.

SHORTLY AFTER I turned thirteen my grandfather gave me a book titled *Grandfather Remembers*. The point of the book is for grandfathers to share basic personal details with their progeny: the family tree, their own childhood and adolescence, their marriage and career, etc., all the way up through the birth of little me, the reader. It's fill-in-the-blanks style—sort of like Mad Libs for memories—a format engineered to eliminate any withholding of information. My grandfather still found a way to avoid answers. An example, from page 17: "I was told I resembled . . .": *"I was not told."*

I can speculate as to what my grandfather felt during the years he lost his mother to madness then essentially swapped roles with her and became the parent himself. I can guess how frustrating it was to spend the little free time he had as a medical student dealing with lawyers and judges and hospital administrators. I can suppose how much resentment he'd felt toward his older brother, Eli, who got most of Esther's love when they were children and then left him most of her troubles in his young adulthood. I can imagine his angst at trying a risky new treatment, the dread that maybe his father would not have approved, and the raw terror when he heard how it had nearly killed her. I can picture him awake at night. I can speculate about these feelings, but I can't know for sure.

I was not told.

No one was told. I found that out when I visited Wilma, Eli's widow, at her home in Oakland, California. Wilma grew up in Oklahoma. She met Eli when he scampered off to the Dust Bowl in the late 1930s. We spent a couple days talking about the brothers. That is, Wilma spent a couple days talking and I spent them listening. She told me how, even as a grown man—and a professional psychoanalyst at that—Dan would never engage his brother in a discussion of what it had been like, on an emotional level, to live in that household as children.

"The thing is, they were on different wavelengths," Wilma said. "Eli did not want psychological jargon. He wanted closeness. And if Eli asked a question he got what he used to refer to as 'the hyphenated words.' Mother-nurturing. All the Freudian words. That's not what you want. Dan had to distance himself from the feeling a little more, I think. For whatever reason, he had to distance himself."

I'd hoped to find some letters there. I knew the brothers had kept up a correspondence. The FBI, which had followed Eli for decades, had intercepted one letter and sent it to me as part of an information request. (Eli lived a very active life. In Oklahoma he was arrested for

being a communist and put through the state's infamous "Red Trials"—chronicled in a book from 2007 called *Books on Trial*—before
being acquitted. He was chums with Arthur Miller and, as a result,
once soaked in a hot tub with Marilyn Monroe. The FBI kept tabs on
his friendship with Woody Guthrie. At his funeral, Pete Seeger played
"To My Old Brown Earth.") Hoping to find more letters, I spent an
hour going through Wilma's cellar until I stumbled upon a thin file
labeled "Dan."

I ran upstairs and opened it frantically. The messages didn't seem
right. I ran over to Wilma and asked her about it. It was some other guy
named Dan. Some guy from Oklahoma. Some guy I never met but will
never forgive.

"There's a lot of stuff that's missing that I know must have happened," Wilma said. "Eli may have gotten rid of them as a protection to
Dan. There was a lot of witch-hunting going on for a lot of years."

Which left us with only her stories. Of two days' worth, one stands
out above the rest. It took place years after the war. Eli and Wilma were
living in Hyde Park, New York, and my grandparents were up visiting from Washington. My grandfather was completing his training as
a psychoanalyst, which required being analyzed himself. He was going
to the analyst but refusing to talk. Wouldn't answer the psychiatrist's
questions. Just lay mute on the couch as if it were a blank space in
Grandfather Remembers.

Eventually the psychiatrist said to him: "If you learn more about
yourself by not talking than talking, it's all right with me."

"Do you think the psychiatrist was giving him an out?" I asked
Wilma.

"I hope the psychiatrist was doing something to make him aware
that you can learn about yourself by what you refuse to do," she said.
"It makes good sense to me. For a grown man who's read as much
Freud as he did, and done as much work himself, to not understand
that you're learning by withdrawing—to me it was eye-opening.
Isn't it?"

I didn't answer, and Wilma kept talking.

"To me it was where I related to him the most," she said. "I thought,

He's recognized it, he's admitting to it. He was always very careful. A psychiatrist has to be careful. Don't they?"

I didn't answer that one, either. Guess it runs in the family. He had his loose ends, and now we have ours.

MY GRANDFATHER REMAINED an intern at Queens General Hospital through the end of 1939. He made his rounds at the hospital then drove back to visit his mother in the Bronx. He kept Betsy very busy. As it happened he kept a number of Betsys busy—most of them nurses from the hospital. (He later advised my father and uncle, both of whom became doctors, not to get married before their internships.) What he called the car in the presence of these new dates, or whatever happened to the original Betsy, is nowhere recorded. Otherwise my grandfather recalled only a single notable instance from that period: that evening at the hospital in September of 1939 when he and some others huddled around a radio in the interns' quarters, listening to news about Hitler's invasion of Poland.

When the internship was over my grandfather called up Walter Freeman. It was 1940 now. He was still intent on specializing in neurology, and a lot of doctors he knew were getting postgraduate training in the basic science of their field. Freeman had already appointed a fellow for the year but agreed to find a spot in his neuropathology lab if my grandfather would do the fellowship gratis.

My grandfather considered the offer for a little while. On the one hand, the move back down to Washington would wipe out the last of his inheritance. On the other hand, this was Walter Freeman. The "godfather of lobotomy." A man who at the very least knew lots of people. Working in his lab wouldn't be an expense so much as an investment. My grandfather agreed to do the fellowship without pay. He left New York once more for Washington—this time, more or less, for good.

Freeman and my grandfather collaborated on a research project soon after their reunion. They prepared a case study for a poorly documented condition called subacute bacterial endocarditis. Considering all the advances going on in mental health at the time, the work wasn't terribly exciting. Still, it was a professional step. On October 3, 1940, my grandfather presented the profile at a meeting of the D.C. Medical Society, and afterward it appeared in a medical journal. His name was getting out there.

That same month he met a girl named Caroline Raifman through an old classmate. She, too, was from New York, and lived in town working for the Census Bureau. One day, he worked up the courage to dial her and she answered the phone. "What makes you think I want to meet you?" she asked. "Because I'm a nice guy," he replied. That was more or less the tone of every conversation they'd have for the next sixty-some years.

In fact their initial attraction was the car named Betsy. Each needed to visit a long-distance love interest in New York on occasion, and Betsy provided a means to get there. Before long they realized they enjoyed the journeys more than the destinations, and decided, in a manner of speaking, to take a shortcut. They courted for the next seven months. He proposed on a drive back down to Washington from her family's home in Brooklyn.

The proceedings took place on May 14, 1941, a few days after his twenty-seventh birthday. They settled into an apartment across from Gallinger Municipal Hospital in southeast Washington. He'd completed his fellowship with Walter Freeman by then and was working as a chief neurology resident at Gallinger. He was making $25 a month.

"When I married him he had a hundred dollars left in the bank," my grandmother later recalled.

"I had a car," he replied.

"And a car," she conceded.

Walter Freeman threw the new couple a cocktail party. By then he was a certified medical star. In late May the *Saturday Evening Post* ran a long story about lobotomy below a huge picture of Freeman and Watts. The writer witnessed a surgery and recorded the dialogue. "Who am I?" Freeman asked the patient in the middle of the lobotomy. "William Randolph Hearst," was the reply. It wasn't so crazy a response if you really thought about it. That summer Joe Kennedy enlisted Freeman and Watts to perform a lobotomy on his daughter Rosemary. Its failure did nothing to dampen Freeman's rising celebrity.

The military wanted a part of him, too. In mid-1940, sensing an international conflict in the offing, the surgeon general had asked the National Research Council to form a number of specialized medical advisory committees. There was a neuropsychiatry committee headed by Winfred Overholser, the superintendent of St. Elizabeth's Hospital, and under that a personnel and training subcommittee with Walter Freeman as one of its members. The personnel subcommittee met several times over the course of 1941 to fulfill its charge: determining which young mental health professionals might best serve their country in time of war.

My grandfather's name begins to appear on lists attached to correspondence between the personnel subcommittee and the surgeon general on March 5, 1941. He was assigned a rating of IV—the lowest on a scale in which a I was a nationally known specialist (Walter Freeman was a I) and a IV was a young doctor still requiring professional supervision. In time the IVs would make up the class of combat psychiatrists assigned to each military division. In prewar 1941, however, the surgeon general's primary goal was screening out enlistees who might develop into mental cases. A War Department circular from March 12, 1941, provided summaries of various psychiatric disorders, from dementia praecox to neurosyphilis, and explained its need for medical officers capable of recognizing these problems during brief evaluations.

My grandfather's loose ends not only felt more tied by the end of 1941 than they had just a few years earlier—they were actively *being* tied, in ways he of course didn't know. He would find out soon enough. On the first Sunday in December the young couple hopped into the car named Betsy and headed toward Virginia to visit some relatives. They were driving on the 14th Street Bridge when word of Pearl Harbor crackled through Betsy's speakers.

"The car radio interrupted the tranquil music program to blare out the shocking news report," my grandfather later recalled, "and we realized that we were in fact in another world war."

Chapter 6

Showa Restoration

The necessity for a thorough and general renovation of
the state was keenly felt, and the loud cry for the Showa
Restoration has been repeatedly heard.

—Okawa Shumei, *Japanese History Reader,* 1935

I N EARLY 1931 a typical day for Okawa Shumei, then in his mid-
forties, began with a horseback ride. One of his favorite geisha
girls, Yoshimaru, usually met him at the stables. He liked to complain to her, and there was a lot to complain about. Japan was entering
the sixth year of the Showa emperor, Hirohito, but the start to this era
hadn't been promising. The country was facing what Okawa called the
"Manchurian problem." China was enveloped in a civil war that threatened Japanese territory in Manchuria. The United States, whose relations with Japan were still strained from the 1920s, seemed prepared to
back China if tensions boiled over. Russia looked poised to exploit the
chaos by pushing its way into Manchuria, too. To top it off, Japanese
politicians jousted for power rather than uniting to resolve the situation. The morning exercise probably helped Okawa's hangover—he
drank heavily during this period—but there was still a lot weighing on
his mind.

On this typical day in early 1931, after his ride, Okawa made his way to the East Asian economic think tank where he'd worked for more than a decade. There his thoughts no doubt turned to Manchuria once more. The region of Manchuria occupied a special place in the hearts of Japanese. They'd been granted territorial privileges in the southern part of the region after their glorious victory over Russia back in 1905. Having a stronghold in Manchuria extended Japan's footprint on mainland Asia beyond Korea. The region was rich in coal reserves, raw materials, and agricultural goods. Like many Japanese at the time, Okawa often referred to Manchuria as his country's economic "lifeline."

The very rope of this lifeline was the South Manchurian Railway company. Run by the Japanese government, the company managed roughly seven hundred miles of prime track, as well as the adjacent properties that stretched through more than a hundred cities. Development along the railway offered a bounty of industrial opportunities and an outlet for Japan's growing island population. Hundreds of companies, and hundreds of thousands of Japanese, settled there during the decade. The South Manchurian Railway moved these goods and people on its freight and passenger trains. The railway zone was so vital that Japan protected it with a military force of roughly ten thousand troops called the Kwantung Army.

Initially hired at the think tank for his knowledge of India, Okawa Shumei had spent his years there studying the broader history of Western colonialism. During this time he'd noticed that modern colonial charter companies advanced the political goals of their home nation far more than historical ones had; they functioned not only as businesses but as de facto governments. The details of colonization absorbed Okawa: he served as a professor at Takushoku University, a Japanese school for colonial studies, and in August of 1926 he was awarded a law doctorate from Tokyo University for his colonial research.

"For a nation to keep going as an independent country in this present age," he later said of his thoughts at the time, "she should possess a territory that is at least self-sufficient."

In Japan's case, as far as Okawa was concerned, that territory was clearly Manchuria. For the past several years, however, Japan's hold there had been slipping. Its influence hit a low point when the Manchurian warlord Chang Hseuh-liang spurned an alliance with Tokyo for one with the Nationalist Party that was advancing east through China. Okawa had tried everything in his power to stem the tide: he'd written letters to the Japanese foreign ministry, he'd even traveled to Manchuria to negotiate with Chang Hseuh-liang himself. Yet still, the fools in the Japanese parliament didn't seem to appreciate the gravity of the situation. Liberals followed a "weak-kneed" diplomatic approach favored by the West after the end of the Great War. Conservatives were a bit more proactive, but they hadn't been nearly forceful enough for Okawa's taste. Japan's lifeline was drifting into the ocean; it was time to retrieve it, not argue over how.

So on a typical afternoon in early 1931, as Okawa left the think tank for home, he thought that salvaging Manchuria with such a divisive and impotent government was "absolutely hopeless." He thought of the potential economic damage for Japan if nothing was done. He thought of the Japanese soldiers who'd spilled blood on Manchurian soil during the war with Russia. He thought of how victory there had announced Japan's arrival as the savior of the East. He thought that Japan stood no chance of winning the inevitable "life-or-death" battle with the United States without Manchuria's natural resources. He thought the empire's great mission was becoming nothing but a great wish.

Above all he thought "this cannot be left alone," meaning the time for thinking was over, and the time for action had arrived.

On a typical evening in early 1931, agitated from another day of government inaction, Okawa Shumei attended a meeting of the Sakurakai, a secret group of young military officers as hell-bent on political reform as he was. The group's 150 or so members were formulating a plan to resolve the Manchurian problem and, in the process, set Japan on a stable political course. "It was our belief that if things were left alone Japan would shortly decline as a nation and as a people," recalled one Army major who attended the very first Sakurakai meeting, "and it was our desire to do our utmost to cleanse politics in Japan and to renovate the country." To achieve these aims they were willing to resort to violence. Sakurakai meant "Cherry Society"; the name referred to the cherry blossom, the traditional symbol of the Japanese warrior, a flower that burst into life and later fell to a pure death.

By the early 1930s, Japan had become a fertile ground for extremist groups like the Cherry Society—particularly those made up of disgruntled soldiers from the ideological right. Beyond the security of Manchuria, they had any number of reasons to lose faith in the country's direction. The global market crash of late 1929 hit Japanese soldiers worse than most, since the military consisted largely of young men from the ailing countryside. Their indignation toward Western-style capitalism and big business rose as agricultural regions and common laborers suffered. Extremists on the left existed, too, in the form of a communist movement, but they were arrested en masse in the late 1920s. And so 1930s radicalism was associated almost exclusively with conservative military patriots.

This faction placed blame for the country's condition on Japan's party politicians. Circa 1930, Japan was still getting used to its relatively young parliamentary system; frequent corruption scandals—like the one in spring of 1930, when forty-nine politicians were indicted for bribery—made party members seem out for themselves. Extremists believed these selfish officials were acting against Japan's best interests, and, beyond that, against the emperor's true wishes.

Still, these radical ambitions might not have erupted without the London Naval Conference of 1930. There, Japanese delegates reached an arms accord with four other world powers that disappointed the country's military-minded conservatives. (Naval leaders had wanted Japan's battle fleet to be 70 percent as strong as America's, but the ship ratios established at the conference missed this mark by a minuscule margin.) These opponents felt the London treaty submitted to the West, crippled Japan's military standing, and challenged the emperor's authority over national defense. When Prime Minister Hamaguchi Osachi got parliament to approve the treaty, the vocal opposition transformed into violent outrage. Hamaguchi was attacked by a young right-wing extremist that fall, and months later died of his wounds.

Revolution was now in the air. Okawa and members of the Cherry Society discussed plans to overthrow the government and place militarists in charge. Many of these young officers saw Okawa as a natural philosophical leader. They knew his ideas through the Kochisha activist group and its publications, such as the journal *Nippon*. (After the London treaty, Okawa wrote in *Nippon* that the United States intended to wedge itself into East Asia and that Japan must make "the U.S. realize, at an opportune time, that it cannot accomplish its ambition.") Others knew his books. The aforementioned Army major remembered reading Okawa's *Various Problems of Asia in Revival* five or six times. Another Okawa work, published in early 1930, suggested that soldiers were better suited than party politicians to lead Japan because they reflected the country's noble samurai heritage.

They named their radical plots for government reform in honor of the Showa emperor: calling it the Showa Restoration.

On a typical night in early 1931, after a Cherry Society meeting, Okawa and his closest friends frequented the brothels and teahouses of Tokyo. From the civilian side, there was Marquis Tokugawa Yoshichika (the final lord of the famed shogun line that had ruled Old Japan) and Shimizu Konosuke (a tough guy and muscleman). From the military side, working for the Army General Staff, there was Lieutenant Colonel Hashimoto Kingoro (a founder of the Cherry Society and a great believer in the great Asianist mission) and Colonel Shigeto Chiaki (who agreed the key to securing Manchuria was reforming the Japanese government). Together this clique poured sake and tickled geisha and whispered revolution and generally roughhoused their way into the wee hours.

Okawa's favored haunt was a place in the Tsukiji district called the Kinryutei Inn. Its proprietor, a Madam Ohashi, later said Okawa often showed up after revolutionary meetings to see his best geisha—a plump beauty named Fumimaru who had the look of a French doll. (Their bond was such that when Okawa died decades later, she died three days afterward.) When Okawa got drunk, he became a completely different person, according to Madam Ohashi. The contemplative philosopher in him disappeared, and the passionate patriot emerged. As the nights got long the talk of action got loud and loose.

Eventually Okawa Shumei found his way home from these typical days in early 1931. Inebriated, charged up from the teahouse chatter, and eager for emotional release, he sometimes threatened his wife, Kaneko. As a former geisha herself she must have been accustomed to rowdy behavior, and after six years of marriage she certainly knew what to expect from her husband. But he'd become an even worse drunk than normal and was beginning to frighten her. He came at her at times. "I would run away to keep from being hurt when he had these dangerous spells," she later recalled. In early 1931 she just thought the alcohol was making him act "like a crazy person," but looking back later on, with some distance and perspective, she began to think that maybe something else had been wrong with his mind.

ONE NIGHT HASHIMOTO and Shigeto divulged that even higher-ranking officers than themselves sympathized with the general idea that the Japanese parliament "should be crushed." That news was the final nudge the Cherry Society needed. On February 7, 1931, at around three in the afternoon, a group of young officers met at Shigeto's home to outline a real coup d'état. Okawa Shumei was not at the meeting, but he'd pledged to recruit civilian support for any rebellious action that might unfold. Encouraged by these developments, the group deliberated throughout the day. By midnight a clear plot had taken shape.

The coup would take place on March 20 to coincide with a highly anticipated debate in parliament over a new labor bill. A civilian mob under Okawa's direction would bombard the prime minister's residence and the headquarters of both political parties. The bombs were practice explosives, capable of emitting only smoke and noise; nevertheless they'd spread commotion throughout Tokyo. Afterward, the mob, roughly ten thousand strong, would march on the parliament building in Tokyo accompanied by a band of guards armed with swords. (Most of the plan's surviving details come courtesy of Major Tanaka Kiyoshi, a Cherry Society member who prepared a full accounting of the events in January of 1932, after leaving the military.)

An assembly of troops, consisting mainly of Cherry Society members, would halt the mob under the pretext of protecting the parliament. At that point a high military leader would demand that Prime Minister Shidehara Kijuro and his cabinet resign. (Shidehara had been serving as interim premier since the attempt on Prime Minister Hamaguchi's life.) "The Nation is now confronted with a grave situation," the leader would state. "We request that proper measures be taken." General Ugaki Kazushige, the sitting war minister, would then form a new cabinet around himself—by virtue of an imperial sanction secured, somehow, before the coup's execution.

"We didn't intend to destroy the Diet completely," Okawa later recalled, referring to the Japanese parliament by name. "Our idea was to set up a new political power and form a cabinet centering around the army."

The final task of presenting the plan to War Minister Ugaki fell to Okawa. The two men had met five or six years earlier, likely when Okawa ran the Daigakuryo academy for young patriots. Major General Koiso Kuniaki, head of military affairs for the General Staff, arranged a reunion for February 11. The date held great symbolic significance: it was the anniversary of the founding of Japan. Most Cherry Society officers believed that, deep down, Ugaki wanted the same type of reform they wanted. Getting his direct endorsement to overthrow the very cabinet in which he served was another matter altogether.

One can picture the excitable Okawa growing animated as he spoke to the war minister about the "really scandalous" state of Japan's political parties—his long arms keeping time with his points, cigarette smoke clouding his thick glasses and dark eyes. He explained that a popular movement had been initiated to "take direct action" against the government. He asked if the Army might conveniently "overlook the matter" on Ugaki's command—meaning ignore the mob marching on the Diet—rather than intervene and destroy the coup's momentum.

The men left the meeting with different impressions of what had

transpired. When asked about it several months later by a high political aide, Ugaki said he called the idea "outrageous," refused a request
to supply the imitation bombs, and generally dismissed Okawa on the
spot. Okawa, on the other hand, came away thinking Ugaki was on
board. He "expressed in very strong words his indignation at party politics," Okawa later recalled. The fact that Ugaki had agreed to meet at
all said *something* about his true thoughts. Whatever was really said that
evening, Okawa heard a tacit approval for the Showa Restoration.

He delivered the encouraging news to Hashimoto that same night.
Boosted by the blessing of the war minister—real or perceived or
somewhere in between—Okawa and the others pushed forward with
their plan to overthrow the Japanese government.

MAJOR GENERAL TATEKAWA Yoshitsugu of the General Staff helped
them acquire the bombs. Tatekawa introduced Hashimoto to the head
of the Army infantry school, who issued a transfer slip for three hundred imitation shells—the type used for artillery practice. Hashimoto
arranged for muscleman Shimizu Konosuke to receive the bombs during an exchange at the Shimbashi train station. The shells were covered
in paper so the drop could occur right on the platform. Shimizu took
the bombs home for safe storage. That left little to do but wait.

This task proved harder than the others. By late February, the fellowship was eroding. Koiso, who'd arranged the meeting with Ugaki,
lost his resolve. Several other top leaders reversed course on the plan,
too. Tanaka, the would-be informant, was upset that the plot focused
on the *destruction* of the old government but not the *construction* of a new
one. He didn't feel comfortable including nonmilitary participants—
especially "a man like Dr. Okawa."

For his part, Okawa did nothing to alter this low regard. He and
Shigeto indulged in "extravagant pleasures" on a nightly basis, Tanaka
recalled, and acquired a reputation for bragging a bit too boldly about
their plans in the presence of the geisha girls. Concern rose when
Okawa staged a rehearsal for his mob, in early March, and gathered
only a few thousand followers. It became clear to Tanaka that "such a

plan as mobilizing 10,000 men was nothing but a mere fantasy," and others agreed.

As the date approached Okawa must have sensed the plan was falling apart. Frantic at the prospect of failure, he tried to set things right from the top down. On March 6, 1931, he composed a note for War Minister Ugaki imploring him "to accomplish the great work of the Showa Restoration." Okawa concluded with a furious call to action:

> If you stand up with a belief that never hesitates, filled with patriotic lamentation, and warm yourself with dedicated blood, forgetting immediate trivial matters, thinking of great things only, and bravely stand and commit yourself to the great cause of your Emperor and Fatherland, men of the same mind would respond to you wherever they are, and a great thing would certainly be accomplished. The time is just ahead for a grand mission to descend on you. . . . Let the Imperial dignity be uplifted within and without the country and let the time come soon, even one minute quicker.

Okawa's desperate effort evidently had the opposite effect. Ugaki later claimed he hadn't realized the severity of the plot until he received this alarming note, at which point he made every effort to dismantle the operation. That explanation smacks of self-preservation—especially in light of their meeting the previous month—but Okawa's latest words clearly shook the war minister's nerves. In mid-March, word came down from Koiso that the coup had to be aborted.

Okawa was not so easily beaten. A day or two before the scheduled date of action, he and Shimizu showed up unannounced at Ugaki's home. Koiso turned them away from the front gate, but before leaving, Okawa made it clear that he intended to execute his part of the plan with or without the military's support. The threat was not an empty one: Okawa and Shimizu still had possession of the imitation shells. A band of ruffians, storming the streets of Tokyo with smoke and noise bombs to aid their anarchy, would be quite hard to disperse in peace.

Koiso sought help from Marquis Tokugawa, Okawa's close friend and drinking companion, and the one person who might keep him at bay. On March 19, sometime in the late afternoon, Tokugawa drove to the Tokyo bureau of the economic think tank where Okawa worked. Sure enough, Okawa was sitting there with Shimizu still hashing out the plan. Tokugawa tried to reason with them. He said the coup was certain to fail and questioned the honor of acting in a fit of passion.

"Now, more than ever, endure as much as possible, and with patience and prudence wait for another opportunity to arrive," said Tokugawa, according to his diary entry for that day.

Okawa had never been one to second-guess a decision. Turning back now might have felt dishonorable. So Tokugawa appealed to Okawa's sense of loyalty. He said that even though he disapproved of the plan, he was willing to stand by his friends. He would go through with it, too, and he would even "die with them," if that's what Okawa wanted.

Something in the words, perhaps the way they echoed the code of the samurai, pierced Okawa's emotional side and reached his thoughtful one. He agreed to let the March coup die a quiet death. When the decision was made the three men clasped hands, and wept.

IN LATE MAY of 1931, Okawa made his way to the Japan Young Men's Hall, in Tokyo, to give a lecture on the "Manchurian problem." Nearly a hundred Cherry Society members filed in to listen. The content of his talk almost certainly previewed that of an article he would publish on the subject a month later. In the article, he offered several familiar arguments for a strong Japanese presence in the region. Some were historical (Japan legitimately won interests there in the Russian war), some social (Manchuria remained Japan's economic and cultural "lifeline"), some Asianist (Japan's mission was to lead East Asia in peace). He no doubt told the crowd at the Young Men's Hall something he soon put down in writing: that the time for resolving the situation by "negotiation, compromise, or diplomacy had passed."

Okawa Shumei would have cut quite a figure in front of an audience at the time. His height gave him natural command of a room and his slightly un-Japanese features gave him an exotic look. His big glasses gave a veil of wisdom to the dark eyes and deep voice that might otherwise have assumed an air of villainy. He'd been a commanding orator since his high school days, when he'd concluded that inflammatory speech was more persuasive than a measured recitation of facts. Since then he'd only enhanced his philosopher-patriot style. As a doctor of colonial studies his rhetorical flourishes carried a scholarly ballast; as a known participant in revolutionary plots they also carried a vision of action.

By the middle of 1931, Okawa had been giving public talks about Manchuria for two years. Back in 1929, during his ongoing frustration with the Japanese government, he'd launched a lecture tour intending to deepen public understanding of the so-called Manchurian problem. (To facilitate this effort, Okawa had convinced the state-owned South Manchurian Railway to drop control of the economic think tank where he worked, relieving him of any government ties.) Okawa thought that if Japanese politicians wouldn't address the Manchurian problem on their own, perhaps the Japanese people could compel them.

During that time he and a team of fellow lecturers had appeared in nearly a hundred places across Japan. Okawa distributed pamphlets to the people, showed them films, and proved adept at shifting his tone and topic to suit a particular audience. The general populace received one presentation, for instance, while military personnel and local leaders received another. Whatever his crowd, Okawa impressed listeners with two key points: first, that finding a solution to the Manchurian problem was vital not only to Japan's economic interests but also to its very *existence,* and second, that the government's weak attempts to solve the problem placed this national existence in jeopardy. The people ate up every word. Okawa roused the audience from his lecture platform until they were ready to brave fire and water for their motherland.

By August of 1931, the speaking crew had toured every prefecture in Japan from Hokkaido in the north to Kagoshima in the south. Okawa's words had reached the ears of nearly a hundred thousand Japanese. That month the tour brought Okawa to Oshima, northernmost of the Izu Islands that stretch south from Tokyo Bay into the Pacific. Mitsukawa Kametaro, his old friend and activist partner, joined him on the trip. There was probably nothing remarkable about the lecture itself—nothing that would distinguish it from the dozens of others Okawa had given in the preceding years. Mitsukawa did find one statement interesting enough to document. Okawa told the audience that "a shocking incident will occur in Manchuria" sometime in the next two months.

SIX WEEKS LATER, on September 18, 1931, the so-called Manchurian Incident did indeed occur. It was perpetrated by the Kwantung Army charged with protecting Japan's territorial interests in southern Manchuria. Just past ten in the evening, a Kwantung officer planted forty-two yellow packages of blasting powder on the tracks of the South Manchurian Railway and lit the fuse. The resulting explosion didn't cause great damage—a 10:40 train to Dairen passed over the blown-out rails without stopping—but the Kwantung Army blamed the blast on local Chinese forces. Then they picked a fight, just as they'd planned to do all along.

In a short time the fight escalated into a full-scale invasion. Within days the Kwantung forces had seized several key cities. Back in Tokyo, Prime Minister Wakatsuki Reijiro, supported by the liberal foreign minister Shidehara Kijuro, tried in vain to contain the conflict. There was little they could do. Kwantung leaders ignored calls from government officials to suspend the hostilities, and instead expanded their presence. They felt certain they were doing what was best for Japan. By the end of autumn, the capitals of three Manchurian provinces were under Kwantung control.

The incident put Japan on notice with the West. Even before it became known that Kwantung soldiers had instigated the incident, not everyone was buying the Japanese side of the story. One American political cartoon—eventually awarded the Pulitzer Prize—showed a Japanese arm holding a torch made of international peace treaties. An American who'd been in Manchuria at the time of the incident, and later wrote about it for *Harper's* magazine, felt certain Japan was in the wrong. He later called the incident a reminder that, in a civilized world, militaries "may be used, if necessary, to enforce, and not to direct, national policies."

What made it difficult, if not impossible, for Japanese leaders to regain control was the enormous support for the Kwantung forces coming from the Japanese public. Editorial writers accepted the ruse that Chinese soldiers had set the bomb. Even the liberal English-language *Japan Weekly Chronicle* agreed that "some bellicose Chinese" probably initiated the incident. Crowds jammed a public park in Osaka for nights on end to cheer news footage of the fighting. People everywhere clamored for an aggressive response.

Such national pride over action in Manchuria was precisely what Okawa Shumei had hoped to achieve with his two-year lecture tour. After the incident, he fanned the fury by renewing his public campaign. In a two-month blitz tour he and his fellow speakers scattered to fifty places across Japan. Back in 1929, when Okawa had made his first speeches, the military had rebuffed his requests for official support; now he spoke with full cooperation of the Army General Staff. The military even sent lecturers to join the propaganda troupe.

The Manchurian Incident is often considered the beginning of a so-called "fifteen-year war" that ended with Japan's surrender to the Allied forces in 1945. In retrospect, the event triggered a slow descent into global isolation. The parts of Manchuria severed from China by the Kwantung Army were given a new name: Manchukuo. While Japanese leaders insisted Manchukuo was independent, the Western world saw it as a puppet government. The League of Nations launched an investigation of the incident, which came down, in due time, against Japan. In response, Japan withdrew from the League, signifying an intention to distance itself from Western-style diplomacy. The Japanese public didn't just embrace this decision—they hailed it.

The exact nature of Okawa's participation in the Manchurian Incident remains unclear. He certainly knew Itagaki Seishiro and Ishiwara Kanji of the Kwantung Army, who engineered the incident, but his privileged insight into their plans might have been limited to the basic fact that *something* would happen. At the same time, his fingerprints were all over the affair. One of his protégés served as liaison between the General Staff in Tokyo and Itagaki in Manchuria. The think tank where he worked supplied high-quality reports that Ishiwara referenced during his years of preparation. Okawa may not have been the "civilian brain" of the incident, as the *New York Times* crowned him during the Tokyo trial, but without question he was its civilian voice.

That all came later on. Many years would pass from 1931 before the world understood the full significance of the Manchurian Incident, and many more went by before its gravity would infect Okawa's own conscience. That time did come. In the moment, though, the blood on the tracks in Manchuria was barely dry before Okawa turned his attention, once more, to the revolution still brewing in Japan.

By LATE 1931, high Japanese leaders were starting to appreciate the ferocity of extreme reformist aspirations. Concern reached all the way up the social ladder to Japan's top advisor to the emperor, Prince Saionji Kinmochi, and Saionji's secretary, Harada Kumao. As Kwantung forces expanded their presence in Manchuria, Harada briefed the parliament on the urgency of the revolutionary movement. "This Manchurian incident has its prelude in the Army coup d'etat," Harada said, referring to the aborted March uprising. "The fact that their plot has succeeded in Manchuria will surely give a certain element of the Army the confidence that they can also do the same in Japan, and there lies the real danger."

If Harada had a tunnel into the minds of Japan's leading radicals, and a tiny envoy to travel it, he could not have offered a more accurate description of their thoughts. Another military coup, this one scheduled for late October, was already being hatched. This one took the March plans to new heights. The cabinet would be massacred, Tokyo police headquarters would fall under siege, various newspapers would be coerced to support the cause, and a new military-led government would be appointed—with the job of finance minister going to Okawa Shumei. The general idea, Okawa later recalled, was to "crush them and set up anew a powerful political power capable of undertaking the solution of important problems."

Military police busted the October plot shortly before its execution. A few punishments were meted out—Hashimoto was detained for twenty days—but disciplinary measures generally ignored the systemic nature of the problem. Since the conspirators had been motivated by the desire to improve Japan, some officials even excused the plot as misguided patriotism rather than criminal treason. Okawa Shumei went unpunished, yet again, but this time not unnoticed. In early November the legal authorities placed him under close watch.

For a brief period he tried to play it straight. In February of 1932 he created a new activist group called Jimmukai. (Legend holds that Emperor Jimmu, the mythical founder of Japan, issued a proclamation in 660 BCE calling for his rule to expand to the "eight corners of the world.") Heavily supported by young right-wing military officers, the group started a popular campaign for government reform similar to Okawa's public lecture tour on Manchuria. Jimmukai patrons wanted political dissent minus the illegal violence. Okawa laid low at his home in Kamiosaki, a neighborhood between the Shinagawa and Meguro wards of Tokyo, just a bit south of the city center.

The passive approach quickly proved at odds with his rising cult attraction. Around this time, a pair of naval sublieutenants named Koga Kiyoshi and Nakamura Yoshio paid Okawa a series of visits to chat about the current state of Japan. The two young officers were part of yet another group of disaffected soldiers who valued the ideas of Asianism and social reformation that Okawa had been championing for years. They believed it was Japan's duty "to lead the Asiatic peoples against the White's invasion of the Orient," as one comrade put it. They were enamored of Kita Ikki's 1919 book on political reconstruction. They thought political parties and financial powers spelled the demise of Japan and that only young soldiers, embodying the country's true spirit, could save it.

On March 27, 1932, Koga and Nakamura came to Okawa asking for some guns and some money. The duo had coordinated a "peasant revolt" that would involve mobs of farmers marching on Tokyo from the countryside. The plan reminded Okawa a bit of his own reform efforts. He recognized that certain public figures might be harmed in the uprising, but he saw those casualties as a small price to pay for the great reward of Showa Restoration. Over the course of three exchanges, from April 3 to May 13, Okawa gave his new friends five pistols, 125 rounds of ammunition, and ¥6,000—the "sinews of the action," he later called these gifts.

That action proved no mere peasant revolt. On May 15, 1932, the extremist crew led by Koga and Nakamura wreaked havoc on Tokyo. One squad invaded the home of Prime Minister Inukai Tsuyoshi and shot him in cold blood. Two other squads ran amok in the city. They bombed the headquarters of Inukai's political party and the metropolitan police office. They assaulted utility stations to cut off the city's power supply. They attacked a high official called the Lord Keeper of the Privy Seal. They scattered pamphlets declaring their discontent with political parties, capitalist interests, "effeminate diplomacy," military disarmament, and a depressed countryside. "Destruction is needed for the future construction," their manifesto concluded. "Arise and build the true Japan."

With their itinerary complete, the soldiers surrendered to military police. Rather than commit ritual suicide they wanted to explain their reasoning to the world through a trial.

The May 15 Incident, as it became known, caused surprisingly little damage aside from the death of Prime Minister Inukai. Of course, the authorities could not ignore the murder of a sitting premier like they had dismissed the thwarted coups that preceded it. In half a year of tailing Okawa, justice officials had seen enough to link him to the uprising. A month after the event, they called him on the phone to come in for questioning.

Okawa said he was leaving that evening on a trip to northern Japan, but that he'd be happy to come in when he returned. When he hung up, the police sprang into action. Ten detectives swarmed Tokyo's Ueno Station to capture Okawa before he boarded his 10:00 p.m. train. They arrived to find Okawa surrounded by twenty associates who'd come to see him off. The detectives didn't want to cause a huge scene, so instead of taking Okawa at the station they got on the train with him. They rode for a while, about an hour, keeping an eye on him.

One can imagine Okawa sitting there, likely in a smoking car, his round glasses pressed toward the window, perhaps contemplating where the choices made over forty-five years had brought him. At Tsuchiura Station the detectives made the arrest. Evidently he'd been too distracted to notice them.

"If I was to be arrested," Okawa told them, "I wish it had been carried out at my home."

His home was their next stop. What the authorities discovered there spoke to the considerable extent of Okawa's influence. The papers seized at Okawa's residence proved "beyond all vestiges of doubt that Okawa moved in the best circles of nationalist intrigue," in the words of a U.S. Army report published after the war. He had correspondence with high officials, high-ranking military officers, soldiers involved in the March and October coups, and general sympathizers of Japanese political reform. He had investigative reports on power stations and newspaper offices throughout Tokyo. He had documents whose mere titles suggested a detailed knowledge of the Kwantung Army, the Manchurian Incident, and, of course, the Showa Restoration.

FOR SOMEONE ASSOCIATED with the cold-blooded execution of a head of state, Okawa Shumei must have felt rather charmed the next few years of his life. The guards and prison warden at Ichigaya penitentiary gave him preferential treatment. They let him bathe first and wear a large straw hat to conceal his face. He studied calligraphy and took some time, at age forty-five, to write his memoirs. He called the work "Bonjin-Den"—or "Autobiography of a Mediocre Man"—with a hint of self-deprecation. The manuscript ran to six hundred pages. When it was done Okawa decided he'd written it for himself and, with the warden as witness, destroyed the entire thing.

A general empathy was extended to all the perpetrators of the May 15 Incident. In the weeks and months before their trial, hundreds of thousands of petitions for clemency flooded the courts from all over the country. War Minister Araki Sadao received a petition enclosed with nine pinky fingers—one from each of nine people willing to meet their death so the plotters could live. Araki himself, as well as Navy Minister Osumi Mineo, publicly praised the accused for their "pure" patriotic motives. When the trials began that support only grew. The accused soldiers used the stand to preach an "eloquent indictment of the evils of capitalist democracy, in terms more severe than anybody before had dared to use," according to a writer who attended the sessions. The villains had started to seem like the victims.

The civilian trial, which was separated from the military proceedings, didn't begin until September of 1933. Okawa's day in court arrived that November. He spoke in detail about the March and October plots (during which time, in keeping with a government-imposed gag on the subject, the courtroom was closed so as not to "disturb the public order"). On the twentieth day of the trial he addressed the May 15 Incident. Far from denying complicity, Okawa gave the impression that his actions reflected a personal ethical code that remained uncompromised.

"It is a matter of course that I shall be punished under the stipulation of the law," he told the court in a final statement. "Even at present, however, I am quite convinced that the motive was right and the result has been favorable for the sake of Japan."

Judge Kamigaki Shuroku did not agree. In early February of 1934, the court sentenced Okawa to fifteen years for aiding and abetting murder and violating a weapons law. The prison term was as harsh as Koga's sentence and five years longer than Nakamura's. Okawa appealed.

At the new trial he stressed that his good intentions should receive more consideration. His lawyers emphasized his intellectual contributions to society—his books, his scholarly achievements, his philosophies about the East. They argued that the esteemed Dr. Okawa certainly deserved a lesser punishment than the ringleaders, and that any punishment he *did* receive should not disturb his "sublime and noble" soul. They reasoned the state would be committing a crime of its own in crushing "the man of extraordinary genius as well as the patriot of noble character."

Judges in the higher courts turned a friendlier ear to this line of thinking. On November 9, 1934, the Tokyo appeals court reduced the sentence to seven years. Okawa announced he would appeal once more—tellingly, so did the prosecution—and three days later he made bail on the condition that he disband the Jimmukai. At a third trial his sentence was reduced once more, down to five years, which he was allowed to postpone for health reasons until the summer of 1936. He used the reprieve to visit his mother in Sakata. He also published a book called *Japanese History Reader*. The "loud cry for the Showa restoration has been repeatedly heard," he wrote, and the "righteous demands" of the people will overcome anyone who tries "to oppose or subdue them."

On June 16, 1936, Okawa finally reported to Toyotama Prison. He slept in a wooden cell about the size of four tatami mats. He ate three bowls of rice with a vegetable side each day. He wore a persimmon-colored uniform whose thickness changed with the season. His only companion was a sparrow chirping outside the cell. His voice grew hoarse from lack of use, so the guards let him shout during his daily half-hour stroll in the yard.

In a strange way he felt liberated by his imprisonment. In mid-August he noted in his diary how ironic it was that he no longer had to work for the necessities of life, from food and shelter to tissues and notebooks, and instead could read any book he wanted. "Prison life is something far removed from supposed life in hell," he wrote.

Free from everyday burdens, he spent time exercising the genius his lawyers had fought to preserve. He expanded his doctoral study of colonialism back to the days of Columbus, da Gama, and Magellan. Every morning and night he worked on this history until the manuscript ran to five thousand pages. (He later published parts as a book titled *A History of Modern European Colonization*.) He argued that the lessons of Western colonialism were particularly instructive for Japan— "the one and only powerful and important non-white nation"—as it tried to establish an empire "on loftier foundations." In a memoir of his prison terms, he wrote that he found it easy to focus on his studies because he felt unencumbered by "moral pains."

"Even I, not the most stout or virile of men, could survive in prison, so don't let anyone tell you that things are *too* severe," he wrote.

In July of 1937 Marquis Tokugawa Yoshichika and Shimizu Konosuke met to discuss their old comrade's sentence. Throughout the summer into the fall they lobbied for Okawa's release. They knew people. Some of these people, like many Japanese by that time, had sympathetic ears. Some were quite powerful, too; after all, Tokugawa was a member of the House of Peers, the appointed upper house of Japan's parliament. He asked Justice Minister Shiono Suehiko for a personal favor, and was granted it.

On October 13, 1937, Okawa left jail a free man. For his role in the death of a sitting premier, Okawa Shumei had been detained about two years and had served an official sentence just shy of sixteen months. "As I recall these years," he later wrote, "I find not a speck of dark memory."

ON OCTOBER 14, 1937, the day after Okawa Shumei came home from prison, a minister in the Japanese cabinet gave a speech about the full-scale war that had erupted between Japan and China a few months earlier. "As one who believes in the mission of the Japanese people, explaining our vital role in facilitating the opportunity for Asia's ascendance is a task after my own heart," the minister said, referring to the conflict as a "holy war for the reconstruction of Asia." Such words might as well have come straight from the mouth of Okawa himself. The idea of uniting Asia behind a great divine mission, once confined to the margins of Japanese society, had entered the light as a mainstream pursuit.

The country that greeted Okawa upon his parole in late 1937 looked an awful lot like the one he'd envisioned upon his arrest in mid-1932. Party politics had been replaced by a so-called "national cabinet" filled with nonpartisan bureaucrats. Prime ministers could no longer rise to that position without explicit Army approval.* Military expen-

---

*Case in point: the Army rejected General Ugaki Kazushige as possible premier in 1937, despite his public popularity, as payback for having abandoned the coup of March 1931.

ditures rose sharply, and extreme right-wing organizations proliferated. Japan's presence in Manchukuo, née Manchuria, was secure; its days in the League of Nations, that instrument of Western rule, were done. Contemporary writers debated whether Fascism had arrived, per se, but no one confused this new system for the democracy Japan had worked toward for so many years.

Meanwhile, Okawa found himself something of a celebrity. In April of 1938, six months out of jail, he and Marquis Tokugawa formed a social club they called the Yamato Society. The name Yamato referred to the native Japanese race; the group's thirty-seven members saw themselves as the last scions of proper Japan. They were joined by the likes of Shiratori Toshio, ambassador to Italy, General Matsui Iwane, commander of the Japanese forces in China, and General Tatekawa Yoshitsugu, a high-ranking cohort from the days of the Showa Restoration. They gathered in various homes and public halls across the city to discuss the war with China and consider the best direction for Japan. Okawa shed the last of his roguish associations and settled into elite company.

Before long, Okawa's presence had pierced the most exclusive circles of government. He hosted a celebration for Itagaki Seishiro upon his promotion to war minister in the summer of 1938. He attended social gatherings with Tojo Hideki, vice minister to Itagaki and a rising military star in his own right, and considered him a close friend. "We were on the very best terms," Okawa later recalled. He persuaded an admiral to join the new cabinet of Baron Hiranuma Kiichiro in early 1939. Japanese leaders knew Okawa's name whether they liked him or not. Prince Saionji, the country's top imperial advisor, said, "Fellows such as Okawa Shumei are absolutely no good," as a way of expressed frustration at the company kept by many Japanese leaders around this time. Okawa was an intellectual star and a notorious convict in one.

His connections propelled his career. Okawa received a professorship at Hosei University, in Tokyo, and returned to his old economic think tank in an advisory capacity. He became head of a special boarding school that recruited twenty middle-school graduates from around the country. The war ministry gave ¥150,000 to start the school and the foreign ministry gave ¥50,000 a month to keep it running. The academy was devoted to the tenets of Asianism; its aim, according to Okawa, was to prepare Japan for leadership of East Asia. Every now and then one of Okawa's powerful friends would give the students an encouraging lecture; Shiratori, Itagaki, Matsui, and Tojo were frequent guests. People called the academy Okawa Juku—the University of Okawa.

Home life settled down a bit, too. He and Kaneko had a young live-in maid but no children. Their chance had passed; Okawa was in his early fifties now, and his wife was only two years younger. Instead, his fatherly instincts drew him closer to his Okawa Juku students. The academy was based in Meguro, just a short walk from Okawa's home, and every morning he gave the students a quick talk. He wrote them graduation poems, too. Sometimes, after a night of drinking, he'd stop by the school and have the headmaster let him into the sleeping quarters so he could watch them in the darkness, as he might his own kids. They were his philosophical progeny, and for a man of the mind that was enough.

An entirely new audience warmed to his Asianist ideology. A rush of Pan-Asian societies emerged—some supported by leading government and military figures. Old books that had sold mostly to extremists were devoured by the greater populace upon reissue. Okawa's survey of Japanese civilization, updated to include a discussion on the ongoing war in China, became a smash bestseller under the new title *2,600 Years of Japanese History*. Okawa argued that the Chinese misunderstood Japan's "true intentions" in East Asia. What Japan wanted was a local partnership based on shared Asian ideals—not imperial conquest. The Japanese had only resorted to arms because China needed to "reexamine her attitude" toward Japan's great mission. He considered the war "the first step in the recovery of all Asia, and this in effect will mean the restoration of the world." It was the same type of thing he'd been saying for years, only now people were really listening.

THE TENETS OF Asianism ultimately put Japan on a collision course with the United States. American officials saw Japanese actions in East

Asia as proof of imperial desires, while Japanese leaders saw them as a defense of their interests and a pure pursuit for cultural unity. The U.S. ambassador in Tokyo, Joseph Grew, marveled at how many Japanese bought into the Asianist rhetoric that Westerners found so sanctimonious. (They're "astonishingly capable of really fooling themselves," Grew wrote.) In 1936, President Franklin Roosevelt warned Japan of abiding "the fantastic conception that they alone are chosen to fulfill a mission," but after the war in China broke out the following year, the Japanese were singing the same tune, with diplomat Matsuoka Yosuke telling a group of journalists that Japan was fighting "simply for her conception of her Mission in Asia."

With the rise of Konoe Fumimaro to prime minister in 1938, Asianism graduated from a popular idea into national policy. First, Konoe outlined a plan for a so-called new order in East Asia. He called on China and Japan to clasp arms, along with Manchukuo, and forge a political and economic bloc on the strength of their Asian heritage that would stabilize the region and, ultimately, the world. Little by little, Japan's expanding presence in East Asia came into conflict with America's own interests in the region. The U.S. government asked manufacturers to stop exporting material to Japan that might aid an attack on civilian populations. In December of 1939, President Roosevelt pushed for the expansion of this "moral embargo" to cover even more of the iron and steel business.

The two sides took things up a notch in July of 1940. Konoe's second administration, now with Matsuoka Yosuke serving as foreign minister, pressed Asianist policies harder by calling for a Greater East Asian Co-Prosperity Sphere. The idea was an Asian union formed by concentric circles: Japan at the core, surrounded by an inner ring of Manchukuo and China, and an outer ring of the Dutch East Indies, French Indochina, Thailand, and other nations of the Pacific. The United States, meanwhile, ordered a naval fleet to Pearl Harbor, and escalated its sanctions on oil, scrap iron, steel, and other war materials. Nevertheless, by mid-1941, Japanese officials behind the scenes were agreeing to secure their new Co-Prosperity Sphere, if necessary, through force.

Throughout that year, Japan advanced into East Asia apace with its broadened concept of Asian cohesion. Western scholars traditionally argue that policies like the New Order in East Asia and the Greater East Asian Co-Prosperity Sphere were hollow inventions—strategic justifications invented to legitimize goals of military conquest. That conclusion has plenty of basis. The ongoing war in China had become a severe drain on Japanese resources, particularly oil, and the nations of East Asia offered considerable reserves. Ideas of Asian brotherhood and colonial freedom formed a convenient moral pretext for cooperation, and an ostensibly nonaggressive one at that. Some Japanese leaders certainly exploited Asianist thinking for just this purpose.

At the same time, at least for some Japanese, Asian unity remained an honest (if naive) motivation. Asianist concepts offered a comforting explanation of a terrifying time; as a result, many people took them at face value. "In retrospect, such slogans are looked upon with disdain and people would say it was mad to have thought that the rest of the world would understand," the poet Yoshimoto Takaaki later admitted. "But as ideals, in principle, the 'construction of the Greater East Asia Co-Prosperity Sphere' and 'the liberation of East Asia' were not inherently evil notions." Rhetoric aside, many Japanese felt justified to do what the United States had been doing for years. Matsuoka Yosuke, who gave many talks during this period at the Asianist academy run by Okawa Shumei, once compared Japan's situation with the Chinese to old American tensions with Mexicans and Indians.

That's not to say all Japanese leaders wanted war, but time and again they proved unwilling to set aside their vision of Asia to avoid it. Many felt encircled by what some called the "ABCD powers"—America, Britain, China, and the Dutch—and believed the only way out of this political stranglehold was to fight. None were willing to meet the chief demand of the United States: withdrawal from China. In mid-October of 1941, now into his third cabinet, still unable to ease the global tensions, Konoe resigned. War Minister Tojo Hideki became the new premier. Tojo was the one figure who might control the military and still make a fresh push at peace negotiations. Then again, his Asianist outlook clouded his judgment. At his formal ceremony, Tojo affirmed that Japan saw the new order in East Asia as part of a greater step toward world peace.

By early December, all hope for such a peace had been abandoned. Tojo struck first, and with a horrible vigor. The Japanese calendar read December 8, 1941, when fighter planes stormed Pearl Harbor. That same day, in a coordinated assault on the Pacific, Japanese forces attacked the Philippines, Malaya, Hong Kong, Thailand, and Midway and Wake islands. News vendors on city street corners rang little bells for a special edition. At noon NHK broadcast the official declaration of war. The Japanese airwaves soon swirled with patriotic songs. Newspapers soon described the fighting as "the great moral and cultural revival of the East" and "full freedom for Asiatics." The government gave the conflict a name: the Greater East Asia War.

These words, bouncing between mouths and ears on the streets of Tokyo in December of 1941, no doubt sounded familiar to Okawa Shumei. He wasn't the most influential figure in Japan during the run-up to global war, but as his country took those final fateful steps, enough truly important figures shared his mind-set that he didn't have to be.

DURING MY VISIT to Sakata, Okawa Kenmei told me a story he'd heard about how Shumei had spent his days leading up to Pearl Harbor. Someone recalled that Shumei had waited by the telephone for President Roosevelt to call, hoping to be the person who helped Japan avert total war. The story seemed a little absurd, but then again lots of what Okawa Shumei did over the years seemed a little absurd, so I asked Kenmei if it was true.

"Who knows?" he said. "Maybe he'd lost it by then."

I didn't pay much mind to this brief unverifiable anecdote at the time, but I was reminded of it a few weeks later, after a conversation I had with a Japanese historian named Awaya Kentaro. Awaya was a professor emeritus at Rikkyo University, and considered one of the world's leading experts on the Tokyo trial. My translator, Chiaki, and I met him in a crowded café in suburban Tokyo. Awaya lit up a Mild Seven cigarette as soon as we sat down, and I handed him a copy of my grandfather's examination of Okawa Shumei by way of an introduction. In response, Awaya slapped the air as if it were Tojo's head.

"People still question whether that was his play or a real insanity," he said.

"What do you think happened?" I asked.

"Depending on who you address the question to, you get a different answer," he said, dragging on the Mild Seven. "He was sane during the interrogation process before the trial started. Then, after he was excused from the court, he regained his sanity and translated the Koran. So some people think he faked insanity."

"What do *you* think?"

"It's very difficult to say," he said.

I got the feeling Awaya hadn't finished his thought, but then our drinks arrived and we got sidetracked, and spent much of the afternoon discussing the trial itself. Awaya has argued, in his decades of work, that the trial's legacy still influences Japanese society (much in the way, it struck me, the Civil War still influences the United States). On the one hand, he's argued, those who reject the trial—insisting, as Okawa Shumei would have, that Japan acted with a pure motive for liberating Asia—represent a dangerous sort of cultural amnesia. On the other hand, those who blindly accept its outcome, believing a "criminal militaristic clique" of Okawa and company led the country into aggressive war, can avoid feeling responsibility for going along with the times. All those people in the crowds who cheered Okawa's lectures about the Manchurian problem, for instance, had some part in the general empowerment of Japan's divine mission. Both sides, said Awaya, continued to complicate Japan's relations with its neighbors in East Asia, especially China.

Awaya drank his coffee in five minutes and spent the rest of our conversation sipping water and stamping out each Mild Seven cigarette half an inch above the filter. He wore his light jacket the entire three hours we sat there, and kept his arms crossed for much of that time, too. I asked if he thought Okawa was as influential to Japan's imperial rise as the Allied prosecution later argued.

"The prosecutors indicted Okawa because they figured he was the one who founded this ideology," he said, referring to Asianism, "but there were many others who talked about it. So there are many others to be blamed."

I told him I'd met several people who didn't think what Okawa did was a crime. He said he thought Okawa probably felt the same. Then he returned to the idea of Okawa faking his insanity, almost out of the blue.

"It was just like a cartoon," Awaya said of the slap. "So some people still wonder whether or not he was mentally ill at that time."

A few minutes later I asked once again what Awaya thought really happened on that wild opening day of the Tokyo trial.

"I don't know," he said. "Nobody knows."

"But you've read the reports. What do *you* think?"

"Well, if I have to say, I've recently been feeling that Okawa might have put on an act."

"Why do you think that?"

"Because the timing is too perfect."

I thought about Awaya's theory for a while after I left the café that day. It wasn't the first time I'd heard it. The timing of Okawa's breakdown—sparing him from the trial itself as well as prison time or worse—was as perfect as it gets. But maybe it just seemed that way because Awaya and others were looking at the curious event in isolation. If you looked at it in another context, as the action of someone who once waited like a crazy person for FDR to call him, the behavior took on an entirely new meaning. What I hadn't considered up to that time was how one might see Okawa's courtroom behavior not as a perfectly timed moment of madness but as the low point on a long downward slope—rather like Japan's decision to attack the United States. Maybe he'd been slipping toward insanity for years, slowly and imperceptibly, the way a minute hand moves on a watch, camouflaging his odder moments under a general guise of eccentricity. Maybe he'd lost it before the war had even begun. I'd never heard anyone suggest this possibility, and if Awaya's own research on avoiding responsibility among the Japanese populace was correct, there was an obvious reason why. If Okawa was a bit crazy before the war, then that meant the country that adopted his ideas must have gone a bit crazy, too.

Chapter 7

╬══╬

The Making of a Combat Psychiatrist

And remember—the essence of our job is to help and treat the individual. To do this, we often have to curb our impulse to kick him instead.

—Captain Daniel S. Jaffe, 97th Infantry Division,
October 9, 1944

THE FIRST LESSON that should have been learned from the Great War was that many men would break. America's armed forces suffered one psychiatric casualty for every four physical wounds over the course of the conflict. The "fifth man," some called him. The military had tapped Thomas W. Salmon, the same physician who'd created psychiatric services for immigrants at Ellis Island years earlier, to establish a mental health program for American soldiers heading overseas. "The extent of these casualties is almost beyond belief," Salmon wrote in June of 1917, upon reaching Europe in advance of the U.S. troops. "I have not yet had access to the official records but apparently the neuroses constitute one of the most formidable problems of modern war."

In a typical case of "shell shock," the term of choice during the Great War, a parade of stressors chipped away at a soldier's stability. Days under fire, nights in a foxhole, little food and water, very little sleep. Then an artillery shell would explode nearby, maybe tossing him to the ground or killing a buddy, and something inside snapped. By the close of the conflict a clear relationship had been established between the intensity of combat and the rate of mental breakdowns. In early 1918 a military psychiatrist saw eighteen cases of shell shock during a full six weeks of low battlefield activity. Then he saw fifty-two cases during a harsh four-day attack, and forty-three more during a rough two-day raid.

Shell-shocked soldiers became noticeably delusional and confused. Some presented with uncontrollable twitches. Some stiffened into fearful statues. Some had haunting visions of the carnage. Some lost memories, or control of their emotions, or motor skills. Some showed a severe startle reflex whenever a door slammed shut, or a plate hit the floor, or a chair toppled over. Often these wounds followed a soldier home from the war. One anonymous soldier, writing in the *Atlantic Monthly* in 1921, wished he could convey to the public "how dreadfully alone a shell-shocked man can be, even though surrounded by those who love him most."

One glimmer of hope during the Great War was the realization that mental casualties who received urgent treatment near the front lines had a good chance of recovering. At first, American soldiers were evacuated hundreds of miles to the U.S. Army General Hospitals positioned far behind the front lines. In severe cases they returned stateside on a hospital ship. This delayed treatment gave the disabilities time to set in and enabled patients to embrace the ailment as a ticket home. On the contrary, soldiers who received hot food, rest, and reassurance close to the lines often made quick and complete recoveries. The best care occurred within a few hours of onset and "within the sound of artillery," wrote Salmon.

In January of 1918 the American military created the position of division neuropsychiatrist to deliver mental treatment on the front lines. These early combat psychiatrists used methods that were as simple as they were effective. They were stationed in frontline triage areas, as opposed to traditional hospitals, to give shell-shocked soldiers little chance to get comfortable outside the trenches. They emphasized the honor of battle and reminded patients that their buddies were still out there fighting. They showed pictures of German prisoners to evoke patriotic responses. Soldiers suspected of malingering were given awful jobs, like digging latrines, to discourage any trickery. The numbers testified to their success: anywhere from 65 to 85 percent of soldiers treated within days of their breakdown returned to combat.

"In hospitals close behind the lines there is still the atmosphere of the front and a mental tone which comes from mass suggestion of men striving shoulder to shoulder," wrote one military psychiatrist at the time. "Out of danger, far from the front, perhaps among hero-worshipping friends, the invalid is unavoidably conscious of himself more as an individual and less as a link in the battle line."

After the armistice, many military psychiatrists—Salmon among them—suggested that only mental weaklings with underlying emotional instabilities had broken down in combat. This thinking emerged from the fact that not all mental casualties in the Great War had been alike. Some soldiers had survived the entire contest with their wits fully intact. Others had cracked after suffering physical injuries, usually concussions, that manifested in nervous symptoms; the term "shell shock" fit these cases well. A third group had broken during artillery fire despite suffering no discernible physical harm (with a subset breaking before they even reached the combat field). Rather than "shell shock," Salmon preferred to call these strictly psychological cases "war neuroses."

The concept of "war neuroses" implied that only those soldiers emotionally predisposed to mental breakdown would actually break down. This thinking held that any neurotic tendencies concealed in the comforts of civilian life would be exposed under the peculiar stresses of the military. "It is believed rather to be a psychological result from disharmony with new and rigid conditions which the neurotic, who is so intensely individualistic, finds it impossible to adapt himself to and so breaks down," wrote Pearce Bailey, who directed military psychiatry alongside Salmon during the Great War. Officials thought they'd discovered a basic law of military psychiatry: stop individuals with mental instabilities from entering the service, and you'd stop soldiers from suffering mental wounds on the battlefield.

In the immediate aftermath of the Great War, military leaders paid little attention to *any* of its mental health lessons. A military medical manual published in 1937 devoted just one of its 685 pages to mental health. Toward the late 1930s, as the prospect of another global war became distinct, military consultants made a critical mistake: they ignored what they'd learned about treatment on the front lines and instead pushed an aggressive stance toward screening out the so-called weaklings. If civilian psychiatrists could eliminate psychoneurotic individuals during enlistment, then division psychiatrists would no longer be necessary during combat.

So it happened that the American military entered the Second World War having forgotten a key lesson from the first one. In late September of 1940, Winfred Overholser, head of St. Elizabeth's Hospital, sent a memo to President Franklin Roosevelt describing the potential advantages of establishing a screening system at induction centers. Money, as much as medicine, encouraged this approach. Overholser estimated that neuropsychiatric casualties from the Great War had cost the country close to a billion dollars. In November the Selective Service System adopted an intense screening program for new soldiers, and in 1941 the position of division neuropsychiatrist was dropped from personnel rosters. By the time soldiers shipped out for World War II, the closest a military psychiatrist could get to the action was the general hospital.

MY GRANDFATHER TRIED to enlist just after the attack on Pearl Harbor. When the Navy refused him on account of his height—he recalls being told he was half an inch too short—he decided to finish his final year of psychiatry training at St. Elizabeth's Hospital. Ten months later, the Army said he'd trained enough. Toward the close of 1942 there were only around twelve hundred psychiatrists in the service; his medical resume, modest and incomplete by civilian standards, nevertheless recommended him for an important post. He was commissioned as an officer in the medical corps with the rank of first lieutenant. On October 24, 1942, he left Washington for Charleston, South Carolina, to serve on the neuropsychiatric ward of Stark General Hospital.

The job satisfied my grandfather's desire to serve. It did nothing to appease his urge to fight. He was twenty-eight, and eager to answer the call of his generation, and couldn't quite shake the thought that treating evacuated soldiers in a general hospital was a lesser fate than fighting the enemy at the front lines. "One had to feel rather helpless in the face of all these monumental events, to be relegated to what seemed like such a minor role, that of taking care of the sick and the wounded from all these battles, in hospitals stateside," he later wrote. "Even knowing how important it is in wars to 'care for him who shall have borne the battle,' as Lincoln urged in his 2nd Inaugural Address, the feeling cannot help but be one of being passed over by history."

His arrival at Stark only increased this frustration. The one chance he had to practice medicine came after a New Year's party. The commanding officer of nearby Fort Moultrie called the hospital in the middle of the night saying he was having a heart attack. My grandfather hustled out to save the officer—to find a simple case of indigestion awaiting him. His country had been at war for about a year, and he couldn't have felt less useful to the cause. When news of his transfer came he must have rejoiced.

On January 14, 1943, he reported for duty as a psychiatric ward officer for the newly improved Valley Forge General Hospital in Phoenixville, Pennsylvania. George Washington had used Valley Forge as a headquarters during the winter of 1777–78, when the Revolutionary Army was in desperate need of rest and rehabilitation. By early 1943, the grounds were home to a newly renovated million-dollar medical campus on 180 acres of land: 100 brick buildings, 2,000 beds, 8 operating rooms (including a mobile X-ray unit), and a chemical and bacterial lab. My grandfather and grandmother took an apartment near the railroad station at Perkiomen Junction to start, lest another transfer loomed.

The first patients were fresh from the rough North African theater. They arrived on March 12, and a few weeks later another group arrived—this batch very disturbed. Patients punched holes in walls and broke locks on windows. Several escaped from the ward, according to records, simply by running headfirst through the flimsy doors. There was an ongoing joke about the "real battle" between the engineers trying to maintain the newly constructed buildings and the patients trying to tear them down.

"We were on twelve hours of duty," my grandfather later said, "and the patients were on twenty-four hours of wrecking the hospital."

Over the course of 1943 my grandfather and the other ward officers handled 980 neuropsychiatric admissions. They diagnosed the wounded soldiers and sometimes administered rudimentary psychotherapy, but their main task was disposing of the patients as quickly as possible. Each case culminated in a three-pronged decision: Should the soldier be discharged with disability, transferred to a specialized psychiatric hospital for more treatment, or returned to duty? This last outcome was rare. Records show that only 52 of the 980 neuropsychiatric patients at Valley Forge in 1943 continued to serve after their release.

My grandfather recalled just a single patient from his time at Valley Forge: a lieutenant who experienced symptoms of depression during combat. The officer had slow vital functions, delusions of unworthiness, and an impulse toward self-inflicted injury. After his release he sometimes dropped by my grandfather's place to play classical records. He never returned to battle.

Very few patients on the psychiatric ward made a quick and full recovery. In a 1945 issue of the *Journal of Nervous and Mental Disease,* Dallas Pratt, who worked with my grandfather on the psychiatric ward at Valley Forge, published the results of a follow-up survey on 142 former soldiers treated there. About two-thirds reacted to noise with a startle five months after their release. A similar amount had dreams about the battlefield. Roughly half still had tremors. Pratt hoped to refute a prevailing wisdom, held by many military leaders at the time, that psychiatric casualties were malingerers who would magically be "cured" with a medical discharge. "The guilt feelings, the devotion to the soldier-self left behind on the battlefield, the consequent sense of apartness from the community—these remain," he wrote. As experience from World War I predicted, problems that might have been treated quickly at the front lines became harder to alleviate by the time soldiers reached the general hospital.

Weeks turned into months. My grandfather had every reason to believe he'd remain at Valley Forge for the rest of the war. He and my grandmother moved into a stone house with a side garden in nearby Kimberton and shipped up their furniture from Washington. They prepared for a long stay. The cases were intense but life outside the hospital was not. Officers played golf at a local country club. Hospital administrators held tea dances for the Duke and Duchess of Windsor and their like. An old medical school classmate, who worked in the hospital's urology section, came over to play Monopoly "every damn night," my grandmother later recalled. They literally lived, as the photographs attest, near the corner of Easy Street and Easy Street—the nexus of the simple life.

In all likelihood my grandfather resigned himself to the lesser glories of military service away from the battlefield. Then, in early November, history came around again and pointed him to it.

THE ORIGINAL WORLD WAR II psychiatric program was, in retrospect, something of a disaster. The plan called for new recruits to endure four or five mental health evaluations, at least fifteen minutes apiece, from the moment they reached their local Selective Service station to the time they joined a unit in training. The actual process proved far less rigorous. Enlistees received a cursory evaluation at the tail end of their general medical exam. Often a psychiatrist didn't even conduct it. Quality was regularly abandoned for quantity. Screeners saw hundreds of potential soldiers a day; one reported doing 135 evaluations in a span of two hundred minutes. Most had time to ask only two or three questions before making a decision and moving down the line. *Do you like girls?* was a common one. *Do you wet the bed?* was another.

The hasty process also lacked uniformity. Psychiatrists applied their own criteria to the cases in front of them. City-educated examiners took one look at rural boys from the South and labeled them schizophrenics. Some psychiatrists believed a few sessions with a psychiatrist, or an institutionalized relative, should disqualify a candidate. Some absolved malingering with the logic that anyone who'd fake an illness to avoid service was, in fact, mentally ill. Some hesitated to dismiss psychopaths because, for one thing, psychopathy was hard to define, and for another, they'd probably make good fighters. Many professionals doubted their ability to identify any but the most obvious mental health cases from such a thin slice of behavior. The psychiatrist C. Macfie Campbell, who'd been a screener during World War I, wrote that "if we are honest we have to admit that we are merely guessing."

Ultimately the decisions made by screeners stood as a testament to their disorganization. In October of 1942, writing in her My Day syndicated newspaper column, Eleanor Roosevelt worried that draftees weren't getting "a sufficiently careful psychiatric examination." Many early screeners indeed functioned as sieves. A memo from March 1943 described a number of severely deficient soldiers who'd been sent into combat. One unfortunate case thought the troopship taking him to Europe had actually gone "somewhere in Brooklyn." The War Department directed medical officers at induction stations to use more caution so that mental "misfits" didn't arrive overseas and disrupt the morale of a unit.

In July of 1943 officials established a policy of discharging anyone capable of rendering only limited duty. However well intentioned in theory, the rule in practice meant those who might once have performed important noncombat jobs were now rejected from the service. Many psychiatrists responded to the new policy by setting the lock too tight. Despite the fact that Tulsa's 1943 football team reached the Sugar Bowl, twenty-four of its players were found unfit for duty.

The result this time was a crisis of confidence in America's young men. In early August, after it was reported that about 10 percent of those who showed up at induction stations were rejected for psychiatric reasons, Secretary of War Henry Stimson ordered an "immediate investigation" into the military screening program. The team of eight psychiatrists who looked into the matter, led by Winfred Overholser of St. Elizabeth's, not only confirmed the validity of the rejections but suggested there be even more. "We find that instead of being too high," the committee wrote, "the overall psychiatric rejection rates are at the present too low."

What's ironic about the fear of enlisting anxious soldiers, looking back, is how well many of them performed in combat. One military psychiatrist categorized the risk of breakdowns in 138 soldiers who'd shown some early psychiatric symptoms. After sixty days in battle only three had been evacuated as mental casualties. Nine had been awarded a Purple Heart and eight a Bronze Star. The numbers were proof that "all neurotics do not necessarily break down in combat," wrote the author. That was a far cry from proponents of military screening, who said such individuals wouldn't hold up at all.

Despite the heavy screening process, mental casualties piled into military hospital beds. By the middle of 1943 neuropsychiatric cases made up 15 to 25 percent of all battle casualties in many campaigns. An annual summary of the problem reported a hospital admission rate of 60 neuropsychiatric cases per 1,000 men in overseas battle, compared to a rate of roughly 17 per 1,000 in the Great War. The disparity was startling. In the earlier conflict screeners had removed just 2 percent of enlistees. This meant that even with an examination process at least four times more rigorous in World War II, the U.S. military had a psychiatric incidence rate nearly four times as high as that in World War I.

As of August 1943, the Army was discharging 115,000 men a year for neuropsychiatric reasons—by far the most of any category. It was an unprecedented pace. From a perspective of military manpower, it was also an unsustainable one.

BY FALL THE entire approach to American psychiatry was being questioned. The underlying principle of the screening program was that everyone who broke down in war had entered service with an identifiable mental weakness, but reports from the field told a very different story. During the rough Sicilian campaign, a veteran division produced more psychiatric casualties than a group of fresh troops. That didn't mean the veterans weren't tough—but rather that the rigors of war could break even strong minds.

"In short, it became evident that anyone could develop a psychoneurosis under certain circumstances," wrote Malcolm Farrell and John Appel, psychiatrists in the surgeon general's office, in a 1943 review. "If screening were to weed out everybody who might develop a psychiatric disorder, it would be necessary to weed out everybody."

A comprehensive military psychiatry program would not only keep abnormal minds out of the Army, it would treat the normal ones in it. This shift in strategy was reinforced through a series of official directives issued between September and November of 1943. The surgeon general circulated a letter to every medical officer summarizing the new stance. Mental casualties would be considered urgent cases, and treated urgently. They should be labeled "exhaustion"—not "war neuroses" or "shell shock" or the like—to soften the stigma of the problem, to underscore its universality, and to suggest imminent recovery. The psychological and physical factors that led to a breakdown should be detected early and, whenever possible, prevented from escalating. General policy was moving away from the elimination of manpower and toward its conservation.

Executing this initiative meant moving psychiatrists up near the action, but high military officials had ignored several calls to reinstitute the division neuropsychiatrist. One early request, made back in April of 1942, had been rejected on the grounds that psychiatrists couldn't perform their job "under the present type of mobile warfare." Another request, made the following March, had been rebuffed by an officer who didn't believe "anything of any real value can be accomplished by psychiatrists with the division in combat." Only after Surgeon General Norman T. Kirk personally took the matter to Army Chief of Staff George C. Marshall—a notorious skeptic of mental casualties—was the position approved.

Shortly before this announcement, a group of military psychiatric consultants from the surgeon general's office convened to discuss the particulars of the new position. A list of potential division psychiatrists had been prepared. The consultants in attendance discussed whether it was wiser to move all the most capable psychiatrists up to the combat zone or to keep some in the general hospitals to treat the severe casualties who returned. The logic that one good man up front could spare many soldiers from reaching the back carried the day. "It will not be satisfactory to send just anyone on this job, for the men must be carefully selected," read the minutes from the meeting. "Our best men must be overseas where they are needed most."

On November 9, 1943, military rosters were revised to include a psychiatrist with each division. My grandfather left Valley Forge General Hospital a week later to report for duty with the 97th Infantry Division at Camp Polk, in Louisiana.

HE ARRIVED DURING the so-called Louisiana maneuvers. These were serious war games—the same that had clinched Eisenhower's rise to the top of the Army ranks—and that meant absolute battle conditions. Soldiers on maneuvers did all the things their counterparts did on the front lines overseas: slept in pup tents, formed chow lines, used their helmets as both food bowl and washbasin, ate K rations. To boot, Louisiana was having one of its worst winters on record. The ice storms got so bad they toppled trees and utility poles. It wasn't quite moving straight from the corner of Easy Street and Easy Street to the foxholes in Europe or the islands of the Pacific, but it must have felt like it at first.

A month into maneuvers he got a reprieve when the Army ordered all sixty of the new division neuropsychiatrists to Walter Reed Medical Center, in Washington, for a three-day orientation. The surgeon general's office had organized a sort of intellectual boot camp in military psychiatry. More than a dozen officials spoke at the event, several big shots among them. Surgeon General Norman Kirk offered some brief words of encouragement. General Howard M. Snyder, from the inspector general's office, emphasized the new Army policy of conserving manpower. An excerpt about division psychiatrists in World War I, from a book edited by Thomas Salmon, was distributed to everyone in attendance.

The proceedings were led by Lieutenant Colonel William C. Menninger, the new chief of psychiatry in the surgeon general's office. Menninger hailed from America's first family of mental health. His older brother was Karl Menninger of the famous Menninger Clinic in Topeka, Kansas. The younger Menninger had a charming knack for putting others at ease. He played piano, told dirty jokes, and spoke with "persuasiveness, salesmanship, and [a] magic touch," in the later words of a colleague. A devoted philatelist, he once asked an Army psychiatrist stationed in Europe to bring back some rare Nazi stamps if the opportunity arose. When Lieutenant John Appel first reported to him for duty, stating his name and rank, Menninger replied: "Oh, come off it, Jack. Call me Bill."

The new division psychiatrists saw plenty of Menninger during their three days in Washington. Many were probably in awe of him: all of them knew about the famed Menninger Clinic; some, like my grandfather, had probably read Karl's *The Human Mind* in their youths. On December 13, William Menninger gave an opening address that turned into a pep talk about the responsibilities of being the "sole representative" for psychiatry among a large combat force. Menninger's ability to inspire was on full display in the early moments of his talk.

"Your records were such that in picking the men for this new and heavy responsibility, you were chosen," he said. "What you do and how you do it we hope will go down in history as one of the major contributions of psychiatry in the American Army."

During his hour-long address Menninger elaborated on the ten duties of the division psychiatrist described in War Department Circular No. 290. As a general rule they would advise command on all matters pertaining to mental health, consult on courts-martial, and maintain a working relationship with the division surgeon. They would also extend psychiatric screening efforts beyond enlistment into the training period. Menninger compared their task to that of a pioneer, a missionary, an educator, and a salesman in one.

Of course, the most critical function of the combat psychiatrist was to prevent and treat breakdowns. "It has become imperative that we do salvage men," Menninger said. On that account, the division psychiatrists were expected to help soldiers adjust to military life. They would reassign rather than discharge those who might be more effective in other units or in noncombat roles. They would track the division's mental health through statistical records and, of course, supervise all neuropsychiatric casualties during combat. They would also design programs to elevate soldier morale—a key indicator of mental health, military psychiatrists were finding—and constantly calibrate the "mental toughness" of the troops.

To do that the psychiatrists would first have to gain a thorough appreciation for the life of a soldier. Ride their vehicles, take their infiltration courses, partake in their bivouacs, Menninger encouraged. He believed that an integral part of the division neuropsychiatrist's task was to earn the other soldiers' respect. "To 'know your job' means to live with the men, to do what they do, to experience their struggles," said Menninger. Each person in that room should be a soldier, an officer, a physician, and a psychiatrist—"in that order," he said. His closing lines echoed the assurance of his opening ones.

"We feel certain that if you are the judicious dynamo we believe you to be, you can be one of the most important factors in a successful division," Menninger said. "We shall think of you literally as our front line representatives and confidently expect you to write a famous chapter in American psychiatry."

WOULDN'T YOU KNOW, but the only living division neuropsychiatrist I could find lived two stops away from me on the 1 train in Manhattan, and wouldn't you know, but he told me in a letter that he remembered my grandfather, too. His name was Bertram Schaffner. He lived in an apartment on Fifty-ninth Street facing the southern perimeter of Central Park. I went there one day trying to contain my excitement at perhaps finding someone with insight into my grandfather's war. At the very least I thought I'd learn something that hadn't made the dispassionate pages of his memoirs.

Dr. Schaffner's caretaker led me to a seat in a corner of the living room with a view of the park. Schaffner himself soon emerged from another part of the apartment and made his way toward me, very slowly, with the help of a walker. He was in his late nineties, born two years before my grandfather. He sat down across from me and hid his catheter under a blanket that covered his lower half. A clutter of items occupied chairs and tables surrounding the window beside us. He wore glasses over inquisitive eyes and had large ears and lips that seemed naturally turned upward in a smile. It was half past ten in the morning.

"You said in your letter you remembered my grandfather," I said. "That was surprising to me."

"I think I do," he said. He spoke slowly. "The person I remember had a very prominent profile. And a very sharp nose. Very handsome, but very—not very sociable. I made efforts, I think, to talk to him. He didn't respond."

"When was this?" I asked.

"I think we met at an assemblage of psychiatrists," he said. "They were being assigned to wherever, whatever division they were going to belong to."

I asked if he meant the Washington conference of December 1943.

"Could be," he said. "He withdrew. He didn't attempt to socialize."

We spoke for about an hour that day. Schaffner had been drafted during the third year of his psychiatry residency at Bellevue Hospital, but deferred active duty until he finished his training, in April of 1941. Pearl Harbor hadn't happened yet but the signs of war were there and the draft was in full swing. He was assigned to evaluate draftees for the Selective Service at Governors Island, off the southern tip of Manhattan. After about a year and a half he transferred to other induction centers in upstate New York to perform the same duties. He told me his psychiatric interviews with each potential soldier lasted about five minutes.

"The Army wanted us to do this," Schaffner said, "because they thought we could detect people likely to break down, and wanted us to eliminate people not likely to stand up under combat."

Later on he served in Europe, and after the war he stayed in occupied Germany as chief of psychiatry at the 116th General Hospital in

Nuremberg. He played a role in the Nuremberg trial that sounded like the counterpart to my grandfather's role in Tokyo. Schaffner was on a commission to determine the competency of Nazi arms manufacturer Gustav Krupp, then acted as a caretaker at the hospital for SS officer Ernst Kaltenbrunner. Krupp's case would serve as a judicial precedent for the insanity of Okawa Shumei—but I only learned that later on.

"My job was to see if Krupp was fit for trial, which he wasn't, and to keep Kaltenbrunner alive so that he could go through the trial, and he did," Schaffner said. Kaltenbrunner had suffered a cerebral hemorrhage and Schaffner was instructed to keep his blood pressure down as he recovered. He also had to keep away the many bitter occupation troops who wanted a piece of the patient.

"We used to joke, we kept the American soldiers from killing him," he said.

Toward the end of our chat I could see Dr. Schaffner getting confused. That was certainly understandable given the great distance between our conversation and the events being recalled. (At one point, when I asked if he remembered any particular patients during combat, he thought for a moment, answered no, then broke into a charming smile and said, "I didn't know I was going to meet you.") Looking back, I was lucky to find him when I did; I visited him once more then found out he'd died a couple months later. I knew before I left that Schaffner wasn't the long-lost guide into my grandfather's past, but I was starting to suspect that such a guide was just a figment of my own imagination. My grandfather hadn't just kept past feelings hidden away; it sounded like he'd hidden them in the present, too. His mind was becoming so curious to me—beyond frustrating, really, and into the realm of the fascinating—the way it defended itself from an enemy who didn't even seem to exist.

"I just remember that he was very aloof," Dr. Schaffner told me. "And we wondered why."

THE WASHINGTON CONFERENCE was thirty years of military knowledge distilled into about twenty-four hours of instruction. Many of the talks focused on preventive psychiatry—fortifying the minds of new soldiers against the hardships they would soon face. On December 13, 1943, John Appel introduced the approach to prevention that he'd been developing since March. It consisted of two main pillars. The first was education. That meant reversing the preconceived skepticism most soldiers held toward psychiatric problems. "Either a man was insane or he was completely normal," Appel later wrote of the typical military mind-set. "The possibility has not been considered that there might be anything in between."

A series of lectures on mental health had been drafted on the subject—six intended for officers, three for enlisted men—and it would be the division psychiatrist's job to lead this instruction in stateside training camps. That afternoon Colonel Bernard A. Cruvant stressed the importance of directing these lessons at the line officers who would serve beside the soldiers in the field. As immediate superiors developed a keen eye for the personality changes, emotional outbursts, and general anxiety signaling mental casualties, the rate of mental casualties would fall.

The second pillar of prevention was motivation. On the afternoon of December 14, General Frederick H. Osborn led an extended discussion on the topic. In 1943 too few American soldiers possessed sufficient morale—defined by one military official as "a will to fight stronger than a will to live." One out of every three soldiers felt their task in World War II was not worthwhile, according to a survey from earlier that year. Part of the morale problem was that American troops didn't know their enemy. When the military asked GIs what the Luftwaffe was, 58 percent failed to identify it as Germany's air force. Many of those surveyed thought it was the national anthem.

Psychiatrists feared this low fighting interest made troops particularly susceptible to the stresses of war. In response, Appel had overseen the production of five Why We Fight films. They were directed by Hollywood's own Frank Capra with the help of a Harvard sociologist, a Yale psychologist, and an engaging writer named Theodor Geisel—better known as Dr. Seuss. An hour a week during training had been set aside for the division psychiatrist to boost troop morale with the help of these movies and whatever other motivational tools he could muster.

The other major topic at the Washington conference was treatment. A strong preventive program might minimize mental casualties, but by 1943 no one suffered the illusion of eliminating them. Once the division psychiatrists shipped out with the troops their focus would shift from preventing casualties to recovering them. During their orientation, the new division psychiatrists received a crash course in the accepted methods of the day. They each got a "restricted" copy of a three-hundred-page book printed that September called *War Neuroses in North Africa*. The book was prepared by a pair of psychiatrists operating in the Tunisian campaign named Roy R. Grinker and John P. Spiegel. In the early years of World War II, it was considered the bible of military psychiatry.

The approach developed by Grinker and Spiegel was rooted in psychoanalytic theory. (Grinker had trained with Freud himself.) They called it "narcosynthesis." Traumatized soldiers received an injection of the barbiturate sodium pentothal to induce sleepiness, then relived their battlefield experiences until they achieved an emotional catharsis. The effect was "dramatic," wrote Grinker and Spiegel in *War Neuroses in North Africa*, with patients spontaneously reenacting vivid battle scenes:

> They talk to unseen buddies, wince at unheard explosions, bury their heads under the pillow when the shells come close and flatten themselves out on the bed, as if they were in the bottom of their foxhole.
>
> The terror exhibited in the moments of supreme danger, such as at the imminent explosion of shells, the death of a friend before the patient's eyes, the absence of cover under a heavy dive bombing attack is electrifying to watch. The body becomes increasingly tense and rigid; the eyes widen and the pupils dilate, while the skin becomes covered with fine perspiration. The hands move about convulsively, seeking a weapon, or a friend to share the danger. Breathing becomes incredibly rapid and shallow. The intensity of the emotion sometimes

becomes more than they can bear; and frequently at the height of the reaction, there is a collapse and the patient falls back in bed and remains quiet for a few minutes. . . .

Grinker and Spiegel claimed to have returned about 72 percent of their twelve hundred or so patients to some type of duty, but they'd operated in the rear-echelon hospitals, so few of their patients made it back to the front lines. The new class of division neuropsychiatrists, with a mandate to preserve fighting power, would be stationed in forward medical areas. To give a sense of the soldiers seen in this nonhospital setting, two speakers came in fresh from the battlefields. One was Martin Berezin, who spoke at length about the fighting on Guadalcanal, a jungle island in the Pacific, which had taken place from the summer of 1942 into February of 1943.

The breakdown rate at Guadalcanal reflected its brutal conditions: rugged mountainous terrain, hand-to-hand cave fighting, extreme heat and daily rain, a relentless Japanese attack. Two of every five men evacuated stateside were psychiatric cases. As division surgeon during the campaign—this was back before the division psychiatrist had been approved—Berezin had noticed a great number of men in what he later called "varying degrees of 'startle' states." His commanding officer wanted to court-martial them as cowards, but Berezin managed to treat some by diagnosing them with blast concussions, which sounded enough like a serious physical ailment for his superiors to accept. A few men returned to combat. In general Berezin's experience stood as a testimony to the difficulties of practicing psychiatry at the front.

The entire morning session of December 15 was given to the second combat speaker, Frederick R. Hanson. Described as clever, energetic, and possessing a "low and calm" voice, Hanson had been way in front of the division psychiatrist curve. He'd recommended the position be created all the way back in an August 1942 communication to the surgeon general. His work in the North African theater, in the spring of 1943, confirmed that fatigue played a leading role in mental casualties. Treat exhaustion, Hanson believed, and you'd improve psychological stability.

As a result, Hanson devised a fairly simple regimen of rest and reassurance for psychiatric cases. He put them to sleep for long periods with barbiturates, awakened them only for meals, then after a day or so discussed the universality of fear and urged them to rejoin the fighting. It was very much in the style of combat psychiatry from World War I, and it was equally effective; Hanson returned 60 percent of his cases to combat within four days, and 89 percent of those remained in action a month later. Hanson's lessons, above all others, would guide the work of division psychiatrists on the battlefield.

My grandfather couldn't have left Washington with anything less than a full sense of the gravity of his task. That he would have to help troops endure the stresses and strains of war while resisting them himself was also becoming apparent. Since the 97th Infantry was still on maneuvers, soldiers separated from their unit had to travel as a "casual," just as they would in actual combat. Returning from Washington to Louisiana, my grandfather-the-casual had to hitch rides with whatever friendly vehicle was going his direction. He spent cold, rainy nights among piles of military mailbags, half trying to sleep, half trying to stick out enough to be seen by any passing mail truck. The staccato, thousand-mile journey—riding for a while, waiting for what felt like forever, riding for a while more—taught him a lesson as important as any he'd learned at the Washington conference.

"After several days I got back to the division," he later said. "But I vowed I'd never be a casual in a combat zone."

As a general rule, the sixty division psychiatrists were greeted by their new divisions with suspicion and granted little in the way of authority—particularly the eight, like my grandfather, who remained relatively lowly first lieutenants. Colonel Menninger began to receive "disquieting reports" within weeks of the Washington conference. Two division psychiatrists said their commanders expected them to make wholesale discharges. Another said he was being used strictly as a physician. Still another was told by his division surgeon that the entire military psychiatry program was absurd. Some were called "nut pickers" who belonged in lunatic asylums, not among units of good old "red-blooded" American soldiers. One new psychiatrist, on maneuvers, had been confined to mess hall inspection.

Menninger had expected as much. He'd warned the psychiatrists in Washington that they might be in for a rude welcome. ("We can forecast with certainty that you will often be expected to 'get rid' of men whom you know we must save," he'd said.) Many officers still felt that psychiatric cases were simply weaklings or malingerers. They saw the division neuropsychiatrist as a tool for disposing of soldiers who didn't meet their models of manhood.

In a letter written in late January 1944, Menninger reminded all division psychiatrists why they were there. "Your main job is to salvage men and not discharge them!!" he wrote. At the same time, he was so concerned about the ability of first lieutenants to establish themselves that he alerted Surgeon General Kirk to the problem. Kirk responded by circulating a letter suggesting that all division surgeons promote these men first chance they got "for the sake of his effectiveness."

My grandfather seems to have been among those division psychiatrists who entered a combat division with plenty of enemies on his own side. He might even have been the one who told Menninger that he'd been relegated to mess duty on maneuvers—the 97th Infantry remained engaged in its war games until the end of January. The nature of his job would have made it difficult to make friends even if he were the extroverted type, and, of course, he was not the extroverted type. "It took quite some time before other officers in the division bonded with me like a comrade or a brother," he later wrote. He made captain in early May.

THE EARLY PROBLEMS experienced by division neuropsychiatrists in World War II reflected a general doubt among military officers about the legitimacy of mental casualties. During fighting in French Morocco, in the spring of 1943, a line officer reportedly leveled his gun at three soldiers who'd been diagnosed as schizophrenics, believing that "a soldier will go to any odds to get out."

Around that time, Army Chief of Staff George Marshall had ordered an investigation into malingering. The results of this inquiry prompted Marshall to draft a press release about the problem, in which he described psychiatric cases as soldiers who developed "an imaginary ailment which in time becomes so fixed in his mind as to bring about mental pain and sickness." Colonel Menninger combed through the release line by line making corrections; in the above case, he suggested the word "imaginary" be changed to "psychological."

Marshall's mind-set was hardly unique. Elliot Cooke, one of the men dispatched by the chief of staff to study the problem, later reported that most commanding officers failed to see mental illness as a genuine medical problem. Instead, they believed all patients were fakers and all psychiatrists were hindering the war effort. "You either believe in psychiatry or you don't," Cooke wrote. A psychiatric consultant in Europe reported in October 1943 that one division surgeon, upon being told that psychiatric cases could be treated effectively at the front lines, said he would prefer to evacuate such men and never see them again. Even those officers who acknowledged the existence of mental casualties were hesitant to put recovered cases back at the front for fear the other troops would no longer respect them.

The topic hadn't really entered civilian discourse until the infamous "slapping" incidents involving General George S. Patton came to light in late November of 1943. Twice that summer "Old Blood and Guts" Patton initiated altercations with mental casualties he'd thought were faking it. On August 3, during a visit to the 15th Evacuation Hospital in Sicily, Patton had slapped Private Charles Kuhl, who was being treated for "moderately severe" anxiety. Two days later Patton had instructed all officers in his Seventh Army to court-martial such cases rather than hospitalize them.

"It has come to my attention that a very small number of soldiers are going to the hospital on the pretext that they are nervously incapable of combat," Patton wrote. "Such men are cowards, and bring discredit on the Army and disgrace to their comrades who they heartlessly leave to endure the danger of a battle which they themselves use the hospital as a means of escaping."

A week later, during a visit to the 93rd Evacuation Hospital, Patton had repeated the scene with Private Paul Bennett. A farm boy who'd enlisted before Pearl Harbor, Bennett was no coward. His nerves had started to fade when his wife sent a picture of their new baby, and he cracked when his best buddy was wounded in front of him. Even as he'd been ordered to the hospital, Bennett had expressed a desire to return to his unit as quickly as possible. When he told Patton he couldn't stand the shelling, the general called him a "yellow son of a bitch" and slapped him in front of all the doctors, nurses, and patients in the tent. Patton ordered Bennett to return to the front or face a firing squad, then drew his pearl-handled Colt and threatened to do the job himself.

The public seemed split over Patton's actions. Some accepted his brashness as necessary to win the war. One letter into *Time* magazine thought the uproar made the country look "soft." Kuhl's own father reportedly wrote his congressman in support of the general. Others weren't so fast to forgive. A senator from North Carolina called Patton's actions "unpardonable." An American Legion post in Iowa questioned the point of fighting Fascism while practicing it: "If our boys are to be mistreated, let's import Hitler and do it up right." One serviceman suggested that Patton be examined by a psychiatrist himself. Patton's own formal apology to Eisenhower revealed a belief, based on personal experience, that only tough love could treat "mental anguish." It closed with the supercilious suggestion that by slapping each broken soldier, Patton had "saved an immortal soul."

THE 97TH INFANTRY trained as much as any division in the American Army. After Louisiana maneuvers they packed up for Fort Leonard Wood, near Rolla, Missouri, to review whatever weaknesses had been exposed in the war games. In midsummer the division left for a series of camps along the southern California coast. First stop was San Luis Obispo for amphibious training on the foggy shores of Morro Bay and Pismo Beach. Next was Camp Callan, just north of San Diego, to practice beach assaults and transport landings on San Clemente Island under the auspices of the Navy and Marine Corps. Then to Camp Cooke, near the city of Lompoc, a bit north of Santa Barbara, for more of the same. None of the men knew for certain what the Army had in store for the division, but the style of their training left most to presume they were headed for the Pacific theater.

"[W]e expected that we were due to invade one of the islands near Japan," my grandfather later wrote. "Resistance by the Japanese could be expected to be as fanatical as ever."

During training my grandfather was attached to the General Staff to coordinate the division's mental health program. Under the California sunshine the other officers warmed to the idea of having a psychiatrist among them. He formed a mutual respect, if not quite a friendship, with General Milton B. Halsey, his ultimate superior in the division, and Kenneth Somers, the division surgeon, his immediate superior among the medics. He became close with Ralph Yarborough, the judge advocate general, who later became a senator from Texas, and Pat Frazier, a medical personnel officer and begrudging bridge partner (my grandfather was awful), and Bill Hill, the dental officer with the devilish sharp mustache. My grandmother followed from camp to camp, in their car named Betsy, and set up houses in the towns nearby.

They formed a small social clique with Albert Waxman, the warrant officer, and Walter Duffield, an adjutant to Halsey, and their wives. Waxman was another Jewish boy from Brooklyn. He was called Waxy so often, and for so long, that at some point he forgot his given name was actually Alfred and had to change it legally to Albert. His wife, Sylvia, was known as Waxy-She. Duffield went by Duffy. He was tall, with red hair, a jovial spirit, a bawdy sense of humor, and a taste for Scotch. Duffy and his wife, Dottie, had a bright cocker spaniel named Georgie. If you told Georgie to take something to Waxy-She, he made the delivery right at Sylvia's feet.

On nights and weekends Waxy ran an informal speakeasy. Officers came in through the front door, favored enlisted men through the back. There was a perpetual poker game and a regular touch football game and in evenings the officer's club. Everyone brought their bottles to the bar and bonded over martinis and manhattans. They drank the local booze when they could; in Missouri it was Griesedieck beer, which I suspect my grandmother forbade, just on general principle.

In August of 1944 my grandfather got leave to visit San Francisco. My grandparents hopped into Betsy and headed toward the bay, where Eli Jaffe was stationed at the time, for a brief family reunion. The three visited Fisherman's Wharf, and the Presidio, and the Golden Gate Bridge. They drove up and down the coast. As usual my grandfather didn't say much. "They've both got much warmth in them even if that brother of mine does sorta keep his light hidden under a bushel," Eli wrote to his wife a few days later. In fairness, my grandfather probably had a lot on his mind. Right around this time, at least according to the math, my grandmother would have realized she was pregnant.

ON JANUARY 7, 1945, my grandfather left his house in Lompoc for the division camp. His light tie was tucked into his dark medical officer's uniform; his dark garrison cap was slightly askew. On his collar and cap were two silver bars to indicate his rank as captain; on his left shoulder was the 97th Infantry insignia patch—Neptune's trident, set in white against an azure Saxon shield. He arrived at Building 6016 at Camp Cooke, shared by other medical officers and a few communications staff, and sat down at the typewriter at his desk. He opened his psychiatric files and pulled out cases and memos going back to December of 1943. It was time to send Colonel Menninger an update on division morale.

The statistical charts he compiled that day show that through the fall of 1944 my grandfather had examined 825 troops for one psychiatric reason or another. Some had come to his attention through his regular screening sessions; others had been referred to him by their line officers with adjustment problems. He handled the lighter cases by reassigning them to more suitable tasks within the division or returning them to duty after a little psychotherapy. About one in seven had a form of psychosis or a neurological dysfunction severe enough to warrant discharge on disability. Three-quarters of his cases were soldiers with either basic neuroses or nothing wrong with them at all—in the parlance of the surgeon general's office, they were "preventable."

Throughout the year, my grandfather had implemented a thorough program of preventive psychiatry. One of the first things he'd done was express the nature and urgency of the problem to his fellow medical officers in the division. "Psychiatric casualties have constituted a major medical problem in this war," he'd written in a circular letter, echoing what he'd learned at the Washington conference. The letter had outlined several keys to handling this problem: removing clearly unfit soldiers, assisting those with moderate neuroses and adjustment problems, and improving division morale as a whole.

"By these means alone we can accomplish a great saving in manpower, aid operational efficiency, eliminate training losses, and reduce the reservoir of potential psychiatric casualties," he'd told his colleagues. Then he'd channeled his inner Menninger and reminded the division medical officers—in what reads like a rejoinder to the Patton school of tough soldierly love—that reassurance, sympathy, and patience were often the best antidotes for anxiety:

> A neurotic symptom is a prop which is helping to support a weak, wobbling structure. Don't try to remove it blindly without substituting some other means of support. . . . If we don't do something to help a man constructively in meeting his problems, or at least to help him "save face" before his own conscience, we can be sure that his symptoms are going to get worse. And remember—the essence of our job is to help and treat the individual. To do this, we often have to curb our impulse to kick him instead.

Medics needed to understand the problem to treat it. To truly prevent breakdowns, however, the line officers who dealt with soldiers on a daily basis would need to appreciate it as well. My grandfather had accomplished that task by designing a series of lectures based on Technical Bulletin No. 12 circulated by the War Department back in February of 1944. The talks provided unit leaders with a small arsenal of mental health strategies—and, more important, digestable aphorisms. Some emphasized the importance of motivation ("Napoleon considered morale three times as important as material"). Some described the environmental stress factors that influence Army adjustment ("The officer should recognize himself as the 'father' substitute . . ."). Some explained the misperceptions about psychological breakdown ("The majority of the mental breaks in the front lines occur in 'normal' individuals").

All in all, the six lectures had been "quite stimulating and encouraging," my grandfather told Menninger. He'd even mimeographed the entire technical bulletin for the line officers to study at their leisure.

His approach with the enlisted men themselves had been "somewhat more difficult," he admitted to Menninger. To prepare for these talks he'd used an article published in the February 1944 issue of the journal *War Medicine.* My grandfather had ordered an overhead projector and showed some of the cartoonish diagrams from the article on a screen. One illustrated the concept of "BROODING" with a dark cloud that hovered just above a man's head, which contained a "THINK BOX" where his brain should have been.

"I tried to make the presentation as simple as possible," he told Menninger.

The first talk in that article described homesickness—how you can overcome it through either humor or toughness, but should never have a "brooding" outlook. The second hit on regimentation, stressing that it was better to gripe about military discipline on occasion than to stew about it in silence. The third explained fear: heroes were "just ordinary men like the rest of us, who are just as much afraid as we are," but who overcame this feeling with good training.

My grandfather explained some of the enclosed statistics, then signed his name and tapped out C★O★N★F★I★D★E★N★T★I★A★L at the bottom of the page before sending it away.

———————

CAMP GOSSIP HAD been spot-on: the military did intend for the 97th Infantry to head for the Pacific. The division had even received clearance to ship out when, at the last moment, the Army reversed course. Allied lines had come under heavy attack during the German offensive known as the Battle of the Bulge. The 97th had already sent about three thousand soldiers, or roughly a quarter of its manpower, as overseas replacements during the battle. Now the Army ordered the entire division to head for Europe and fortify the weakened front.

As the departure date drew nigh, a saying began to circulate among the barracks: "If you want to miss the shippy, see Jaffe in a jiffy." My grandfather developed a standard reply: "If I go through, you go too." Go through they did. On January 30, 1945, troop trains began the cross-country trip from California to Camp Kilmer, in New Jersey. His months of training in preventive psychiatry seemed to pay off in the days leading up to the division's departure. Only three cases of last-minute battle nerves were referred to him there. None was left behind.

How he handled his own separation anxiety is not recorded in the statistics. At some point he said good-bye to his wife—maybe rubbed the six-month bulge in her belly one last time. When it came time to ship out he limped onto the gangplank. He'd injured his knee playing touch football. The fighting hadn't even started and he was falling apart.

On February 18, 1945, the division crossed the Hudson by ferry toward New York Harbor. Troops loaded onto the USS *Monticello* as the 97th band played and the Red Cross handed out coffee and doughnuts. The *Monticello* had once been an Italian luxury liner, but the ship's finer potential wasn't on display for the soldiers. There was a 50-cent bounty for every rat killed, paid in chit to the ship store, according to the division newsletter (datelined: "Somewhere at Sea"). The division sailed in a large convoy of ships protected by destroyers and submarine chasers; still, to avoid attack by German U-boats, the ships zigzagged across the Atlantic and the destroyers dropped depth charges.

The division disembarked at the French port of Le Havre on

March 3. From there it proceeded to Camp Lucky Strike—one of several Army "cigarette" camps, including Old Gold, Camel, Chesterfield, and Pall Mall, that ringed the port city—five miles northwest of Cany-Barville. They stayed put at the staging site for about three weeks. My grandfather got some late training in mines, booby traps, and trench foot. He slept in pup tents. The cold hard ground aggravated an old shoulder problem. Toward the end of March the pain became so great that he began to run a fever. Colonel Somers, the division surgeon, told him to report to the field hospital at Dieppe.

He didn't want to go. He recalled the awful experience he'd had as a "casual" traveling from Washington to Louisiana during the war games, and figured it would be many times worse in an actual war. Finally he agreed to get treatment on the condition that Somers send an ambulance for him the moment that orders arrived to advance to the initiation point.

Somers drove him to the field hospital in a jeep and left him in the hands of a young physician who'd worked at the Mayo Clinic. The problem was bursitis—an accumulation of fluid in the deltoid bursa that my grandfather later described as "a variety of sheer Chinese torture." The Mayo-educated medic filled a needle with Novocaine and punctured the bursa "like a hot poker." My grandfather jumped off the patient table and found, a moment later, that he could finally lift his arm above his head. A moment more and he heard an ambulance roll up outside, come to take him to the combat zone.

Chapter 8

A War for Asian Liberation

The intention of the Greater East Asia War is to rid Asia of foreign, European aggressive powers, sweeping them from our land by building our New Order in East Asia.

—Okawa Shumei, *The Establishment of Order in Greater East Asia*, 1943

T HERE WERE 6.6 million radios in Japan in 1941—fourth most in the world, behind only the United States, Germany, and Great Britain—and Dr. Okawa Shumei's broadcast on December 14 could be heard through them all. It was the Sunday after Pearl Harbor. Half past six in the morning. The Greater East Asia War was only days old, but the Japanese people were already flush with courage. The military had quickly established a dominating presence in the Pacific. In one week alone they'd seized Guam and southern Thailand, sunk two British battleships off the coast of Malaya, and made strong advances in the Philippines. Meanwhile, officials on the home-front had arranged a coordinated mass media assault. Newspapers ran cartoons of a Japanese fist connecting with the faces of Uncle Sam and Winston Churchill and Chiang Kai-shek.

Few public figures could fan the euphoria like the philosopher-patriot who'd made his name urging Japan to liberate the righteous

East from the oppressive West. For six straight days the airwaves sizzled with the logical arguments and jingoistic flourishes that formed Okawa Shumei's singular style. The purpose of the radio series, Okawa told NHK listeners that first morning, was to illuminate "the essential character of our enemy." He opened the program by reminding the audience of the great prophecy he'd delivered back in 1925—that one day America and Japan would meet in a "life-and-death struggle" for global supremacy. Once again Okawa heralded triumph for the "bright dawn" of day over the "dark mists of night." Imaginations were left to conjure some personified Japanese sun, rising into the blue sky with its red sword drawn, slashing down American stars one by one.

"The renaissance of Asia will pave the way for the establishment of a new world order and realization of a higher standard of life for the whole of mankind," he said. "But world history will never enter this stage now without passing through the Japan-American war, or to be more exact, without Japan's victory in the war."

Okawa called the broadcast "America's Great East Asia Invasion History." At each stop on this history tour he planted little oratorical flags to map America's long trail of advancement into East Asia. Okawa began his talks with the voyage of Commodore Matthew Perry, back in 1853. He spent much of his first show recalling how Perry had "audaciously" compelled Japan to open its trading ports against its will, operating under the white man's assumption that "the world was created for their own benefit." The next broadcast centered on the late-nineteenth-century American industrialists who saw China as a vast and vulnerable land filled with natural resources they didn't care to share with the Japanese. Okawa wanted to trace the current conflict to its earliest roots.

His next three talks enumerated the hypocrisies of American diplomacy in the Far East over the years. Even as U.S. investors enjoyed privileged access to Latin America under the Monroe Doctrine, American officials issued a "violent protest" about Japan's desire for "special interests" in Manchuria. Even as U.S. officials demanded entry into East Asia, American politicians restricted the rights of Japanese immigrants. Even as U.S. statesmen promoted peaceful relations and disarmament, American delegates insisted on naval treaties—first at the 1921 Washington Conference, and again at the 1930 London Conference—that gave Japan unfavorable fleet ratios.

"These were a few outstanding examples of America's manifestation of insatiable egotism and greed," Okawa said at the close of his fifth broadcast.

Ever one for rhetorical showmanship, Okawa massaged his words to fit his greater message. He blamed the Manchurian Incident of 1931 on Chinese insurgents when in actuality—as he well knew—Japan's own Kwantung Army had provoked the conflict. Okawa portrayed the incident as an example of Japan "maintaining peace and order in the whole of East Asia" when it had really been an aggressive expansion onto the mainland. He said Japan "never even dreamt of appealing to arms" in Manchuria when he himself had been among those who'd dreamed up the forceful response. In his final show, Okawa faulted President Roosevelt for mistaking the war in China as a violation of international peace treaties instead of recognizing it as a legitimate new order in East Asia.

But throughout his broadcasts Okawa also employed a shrewd persuasive device that made his arguments difficult for opponents to dismiss. He didn't use Japanese allegations to suggest American aggression—he used historical quotations made by Americans themselves. So rather than accuse American parties of injustice at the 1930 London Conference, for instance, he quoted Secretary of State Henry Stimson, who'd told a Senate committee at the time that Japan had bravely agreed to a naval treaty that "would bind their own limbs until their enemy would surpass them." He flipped the Western narrative on its head this way throughout the program. The effect was to force his detractors either to concede his point or to disavow their own words.

By December 19, 1941, Okawa had made an exhaustive case that the Greater East Asia War was being fought not to expand Japan's empire in East Asia but to eliminate America's own. His patient line of argument culminated in a burst of passion. In the thirteenth century, he told listeners, a Japanese commander by the name of Hojo had repelled an attack by the Mongols from the north. "When the enemy came from Ho [north] *Hojo* defeated it and when it comes from To [east] *Tojo* is going to defeat it," Okawa said, just before signing off. "It is not mere coincidence but a blessing from Heaven."

After those first six shows he launched into the "invasion history" of Great Britain without so much as a day's break. When the twelve-part program concluded, with the first flames of war still warm, the fifty-five-year-old Okawa had reached the height of his fame. The broadcasts proved so popular they were compiled into a book the very next month. (Two years later they were translated into English under the title *The History of Anglo-American Aggression in East Asia.*) Okawa was no longer just some curious apostle of Japan's divine mission. He was the voice inside every ear accepting it across the land.

THE CONFIDENT PUBLIC tone Okawa struck during those first days of war betrayed a nervous private mind. He wrote his mother in Sakata to make sure she was all right and enclosed enough money for her to subsist for several months. He confided to his students at Okawa Juku, the Asianist academy, that he didn't think Japan could defeat the United States and Britain while still waging an assault on China. He composed a poem called "On War" whose tone contrasted every ounce of exuberance he'd displayed on national radio.

"On the road to death, the firs planted before our houses are like stones marking the miles," he wrote in this poem. "There is no joy, there is no joy."

Okawa's doubts had been growing for years—ever since his release from prison in the fall of 1937. Soon after getting home, he'd traveled to Nanking, just as Japanese troops were invading the Chinese city. The trip coincided with the notorious "rape of Nanking": weeks of heinous atrocities committed by Japanese soldiers against Chinese civilians. Women were abducted, violated, and brutalized by soldiers; children and ordinary, unarmed men were massacred with rage. By some estimates the death toll reached six figures.

Okawa hadn't witnessed the worst of that inhumanity, but he'd been an accidental victim of unruliness one day, when two Japanese officers mistook him for Chinese and tried to rough him up. They begged forgiveness and fled as soon as Okawa told them who he was, but his ego was badly bruised. If his belief in Asianism were as genuine as he always claimed, Okawa might have been shocked to discover that years of preparing Japan to lead Asia had bred a violent sense of racial superiority. In any event, he became terrified that Asian unity was far out of reach—which meant, by extension, the East was not yet ready to meet the West in the great global clash. By early 1938 he'd begun to question whether the time for Japan's divine mission had really arrived.

After that, Okawa had become obsessed with delaying a fight against the United States until Japan had won the war in China. He made a bizarre attempt to ease international tensions by arranging a business partnership with American real estate mogul Harry Chandler called the Pan-Pacific Trading and Navigation Company. Okawa believed, with a startling degree of naivety, that this company alone might divert the heavy flow of American money into China's military. He became so desperate that in July of 1940 he appealed to his old friend Tojo Hideki for help with the trade agreement. Tojo had just been made war minister and held increasing political sway. In a letter to Tojo, Okawa said this U.S.–Japan trade agreement would be a "lightning stroke" ending the war in China.

"This I believe is the only solution to the present critical situation," Okawa wrote.

Evidently nothing came of this request, because Okawa followed up his letter by confronting Tojo in person. Again Okawa reiterated his belief that Japan must end the war in China before expanding its presence in East Asia. Otherwise it risked upsetting the West and draining precious resources. Tojo dismissed this idea out of hand and wondered, in a mocking tone, what the souls of the dead soldiers would think if Japan left China before achieving a clear victory. Okawa was so frustrated with this reply that he severed his friendship with Tojo for good.

So it was that some part of Okawa Shumei came to oppose the very War for Asian Liberation he'd long championed. His international trading venture had failed by the spring of 1941. (The U.S. State Department suspected the company was a ruse.) By then his confidence in

Tojo as a leader had evaporated, too. (Okawa henceforth referred to Tojo as geta, or Japanese clogs, to suggest he was better placed at the foot of the government.) He kept up a patriotic appearance when called to give his war broadcasts but remained haunted by these personal reservations. He'd been sleeping poorly ever since his return from prison. He'd retire to bed, complain to his wife that his head wasn't clear, and get up again, as if his soothing old dream of one Asia were lost forever.

So FROM THE start of the Greater East Asia War, Okawa Shumei was torn between his country and his conscience. He heard news of Japanese victories piling up one after another. Hong Kong fell in late December of 1941. Singapore surrendered in mid-February of 1942. By March, General Douglas MacArthur had no choice but to retreat from the Philippines to Australia. In late May the last of the British troops evacuated Burma. With each passing week the Japanese empire stretched across more of the Pacific arena. Okawa watched his fellow citizens show their solidarity on the streets and trains of Tokyo. Men wore a khaki outfit with a peaked cap that gave them a soldierly look; women donned baggy pants called *monpe*; everyone sang songs. He rejoiced as the flag of the rising sun flew over a considerable swath of Asia by the spring of 1942, but still felt uneasy at heart.

The patriot in him celebrated the war in a glowing light. For three days in July, and again in September, he went back on the radio to discuss the global significance of the ongoing battle in China. The philosopher in him grieved as the Japanese military—still as outrageous and undisciplined as he'd found it back in Nanking in 1937—caused faith in Asianism to deteriorate across the region. After Indian leaders Gandhi and Nehru denounced Japanese expansion, Okawa wrote them open letters insisting that the fundamental roots of Asian unity were legitimate and that Japanese interest in Asian liberation was sincere.

Tojo continued to rankle him. In November of 1942, the prime minister established a new cabinet department called the Greater East Asia Ministry, whose purpose was to coordinate oversight of Japan's so-called Co-Prosperity Sphere in the region. Okawa found the ministry hollow and pernicious. He considered it indistinguishable from the offices Britain had set up to control colonial India and felt it would antagonize the people of Asia. "I do not believe Tojo was capable of grasping the idea of Greater East Asia," Okawa later said. The distrust broke both ways. Tojo put a tail on his former friend; in surviving photos of Okawa from the era, two policemen lurk in the background. "He persecuted me," Okawa recalled.

The good fortunes of the Japanese military began to turn that summer, when U.S. troops emerged victorious at the Battle of Midway, sinking four Japanese carriers in the process. By February of 1943, Marines had forced the Japanese to withdraw from Guadalcanal in the Solomon Islands. Still, Okawa held fast to the government line. In late February he went on the air again to rally Asian unity. (He would broadcast some thirty shows in all during the war.) That same month, in *Sunrise* magazine, he encouraged all countries in the Greater East Asia Co-Prosperity Sphere "emancipated from Western domination" to cooperate with each other, and promised that "all will end well" if they did. He was hard at work on a new book glorifying the empire's great mission. *The Establishment of Order in Greater East Asia,* published in August of 1943, defended every Japanese policy move of the wartime period.

"The intention of the Greater East Asia War is to rid Asia of foreign, European aggressive powers," Okawa wrote, "sweeping them from our land by building our New Order in East Asia."

He knew that many Asians felt more persecuted than liberated by the Japanese, but he wouldn't let himself accept it. In this he wasn't alone. Many leaders of national independence movements across East Asia initially welcomed the war as a step toward freedom from colonial rule. In November of 1943, Prime Minister Tojo convened an Asiatic conference in Tokyo. The participating parties—representing Japan, Manchukuo, Burma, the Philippines, Thailand, India, and the collaborationist government in China—made a joint declaration to construct a unified Asia. "My Asiatic blood has always called out to other Asiatics," said the Burmese delegate Ba Maw. Okawa attended the conference as a guest. Once again he'd refused to reconcile his mixed emotions.

As the war evolved, though, the Japanese presence in Asia felt every bit as oppressive as the old Western imperialism. Military leaders ravaged the region for war materials, imposed Japanization programs aimed at converting natives into subjects, forced young girls into a new life as "comfort women" for soldiers. The lofty ideals of Pan-Asian brotherhood had become, in practice, a grotesque form of exploitation. Ba Maw later admitted that the strength of Japanese nationalism made true cultural understanding impossible. "[M]ost of the Japanese military leaders were men without a truly Asian vision," he said. Reality defeated the illusions of Asianism one by one, until only a few diehards like Okawa Shumei remained.

ALL THROUGH THE war Okawa Shumei believed things might have been different if only he'd started his Asianist academy earlier. Okawa Juku had been established back in 1938 as a grooming ground for the future ambassadors of Asian unity. The institute recruited seventeen-year-old students who possessed a strong will, a keen sense of responsibility, and a robust constitution. Okawa supervised the strict selection process himself. Applicants who met his criteria and passed a tough entrance exam moved to the Meguro ward of Tokyo, right near Okawa's own residence, where their living expenses were covered for the duration of the two-year program. Until the war broke out, twenty young men from around the country were accepted into each class.

Okawa Juku students were immersed in the intricacies of East Asia from the very start. Upon enrollment they were assigned a particular focus country from a list that accorded with Okawa's broad concept of Asian civilization: India, Siam, French Indochina, and Dutch East Indies in the Far East; Afghanistan, Turkey, Arabia, and Persia in the Middle East. Graduates were embedded in a country with the help of the Japanese government or Okawa himself. Some ended up at consulates, some at commercial firms, some at newspapers. Okawa hoped they'd remain there for a decade, learning the culture of the place from the inside, and asked in return that they make occasional reports home.

If they found some way to aid the liberation movements of the host country, even better.

Students left Okawa Juku with a first-rate education in foreign service. They studied the native language of their focus country as well as English and French. Their course load included Japanese and European history, international politics, and the economics of East Asia. The program was run with a military-style rigor. Student lives were scripted from the moment they awoke at 0530 to lights out at 2200. Classes began promptly at 0900, flag-raising promptly at 0750, more classes promptly at 1300, bathing promptly at 1630. They learned aikido, a style of martial arts derived from jujutsu, from the great Ueshiba Morihei himself.

In addition to giving morning talks, Okawa taught colonial history and the Japanese spirit. His most popular lessons were later compiled into a book called *The Founders of Asia*. Okawa retraced five independence leaders—Gandhi and Nehru of India, Ibn Saud of Arabia, Mustafa Ataturk of Turkey, and Shah Pavlavi of Persia—who'd overcome trials and suffering to "lead Asia to the right direction." The idea that a single person could carry the hopes of an entire nation against the forces of oppression was inspiring to the young men who'd soon become lonely representatives of Japan's great mission in a foreign land. "Students of the Juku adopted this way of thinking," one graduate later recalled. "To become a stepping stone of Asian independence."

The Greater East Asia War sapped the program's virility. Young men who might otherwise have considered Okawa Juku joined the Japanese military; while records are spotty, enrollment declined considerably after 1941, according to Okawa's chief assistant. Graduates already posted in various Asian countries were conscripted into the Army. Many were given special missions that exploited their unique knowledge of the region and its rebellious factions. Twenty died in battle.

Over the course of its existence Okawa Juku acquired a reputation as a spy school. The war ministry partly funded the institute, after all, and its mission was closely tied to the government's "new order" agenda. Recruitment pamphlets emphasized personal qualities typically associated with spy training: a common family, anonymous features, an ability to keep secrets. A cofounder of the institute, Iwakuro Hideo, had pioneered the Army's famed Nakano spy school. General Tanaka Ryukichi, a high Army official, gave guest lectures on sabotage to Okawa Juku students. That the institute failed to hide its relations to espionage was perhaps the strongest reason to doubt that it had any relation to espionage.

Okawa resented this connection and always denied it in strong terms. He maintained that neither the war ministry nor the foreign ministry, which also contributed funding, had control of the school's curriculum. (Foreign officials, for their part, did see graduates as potential intelligence gatherers, though not necessarily covert operatives.) Okawa believed his students served a dual purpose: to accumulate cultural knowledge that would help Japan lead East Asia on the one hand, and to represent Japan's genuine concern for Asian liberation on the other. When he told students the war might have gone differently if he'd started the academy earlier, they took him to mean that as the bonds of Asian community grew stronger, the chances of the East defeating the West rose.

By late 1943, though, Okawa seems to have grown resigned that this chance had passed. He wasn't alone. Much of the country recognized that the tide of war had turned against it. In mid-April, Admiral Yamamoto Isoroku, commander of the Japanese fleet, was shot down and killed by American fighter pilots. By the end of May, the Japanese had also lost the Aleutian Islands. A Japanese stronghold in the Gilbert Islands called Tarawa fell in November. Okawa often communicated with graduates by mail. During that ominous year he wrote to his old students stationed abroad, telling them to prepare for defeat, and also for death.

TOWARD THE FALL of 1944 Okawa returned to his hometown of Sakata. He always visited his mother during these trips, and he liked to see his nephews, too. On occasions when his wife joined him the whole family would pose on the lawn for a portrait. Around the house Okawa sometimes wore a dark kimono, and sometimes a Western suit with a bow tie. Often he invited over military friends and sat with them across a table beside a window facing the mountains. Everyone in town knew him—he was a local legend—and on this particular visit a men's group invited him to give a talk. He accepted.

By late 1944 there was no doubt the Allied forces had control of the war in the Pacific. Back in February, American troops had conquered the Marshall Islands, and later that month an air attack had destroyed a Japanese naval base on the Caroline Islands. Afterward, Japan had mustered one final major offensive in eastern China, but it was far too little too late. That summer the American forces had invaded Saipan, in the Mariana Islands, and clobbered the Japanese Navy. With Tokyo officials clamoring for a change, Tojo Hideki resigned as prime minister in mid-July. Tojo's replacement was General Koiso Kuniaki—the very same who'd worked with Okawa during the aborted coup attempt, back in March of 1931.

Perhaps it was Koiso's appointment that got Okawa thinking about the past, for he certainly had a nostalgic mind-set when he arrived at the Kian Temple in Sakata for his talk at the end of September or the beginning of October. He'd decided to talk about things he'd never talked about in public before—events from his past that everyone knew of but never discussed. He might not have been aware that one of the members of the audience was Haga Saburo, a reporter for the Sakata bureau of the *Mainichi Shimbun,* a Tokyo newspaper. Then again, at that point he may not have cared.

Okawa addressed the men's group in Sakata with unusual candor that day. He talked about the uprising of May 15, 1932, that resulted in the assassination of a sitting premier. He expressed regret over his role in the Manchurian Incident that marked the beginning of Japan's imperial path. "I feel keenly the responsibility for leading Japan into an unexpected direction, with the Manchurian Incident as the starting point," he told the crowd. He said it was up to future generations to weigh the good or evil that had come from his plotting these transformative events.

Okawa also shared his disappointment with Tojo's unwillingness, as war minister back in 1940, to end the military campaign in China. "He laughed at my plan and refused to accept it," Okawa said. It was as if he were hoping to exchange an admission of guilt for a moment of forgiveness.

After the talk, Saburo, the *Mainichi* reporter, was puzzled by what he'd seen and heard that day. This wasn't the Okawa Shumei that everyone in Sakata remembered. Despite his outward composure, Okawa seemed plagued by the misery of his memories. Later, looking back on that day, the reporter wondered if he hadn't seen the first signs of the pressure building inside the mind of Okawa breaking free.

OKAWA KANEKO SAW her husband start to slip right around the same time. The couple bought a home in the Aiko district of Kanagawa prefecture just southwest of Tokyo. It was a very quiet place, set on a hill overlooking the river below and the mountains beyond, far back from the main street. There was a fine Buddhist temple just a short walk away. Still, Okawa Shumei struggled to find peace there. Kaneko noticed her husband becoming very moody. One minute he'd be in great spirits, and the next he'd be in terrible ones. He began to dress sloppily—a very uncharacteristic change, since he was normally so neat and proper in his manners and appearance. He was forgetting things he would normally remember. Whatever had troubled his mind at night was now also distracting him by day.

Everywhere he looked there was more misfortune for Japan. In late fall of 1944, shortly after Okawa's talk in Sakata, MacArthur made a triumphant return to the Philippines, leading the invasion of Leyte, which resulted in yet another decisive American victory. By early March of 1945, the Allies had seized the Philippine capital of Manila, and later that month the British liberated Mandalay, in Burma. In the spring the Americans invaded the islands of Iwo Jima and Okinawa, knocking on the doorstep of Japan's main island. Japanese forces began to withdraw from China in May.

The heavy bombing of Tokyo also began in early March of 1945. American B-29s swept through the sky hundreds at a time and dusted the city with a deadly confetti of oil and phosphorus and napalm bombs. The attacks came every few days and made little if any effort to distinguish industrial military targets from civilian residential areas. Thousands upon thousands of Japanese were killed. Survivors struggled through the wreckage to find food, clothing, and shelter. In the coming weeks millions of people fled Tokyo for a glimmer of safety somewhere outside the city.

On May 24, 1945, hundreds of bombers laid waste to areas of the city just south of the imperial palace. Okawa heard the planes overhead. One of his first thoughts was whether they might strike the Okawa Juku academy in Meguro. He soon learned that the school's main office, along with its records, had been reduced to a pile of ashes and rubble. The last hope of any greater Asianism rising up to rescue Japan faded for him like the final orange pulse of an ember.

The war that began for Okawa Shumei with a radio broadcast ended with another one. A strange voice crackled through the airwaves at noon on August 15, 1945. Like the rest of his countrymen, Okawa had never heard the Showa Emperor speak. In the previous ten days atomic bombs had eviscerated Hiroshima and Nagasaki; everyone knew the end was near, but it could only arrive with the emperor's blessing. In his unprecedented recorded speech, Hirohito told the Japanese people that he'd agreed to accept the Allied terms of surrender. "Indeed," he said, "we declared war on America and Britain out of our sincere desire to ensure Japan's self-preservation and the stabilization of East Asia, it being far from our thought either to infringe upon the sovereignty of other nations or to embark upon territorial aggrandizement."

Okawa couldn't have missed the echo between his own message at the start of the war and that of Japan's beloved leader in its final hour. He listened to the speech then went over to his diary and made a brief entry. Forty years of work toward Asian revival, he wrote, "has vanished like a soap bubble."

JAPANESE MEALS OFTEN consist of what gets translated as a "set." A standard dinner set might include miso soup, a bowl of rice, separate plates of tempura and grilled fish and sushi, a dishlet of pickles, a pad of sweet tofu for dessert. Even a nonpicky eater would struggle to finish the whole thing, and I'm an extremely picky eater. I frequently got the impression, based on vocal inflections and hand gestures, that my translator, Chiaki, was apologizing to a waitress who was either offended or confused that I'd left so much food untouched. In several meals together she never once left a morsel.

"I don't know how you all stay so thin," I said to her one night in Sakata. We were in a local sushi shop, drinking sake with the set. The customary way to drink sake is to fill the other person's cup once it's low. You aren't supposed to fill your own.

"It's all healthy foods," she said.

Chiaki got a lot of exercise pouring sake that night. We'd met a number of people very familiar with Okawa's life and work by that time, but the mysteries about him only seemed to multiply, and his curious nature was starting to bother me. Some saw his Asianism as an honest desire. Some saw it as a masquerade for nationalism or anti-Westernism. Some really believed he'd wanted to avoid a war. Some only believed he'd wanted to avoid a war Japan couldn't win. Some thought he really went crazy. Some saw his insanity as a little too convenient. Okawa was like an intellectual chameleon blending into all the backgrounds of history. I tapped my empty cup and Chiaki filled it again.

"Okawa will confirm whatever opinion you already have," she said.

I found out just how right she was shortly after we returned to Tokyo from Sakata. A couple days later we visited the campus of Tokyo Women's University to meet Usuki Akira. We met him in a conference room lined with what I can only assume was an eclectic collection of works, if the two English titles I noticed—Alex Haley's *Roots* and a book called *Circumcision*—were any indication. Usuki had recently published a well-received book about Okawa's pioneering role in Japanese studies of Islam. That role had culminated with the translation of the Koran he completed after his removal from the Tokyo trial. He'd finished it after recovering his faculties, which led some people to believe he'd never lost them.

"When I was a student, my impression of him was very bad, because he's a right-wing politician, and he was in the international tribunal, and he went mad," said Usuki. "But he recovered soon—why?"

Professor Usuki spoke in English and only turned to Chiaki a few times for help with a particularly tricky phrase. He had the quintessential scholar's look, with a full white beard and eyeglasses hanging around his neck by a long black string. We sat on opposite sides of a long table shared by several small stacks of Okawa's books pulled for reference. Usuki fumbled around for a specific work—"For example, this book; no, not this one, this book; no, not this book . . ."—and finally found a little journal from 1908. This was the first thing Okawa had ever written about Islam. He'd been in his early twenties at the time.

Usuki had a theory about Okawa's intellectual development that all started with this journal article. The topic had been a mystical sect of Islam called Sufism. Usuki believed the work reflected Okawa's youthful attraction to spirituality and idealism. He put down the journal and fumbled around some more for another book. This time he picked up a thick compilation of works, flipped to a page in the middle, and held it up to show me. The page was blank. Usuki explained that Okawa had tried to write an article about Sufism after the war but had never submitted it. The theory was that Okawa's years of involvement in the messy practical politics of prewar Japan, and the even messier Asianist policy of the war itself, had left him out of touch with his spiritual core.

"During his life, he's always a contradiction, on many levels," Usuki said a few minutes later. "He's always divided within himself. He cannot unify himself from within. That is why he had to become mad during the tribunal."

"You think that was the reason he went crazy?" I asked.

Usuki gave a nervous laugh. "Of course he patted Tojo on the head, but after he was hospitalized his madness was not so strong," he said. "Anyway, his contradiction on an idealistic idea and Japanese reality caused him a catastrophe. I think."

Usuki was certainly right that Okawa's life was full of contradictions. He cooperated with the invasion of Manchuria but advocated Asian unity. He maintained an unshakable belief in Japanese superiority but denounced imperialism. He professed deep hatred for the West but steeped his brain with the works of Western thinkers. He imparted the loftiest goals of human harmony to his Okawa Juku students but spent his nights getting drunk with geisha and military officers. His life was an endless series of internal conflicts between sacred ideals and profane execution.

"There's always two trends," said Usuki a little while later. "On the surface the political life, and inside himself the spiritual life."

He held his hands apart to represent both lives then clapped them together.

"And they clashed," Usuki said. "In the daily life he oppressed spirituality, so after World War Two he destroyed himself." He meant "suppressed," I think, but the mistake might actually have been more accurate.

"So you think part of his madness was caused by the fact that he was such a contradiction of suppressed thoughts and vocal thoughts?" I asked.

"That is why he couldn't write on Sufism at the end of his life," he said, fishing out the book with the missing article. "It's blank."

We chatted about the various sides of Okawa Shumei for hours. "Many faces, but he is one," Usuki said. Chiaki had hit the nail on the head: Okawa *could* confirm most any opinion of him, because his character shifted so often. Just before we left, Usuki said something to suggest that his own youthful opinion of Okawa the patriot—right-winger, war criminal, and Tojo slapper—had changed over the years as he'd become more familiar with Okawa the philosopher.

"Okawa is a fascinating man, so please explain him from a positive side," Usuki said. "Of course, he has a very negative side. Contradictions. But in general, he is very, I think, a good guy."

"So you can overlook the coups, and May fifteenth, and Manchuria?" I asked. "You see that as not as important, when it comes to understanding Okawa?"

"Most Japanese—" He turned to Chiaki and said a phrase he couldn't quite put into English. Then she turned to me.

"The people who haven't tasted the food, they hate the food," she said.

Chapter 9

⊣═══⊢

Breakdown

> In retrospect, during combat it was surprising to see that men who had seemed so normal during training broke down under the stress of battle and came to me looking for all the world like the cases of schizophrenia that I had observed in civilian life.
>
> —Daniel Jaffe, "Memoirs of a Combat Psychiatrist," ca. 1996

THE 322ND MEDICAL Battalion left Camp Lucky Strike for the front lines on March 27, 1945, in a motor convoy that took very few breaks. They drove across northern France then straight through Belgium and into the Dutch city of Maastricht, at the southern tip of the Netherlands, on their way toward northwest Germany. The jeep carrying my grandfather reached the border around nightfall. No sooner had his car crossed into Aachen, the first German city captured by Allies, than he heard the bark of gunshots nearby and the whistle of bullets overhead. They hadn't even arrived at the front lines and they were already under attack.

In training my grandfather had been part of the General Staff, but in combat he was attached to the 322nd Medical Battalion. An Army division during World War II had several layers of medical support. Infantry and artillery units had their own tiny medical detachments for immediate battlefield triage. These are the medics dodging bullets right up beside the ground troops in movies. Divisions also had a larger dedicated treatment unit that provided intermediary care between these frontline aid stations and rear-echelon general hospitals. For the 97th Infantry and its fourteen thousand soldiers this intermediary unit was the 322nd Medical Battalion. The battalion broke down into three collecting companies (lettered A, B, and C), each supporting one of the division's three infantry regiments. Collecting companies funneled casualties back to the clearing company (D), stationed in a makeshift hospital two or three miles behind the front lines.

The 322nd reached Europe with about four hundred enlisted men and two dozen medical officers. Enlisted men engaged in a variety of jobs. Litter bearers, nicknamed the "weak mind, strong back" crew, conveyed the wounded. Ambulance drivers and orderlies conveyed the litters. Technicians assisted medical officers during the treatment process. Most officers had been doctors or surgeons or dentists in civilian life, though some with strictly administrative roles had never practiced medicine. Only one was a psychiatrist. He spent most of his time at this clearing station, more or less attached to D Company, in case a collecting company brought back a soldier who'd broken down on the battlefield.

My grandfather must have had a very tense moment there in Aachen, hearing that first gunfire, before he realized he wasn't in any real danger. Medics didn't carry weapons (at least not officially) and their only protection from enemy fire (at least enemies who honored the Geneva Convention) was the red cross on their jeeps and helmets and armbands. The gunshots in Aachen were tracers—friendly little reminders, fired back at them by members of their own division, to observe blackout rules in the combat zone. They'd been driving with their headlights on by mistake. They switched them off and rolled onward into a dark new reality.

ON APRIL 5, 1945, the members of the 322nd Medical Battalion drove fifty-some miles south along the Rhine River, away from a German stronghold at Düsseldorf. It rained on and off all day. They traveled through flat industrial river towns and the cities of Cologne and

Bonn until they reached Bad Godesberg. There they crossed the Rhine atop a set of pontoon bridges that bobbed under the weight of the jeeps. The division's objective was to press back up toward Düsseldorf on the other side of the river. They started north again. As the infantry moved toward the established front line my grandfather's company stopped a few miles back to set up a clearing station. They found a magnificent estate house that stood on a ridge overlooking the river. This was the Schloss Birlinghoven. The men of the 322nd just called it "the castle."

The castle at Birlinghoven was a wide redbrick structure flanked by white towers and topped with a black roof raised upward in a conelike fashion at the center, as if the main section of the building had put on a witch's hat. The Germans had abandoned the building just a few hours earlier. Some of the 97th Infantry units had come through to secure it, and judging by the condition of the crystal chandeliers, a few of the troops had stopped to take some target practice. There was a ballroom just off the main entrance that would serve as a treatment center. The clearing company set up supplies in different corners. Medical equipment here, surgical there, dental here, psychiatric there. They flew a red cross flag outside the castle. Then they waited.

By April of 1945 the Allies had encircled Germany's Army Group B in an area roughly eighty miles in diameter known as the "Ruhr pocket." The Ruhr Valley had been the industrial heart of the Third Reich. Rich in coal and steel—one member of the 97th later called it the "Pittsburgh of Germany"—the Ruhr was the last major source of war material left to the reeling Wehrmacht forces. The commander of Army Group B and its 325,000 trapped troops was defensive mastermind Walter Model. Hitler had called Model his "best field marshal," and the region's network of rivers and thickets made it particularly suitable for delay tactics, but supplies were fading fast and so was Nazi morale. If the Allies could sew up the pocket and force Model to surrender, they would sever the Ruhr's resources from all remaining German armies and take a major step toward ending the war.

From the castle towers the medics of D Company could easily view the front lines three or four miles away. By that time the 97th infantrymen had aligned at the Sieg River, the southern cordon of the Ruhr pocket, and were determining how to cross it safely. The Germans had blown up the bridges and amassed along the steep northern banks. The river itself was maybe five feet deep and quite swift. A division intelligence report estimated the strength of the German forces at roughly seventy-five hundred troops.

The toughest resistance was expected from the 3rd Parachute Division under Colonel Karl-Heinz Becker. The colonel's ferocity was such that, in a pinch for men, he was said to strip his medics of their red crosses and send them to the front. Supporting the German troops were at least two artillery battalions armed with 88-mm guns normally reserved for fighting aircraft and tanks. "That probably was the meanest gun the Germans had," a 322nd medical officer later recalled.

Division command decided the most effective way to ease the infantry's entry into the Ruhr pocket was to cover the banks of the river with heavy artillery fire. That put the medical clearing station, red crosses or not, in the thick of the action. The 97th artillery had set up a few miles back of Birlinghoven and directed its 155-mm howitzers, capable of firing rockets nearly nine miles on an arc, right over top of the castle toward the north side of the Sieg. On April 7, at 1100 hours, its assault on the riverbanks began. The Germans responded with 88-mm shells of their own. The volleying continued through the night. Shrapnel rained down on the treetops beside the castle. German gunners were probably targeting the 97th artillery and falling short, but the medics feared they had the castle itself in their sights.

The psychological effect of the bombardment was immediate. Privates on guard duty, tasked with patrolling the castle grounds, refused to venture out beyond the protection of the walls. One technician slipped down into the basement and wouldn't come back up. My grandfather found it impossible to get any rest. "The nerve-shattering impact of being under fire has to be experienced to be known," he wrote in his memoirs. A cargo truck driver named Roy Peterman was keeping an eye on his vehicle from a small house just off one of the towers when he saw a soldier pacing nearby and a medic consoling him. When Peterman asked what was wrong, the medic said the soldier was "just a little shell-shocked," and left it at that.

———————

I BROUGHT A blank check with me to visit Roy Peterman. He lived in Oakland, Maryland, two-hundred-some miles west of Washington, D.C., near the West Virginia line. It was a midsummer day and temperatures threatened triple digits. Little heat fires sprouted in the grasses at the sides of Interstate 70. They kicked up a blinding smoke that brought drivers on the highway to a dangerously slow speed, and there was a bad stretch when a collision became less a matter of driving skill than of luck before I broke through the cloud.

The blank check wasn't for Peterman—it was for his neighbor. Peterman had served in D Company of the 322nd Medical Battalion with my grandfather. The company had only about a hundred men, but Peterman was an enlisted driver in the motor pool and my grandfather was a medical officer. Even if my grandfather had been the social type, their interactions would have been minimal at best, and, of course, my grandfather wasn't the social type. Peterman told me on the phone he didn't remember him, but there was this company diary that might be useful to me. Only problem was he'd loaned it to a neighbor many years back, and the neighbor had since died, and the neighbor's widow either couldn't find the diary or wasn't really looking for it.

"I was hoping I could get that, and give you information pertaining to your grandfather," Peterman told me on the phone. "I can't seem to get it out of her."

So I'd brought the blank check. I'd also deduced the address of the woman based on her last name (which Peterman had mentioned) and her proximity to the Peterman household (a five-mile drive down one road). Because my grandfather had destroyed all his war letters I knew only the basic outline of his service. Following his movements based on that vague general information was a little like driving across the country through a series of highway smoke patches. Lots of hoping and wondering. That was no way to write a history. Finding the diary wasn't really an option. If Peterman couldn't get it out of her, maybe my blank check could.

Peterman was sitting on a chair on his front porch when I arrived.

There were two American flags hanging above him and two more waving beside the words "Proud American" on his shirt. He was in his late eighties when we met and said he had sat out there just about every morning since he'd retired. He had a round nose and a good amount of white hair at the sides and back of his head, and a hard stare I wouldn't have wanted to test sixty years ago. His handshake was very firm.

I took a seat opposite him at a little patio table covered in a red-white-and-blue cloth and with a few photographs sitting on top.

"Our home here burned some years ago, and we lost an awful lot of stuff, but I had a box of pictures that didn't burn totally down," he said. "We put them back in the garage back there, and I was going through them yesterday and I did find a couple pictures of where we were set up when we were fighting the Germans. What they called 'the castle.'"

The pictures were from a visit he'd made with his family in 1985. By then the castle was home to a big computer company. Peterman had walked the fenced perimeter and seen through an opening that this was the place he'd been during the war. Peterman's son had a brief exchange with the guard—"My father was here in 1945, you know"—who then let him in.

"How different did it look?" I asked.

"The same," he said, without hesitation. "Exactly the same. To this day I can still picture that place. I can picture the very interior of it. Because the first guy I was working on there, one of our sergeants, infantry sergeants, was shot, he died right there, and I know the exact spot I was there when we was working on him. But he died anyway."

We looked at the pictures and chatted about the castle for about an hour. Afterward I took out a piece of paper and we diagrammed a hierarchy for D Company. A few minutes later we got down to a first sergeant named Baumann and Peterman's hard stare returned. This was the guy who'd written the missing diary. Peterman vented about the neighbor he'd loaned it to, the one who'd since died and whose widow evidently wasn't giving it back.

"Well, I didn't want to bother his widow at the time, but he had my diary of my first sergeant there," he said. "So I give her some grieving time, and I finally called, might have been a year, couple years later. She had never gone through his stuff yet. Gave her some more time. Got information with you here. Called again. She never found it. So I know now: anything you want to keep, don't ever loan it."

When we'd put together a decent company tree I asked if Peterman had an official portrait—something to help fit faces to names. He called inside to his wife, Jean.

"I had a picture rolled up—I believe it might have been the company," he said. "Any idea where that is?"

"Probably in the garage with the fire stuff," she said. "I'll go back and look."

I could tell by Jean's tone that she'd made this trip to the garage before and knew what she was—or, in this case, wasn't—going to find there. As helpful as it had been to meet Peterman, it was becoming clear that I'd have to visit his neighbor the widow. I tried not to think about what I might do if she refused to look for the diary, or if she asked for more money than I had. What was the most socially acceptable form of revenge you could take on an elderly woman? A couple things involving her flowers and/or mailbox came to mind, but I worried that wouldn't be enough to ease the pain. My frustration was building when Jean emerged, about ten minutes later, with a sooty box and some moist wipes.

"I don't know what you're wantin', but this is what is back there," Jean said, setting the box on the far side of the porch. "That stuff is dirty. It is *dirty*."

Peterman went over to dig through the items while I shut down my computer in anticipation of the messy material. He began narrating his findings aloud. A few division Trident insignia patches. A few rusty envelopes.

"He hasn't been in that box of stuff, I'll bet you, for twenty years," Jean said. "But I didn't see the one all rolled up."

There was a long silence as Peterman processed a large piece of mail. "I didn't know I had this," he said. I walked across the porch to see. He emptied the contents and handed me the envelope. It was postmarked 1973. Then he handed me the sheets.

"Is this the diary?" I asked.

There it was underlined in the top corner: "Diary"—spelled "Dairy"—of First Sergeant August J. Baumann.

"Yeah!" Peterman yelled.

"Is that it?" Jean asked. "Is it really?"

"I must have had another copy," Peterman said. His hands were dark with soot, and his hard stare had been replaced by a sheepish grin.

"Dairy" [sic] *of First Sergeant August J. Baumann*
Company "D" 322nd Medical Battalion
5 April 1945—At Burlinghovon [sic] *we set up in the famous*
Oppenheiser [*probable* sic] *Castle that we called the Castle. . . .*
Capt. Jaffe joined us here and began the care of N.P. cases.

One of the first neuropsychiatric casualties my grandfather treated at the castle was Private Johnson from G Company of the second battalion of the 386th Infantry Regiment. After the shelling on April 7, the 386th crossed the Sieg on pontoon bridges against light resistance. They were greeted on the other side with the burp of M42 machine guns and the burst of 20-mm flak, but by night they'd pierced the Ruhr pocket and captured several towns. Early the next morning the second battalion resumed its advance with G Company in the center. Heavy salvos greeted them: a barrage of 20-mm shells paired with the dreaded 88s. The artillery assault was "more intense than any we had received to this date," recorded Private First Class Durig, a company rifleman, in the battalion diary. The men were ordered to continue the battle into the late hours.

The Germans disappeared into the dense woods. Battalion intelligence feared they might "infiltrate or probe our lines during the night." That concern proved deadly accurate. Under cover of darkness an enemy squad waylaid a second battalion command post and shot a first sergeant, who had stepped outside to relieve himself, right in the head. The other Americans held off the raiding German party, then pushed forward at an incredible pace. On April 9 they captured sixteen towns. Frightened civilians flew white bedsheets from their windows. On

April 10 the battalion took fourteen more towns in the face of strong resistance: sniper fire in the villages, artillery fire and machine-gun cover in the open areas. Flak from the 20-mm German guns was even heavier than it had been days before.

The movement quickened even as the men of the 386th "were practically dead on their feet from weariness," according to an official regiment history. Early on April 11, supported by the division artillery, G Company launched an attack on a river near the town of Much. At precisely 0942 hours, the infantry reported a German artillery response. Three minutes later, with the shells still pounding overhead, Private Johnson was evacuated to the clearing station with "exhaustion."

The 386th Infantry Regiment was assigned to B Company of the 322nd Medical Battalion. If protocol held, then a B Company ambulance collected Johnson from the battlefield aid station, deposited his litter at the castle entrance, and turned back around for the front. As the litter bearers carried Johnson into the castle, an admitting officer, typically Captain Ainsworth, directed them to my grandfather's corner. "The men who were brought in with combat fatigue or shell-shock had been seemingly normal up to the point of breakdown, then manifested the signs and symptoms characteristic of the acute schizophrenic cases seen in civilian life," he wrote in his memoirs. The cases he'd seen in medical school, and St. Elizabeth's Hospital, and, of course, his own home—only now wearing a uniform.

No MATTER THE theater, no matter the division, no matter the experience, soldiers who broke down on the battlefields of World War II made their way back to the clearing station looking eerily alike. They were disoriented, incoherent, delusional, hallucinatory, or some combination of each. Case records from the war reveal idiosyncrasies—the private with a tic in his arm that wouldn't subside, the staff sergeant who had to pull out his dog tags when the doctor asked his name, the technician who'd earned a Bronze Star for bravery but came in weeping and trembling—but the general loss of control remained the same.

They said the same things, too. A soldier in the 88th Infantry told the psychiatrist at clearing: "I just can't take that damn artillery." A private in the 85th Infantry said he shook "every time them shells came in." A private first class in the 36th Infantry said he couldn't return to combat because "just drop a couple shells in there and I'd be no use." A staff sergeant in the 91st Infantry didn't have to say a thing: he jumped so violently at even the slightest noise that medics in the clearing station could hardly approach him. William Menninger, who oversaw military psychiatric services for the surgeon general's office during World War II, summarized this universal condition a few months after the fighting ended.

"When the final straw is placed on the soldier's back," Menninger wrote, "the immediate result appears very similar in all cases."

Captain Etter, one of the highest officers in the 322nd Medical Battalion, kept a general accounting of the thirty-eight neuropsychiatric cases that reached D Company during the division's forty-some days of combat. Nearly half were matters of clear combat fatigue—the sort of physical breaking point reached by Private Johnson—or a mild anxiety prompted by shell fire. For these cases my grandfather administered a fast-acting and long-lasting sedative called sodium amytal, varying the dosage depending on the severity, and let them sleep anywhere from thirty-six to seventy-two hours. When they awakened he took a brief patient history and offered some light reassurance about their recovery. At that time, at least according to protocol, they were ordered to shower and eat a hot meal. Most soldiers who received this basic three-day regimen returned to combat duty immediately afterward and stayed there. Captain Etter reported the division suffered "few recurrences."

For some soldiers this treatment course wasn't quite enough. A little less than half of incoming neuropsychiatric cases were sent to a division rest camp for several days of additional observation and treatment under the care of less-harried medics. These men were generally reassigned to noncombat duties; they didn't see action again. Seven soldiers from the 97th Infantry presented a psychosis so severe at the clearing station that they were evacuated to a hospital in the very rear of the theater.

In a few tough cases my grandfather performed a rather intense procedure known as "narcotherapy." He'd learned about the method at the Washington conference for new division psychiatrists back in 1943. He relaxed patients with a barbiturate, established a comfortable rapport, then teased out their traumatic experiences until they achieved a clinical point of release known as abreaction. In one extraordinary case, according to Captain Etter, my grandfather used narcotherapy to recover the vision of an officer brought to the clearing station with hysterical blindness.

The records of the second battalion of the 386th Infantry Regiment indicate that Private Johnson returned to active duty with G Company after his bout of "combat exhaustion." Every casualty who reached the clearing station from this particular battalion, which comprised companies E through H, likely caused my grandfather a rush of worry. One of his closest friends during training had been Captain Walter Duffield. Initially Duffy had been part of the General Staff, but shortly before the division embarked for Europe he'd requested and received a transfer to a fighting unit. General Halsey placed Duffy in command of F Company of the 386th. (Waxy, his other close friend, remained back at division headquarters, far removed from the action.) My grandfather never quite put it this way, but he must have kept a strangely conflicted heart at the clearing station: wanting very much to see his good friend again, but knowing too well what it would mean if he did.

COMBAT PSYCHIATRISTS OVERSAW a three-tiered forward-echelon system during World War II. The first thing they did was encourage battalion surgeons up at the battlefield aid stations to treat mild breakdowns at the immediate point of medical contact. They were present themselves at the second level of treatment, the division clearing station, to handle moderate cases. Soldiers who needed additional recovery time went back a short ways to the third level, known as the division rest area, which had much more room and medical staff. Frederick Hanson, who's credited with conceiving this network, wrote that by late 1944 it was operating at an "optimum plane."

Those in charge of the military's psychiatric program believed soldiers who stayed within this treatment triangle stood the best chance of returning to action. Broadly speaking, they were correct. Before the addition of division psychiatrists, when mental casualties were evacuated to field and general hospitals at the rear of a combat theater, only about 5 to 10 percent returned to duty. By March of 1945, frontline psychiatrists returned some 60 percent of psychiatric cases—not counting those treated at battlefield aid stations, which didn't keep close records—usually within two to five days. By that time only one in ten soldiers who broke down had to be evacuated from a theater of operations. This return rate was accomplished despite a severe shortage of personnel: in the European theater there was one surgeon for every ten surgical cases but only one psychiatrist for every twenty-three psychiatric cases.

The success of combat psychiatry during the Normandy invasion alone was worth the effort of implementing the program. In the two months after D-day, there was an average of one psychiatric hospital admission for every two medical admissions in the First Army. Without a system in place to treat and salvage mental casualties, American manpower would have been severely crippled—with divisions losing at least a fifth of their strength, according to one estimate. Instead, combat psychiatrists maintained the momentum from the beaches. One rest center established for D-day salvaged 80 percent of psychoneurotic cases for full or limited duty. All told, the First Army reported 11,000 psychiatric admissions during June and July of 1944. Of these it lost only 4,000 men. That isn't to say the Allies would have lost this crucial battle without the work of division psychiatrists, but winning it would have been considerably tougher.

The key to the division psychiatrist's work was a promptness that left no time "for symptoms to become fixed," in the words of the surgeon general's office. Most mental casualties treated at the front lines received little more than a sedative for rest and a chat for reassurance. The rest revived a soldier's physical condition—the theory being that "combat fatigue" was truly caused, in large part, by extreme fatigue. The reassurance restored his mental faculties. Ideally the psychiatrist used a tone kind enough to establish therapeutic rapport but firm enough to maintain military authority. He convinced the soldier, in the simplest possible terms, that the experience was a normal reaction to the strains of combat. "In appropriate cases it was stressed that the reaction was situational, that it would be short-lived, and that it had no relationship to 'insanity,'" wrote military psychiatrist Stephen Ranson in a postwar review of treatment at the clearing stations. He made it known that a full return to duty was both expected and imminent. (Clear neurological injuries like blast concussions usually improved in a few weeks, though these cases often involved psychological components, and were treated appropriately.)

The very setup of the clearing station left the soldier comfortable enough to recover but not so comfortable he wouldn't want to return to battle. He got a good meal and a shower and a shave, but he stood on the chow line himself and hit the latrine unassisted. He got attention from medical technicians, but they were men wearing fatigues not nurses in hospital uniforms. At the rest areas a few miles back, this climate of recovery was maintained. After a few days there patients took part in marches and other basic drills. Only those who failed to improve after a week were evacuated to a traditional hospital. Even there the goal was to salvage soldiers for noncombat duty. The entire system was designed to conserve manpower. The term "combat fatigue" itself was imprecise by civilian standards—there was almost always more to these cases than mere exhaustion—but quite practical by military ones.

There was a legitimate theoretical reason for treating mental casualties in this manner. Keeping soldiers close to the front reduced what psychiatrists referred to as "secondary gain." Most soldiers faced competing desires: to avoid further harm on the one hand, and to rejoin their comrades on the other. In a comfortable hospital the incentive to avoid harm might win out. In a military-style clearing station the psychological bond with fellow soldiers remained strong. Division psychiatrists often reminded a soldier of his loyalty to the unit during the "reassurance" phase of his treatment. "Men who have lived together and faced dangers together form bonds that become more important than any other force, including that of self-preservation," my grandfather wrote in his memoirs. The same environment that produced enough stress to trigger a breakdown also often produced enough comfort to heal it.

The rest-and-reassurance approach, simple as it may seem in retrospect, proved remarkably durable. One postwar study of psychiatric cases found that soldiers who received sedation served an average of eleven months after their initial breakdown. This wasn't just a body in the field: three-quarters of this group had a quality of service deemed "good" or "satisfactory." In its final annual review the surgeon general's office declared that the effectiveness of the division psychiatrist had been "completely and definitely established." Still, battlefield psychiatry wasn't a permanent fix. Fifteen to 20 percent of mental casualties who received frontline treatment suffered a recurrence. Psychiatrists knew some cases would have been better helped with individualized civilian-style therapy, but the exigencies of combat didn't allow for it. The time involved in such an approach was simply too great.

Military psychiatrists in World War II relieved symptoms to salvage soldiers. What that meant for their long-term health no one knew. "The permanent effect of the Army experience, and specifically that of combat, on their personalities will only be known with the passage of time," William Menninger himself later admitted. It was something better discovered once the war was won.

As the 97th Infantry advanced toward Düsseldorf the wounded piled up back at the castle. The division scrapped with the nasty 3rd Paratroop Division on the streets of Siegburg then pushed north to Troisdorf, where the Germans gave them "one of the toughest battles we had in the Ruhr Pocket," according to General Sherman Hasbrouck, the artillery commander. Casualties ran three shrapnel victims to every one gunshot wound. The castle could treat maybe a hundred fifty injured soldiers at a time, but by mid-April the medical officers alone couldn't quite handle the load. The situation required the battalion's high command to set aside their authoritative roles and partake in treatment themselves. Anyone with a medical or surgical background was pressed into general emergency service—my grandfather included.

Daniel S. Jaffe, MD, entered the medical corps of the U.S. Army as a first lieutenant in 1942, at age twenty-eight, eventually rising to major. Trained in neurology, Jaffe spent nearly a year treating evacuated soldiers on the psychiatric ward of Valley Forge General Hospital. In late 1943, as part of a military effort to improve mental health on the front lines, he joined the 97th Infantry as a combat psychiatrist.

1

2

Esther and Harry Jaffe, shown here circa 1920, were Russian immigrants who settled in Brooklyn to raise four children, Daniel being the third. Daniel later said he became a doctor to fulfill the dream that had been denied to his father. His decision to focus on the mind, however, was likely the result of his mother's psychiatric troubles—as Esther suffered a series of tragic breakdowns and spent much of her life in mental institutions.

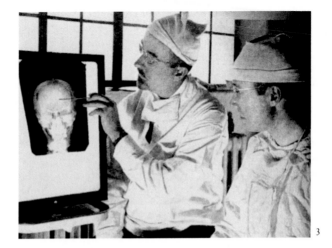

3

Drs. Walter Freeman (left) and James Watts, shown here circa 1941, performed the first lobotomy in the United States in 1936. Both men became mentors to Daniel Jaffe—first while he was a medical student at George Washington University, and again during his postgraduate studies in Freeman's lab and D.C.-area hospitals. This training occurred during a bold era in mental health treatment that exchanged passive asylum care for proactive interventions.

4

In early 1943, Daniel Jaffe (far right) was transferred to Valley Forge General Hospital, where he treated soldiers who'd been evacuated from the rough North African theater. Most patients who ended up on the psychiatric ward were discharged or sent to specialized hospitals for more treatment. Hospital records show that only 52 of 980 neuropsychiatric patients at Valley Forge in 1943 continued to serve after their release.

General George S. Patton, shown here in March 1943, brought the mental health of soldiers into the public light later that year by slapping two infantrymen who'd suffered breakdowns on the battlefield. In November, the military added one psychiatrist to each infantry division. Soon after joining the 97th, Daniel Jaffe was sent with the other new combat psychiatrists to Washington, D.C., for a three-day crash course in frontline treatment.

5

6

Caroline Jaffe followed her husband across the country, from camp to camp, as the 97th Infantry trained during 1944. During this time, Daniel orchestrated the division's preventive psychiatry program, designed to prepare soldiers mentally for combat. Shown here during a late-summer furlough in San Francisco, the couple would soon learn Caroline was pregnant—followed closely by word that the division was shipping out.

7

During combat in Europe, Jaffe was attached to the clearing company of the 322nd Medical Battalion. The company established makeshift hospitals just behind the front lines in buildings such as the Schloss Birlinghoven, shown in present day, which the medics called "the castle." By treating combat breakdowns quickly with rest and reassurance, combat psychiatrists returned most soldiers to battle within a couple days—preserving military manpower.

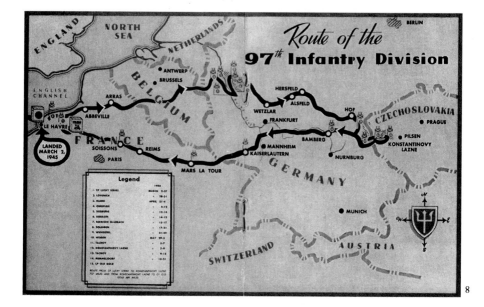

8

Altogether the 97th Infantry was considered the most traveled division in the army, covering some thirty-five thousand miles of land and sea. The infantry chased the Germans east toward Czechoslovakia and was credited with firing the final shot of the European theater. Afterward, the 97th raced back across Europe and returned to the United States to prepare for occupation duty in Tokyo, Japan.

Okawa Shumei was one of twenty-eight Class-A war crimes defendants at the International Military Tribunal for the Far East that followed World War II—better known as the "Tokyo trial." Shown at his arraignment in May 1946, at age fifty-nine, Okawa was indicted as the brain trust behind Japan's aggressive policy of expansion. His Asianist ideology encouraged Japan to lead the Far East in opposition to Western imperialism.

9

10

During World War I, Okawa (left) befriended several Indian dissidents who opposed British rule from the safe confines of Japan, including the rebel Rash Behari Bose. Okawa started a series of activist groups bound by the tenets of Asianism, sparking a broad underground movement. Tokyo trial prosecutors later called his 1922 book, *Various Problems of Asia in Revival*, the "standard Pan-Asiatic handbook of the Japanese nationalists."

11

In 1925, Okawa wrote that America and Japan would one day meet in a "life-and-death struggle" for world supremacy. Shortly after the Japanese attack on Pearl Harbor (here, flames engulf the battleship USS *West Virginia*), Okawa repeated his prophecy during a popular radio lecture called "America's Great East Asia Invasion History." The six-part propaganda series made the case that Japan's war was being fought in response to decades of American aggression in East Asia.

12

General Tojo Hideki (center) was close to Okawa before the war, often lecturing to students at Okawa's Asianist academy. As prime minister for most of the war, Tojo adopted Asianist ideas as part of his official policy (here at a meeting of the Greater East Asia Conference in 1943). But Japan's poor treatment of fellow Asians during the war left many believing that Eastern unity was really Japanese superiority in disguise.

13

American bombardments in 1945 obliterated Tokyo, destroying some 65 percent of all homes, as well as the headquarters of Okawa's Asianist academy. After the war, displaced and hungry Japanese soldiers found shelter alongside widows and orphans in railroad stations and abandoned ruins. When the emperor surrendered on August 15, 1945, Okawa wrote that forty years of work toward Asian revival "has vanished like a soap bubble."

14

Occupied forces arrested Okawa in late 1945 and held him at Sugamo Prison with the other war crimes suspects. In early 1946, right around the time the Allies announced their indictments, Okawa began to act strangely—scribbling nonsense in books and asking to be released. While fellow inmates thought he was suffering a mental breakdown, some American guards believed he was faking madness.

15

Okawa Shumei (back row, center) stands in the dock with the other Japanese defendants at the Tokyo trial arraignment on May 3, 1946. Far taller than the others, and wearing a light pajama shirt rather than a dark suit, Okawa also stuck out as the lone civilian on trial. Okawa often described the Tokyo trial as a psychological "continuation of the war," implying that its goal was not to uphold justice but rather to dispense punishment.

16

Moments after slapping Tojo Hideki at the arraignment, Okawa sits subdued by Colonel Aubrey Kenworthy. Okawa was transferred to the 361st Station Hospital, where Daniel Jaffe determined him mentally incapable of standing trial. Okawa was set free as a result and later recovered his faculties—sparking an ongoing debate about whether or not he faked his insanity to avoid prison or execution.

"This was the first real touching casualty scene," wrote Sergeant Baumann in his diary, "where every man worked until he could hardly move."

My grandfather didn't write much about the medics who served with him at the castle, but various records and memories offer a portrait of the men he spent so much time working beside. The commander of the 322nd Medical Battalion was a chubby-faced, beady-eyed, foul-mouthed physician from Tennessee named Lieutenant Colonel Herd. In official division pictures from the period Herd wore circular glasses with thin frames. He'd joined the 97th Infantry back in February of 1944 after an infamously rough campaign against the Japanese on the island of Guadalcanal. His peers called him an excellent surgeon despite an awful technique. Those who knew him well also called him a first-rate drinker—capable of polishing off a fifth of whisky without showing it.

The battalion's executive officer, or second in command, was Major Gilliatt. The major had a staccato laugh and enjoyed the privileges of his rank, but he was also a compassionate guy by nature, once saving a breakfast line by catching another soldier's vomit in his own helmet. During the patient rush at the clearing station, Gilliatt handled most of the medical casualties: nonsurgical wounds, illnesses, and the like.

Major Rich, who happened to be very wealthy, was technically in charge of D Company at the start of the war, but according to Baumann's diary, Captain Etter assumed day-to-day command of the clearing station. Etter was a classic Texan with a slight temper. He was a great surgeon—and, at least according to rumor, equally proficient with women—and split the hardest cases with Herd. He'd known my grandfather in civilian life, trailing him at George Washington medical school by a few years.

Captains Miller and Todd, who'd been with the outfit from the very start, were close drinking buddies. They never could get Captain Morterano, the Protestant chaplain, to join them—even if they promised to go to chapel in return. Captain Ainsworth was a dentist who doubled as a tireless admitting clerk at the clearing station. Staff Sergeant Farley was so overwhelmed by the flow of patients at the castle, according to Baumann, that he "gave out and had to be put to bed."

Fifty years later my grandfather still recalled the first soldier he watched die on the litter during the war. It was an old sergeant with a bellyful of shrapnel. "With his vital signs dropping, I bent over him, rushing frantically to insert the needle and get the plasma going," my grandfather later wrote. "As long as I live I shall never forget his last words, as his life was ebbing away: 'Tell me I'm going to make it, doc— I've got a wife and four kids waiting for me back home.'"

FEW SOLDIERS REMAINED at the clearing station long, but most who did arrive needed immediate attention. Doctors and technicians at the castle fashioned pressure bandages and tourniquets, changed dressings prepared at the battlefield aid stations, applied or adjusted splints, even made full blood transfusions when the case demanded. Their goal was not so much to heal the wounded soldier as to ensure he could survive the seventy-five-mile-or-so evacuation back to the general hospital at the rear.

The medics at the clearing station also had the uncomfortable duty of treating German soldiers and civilians in the area. Many of these cases were medical; an outbreak of typhus from Cologne reached the castle at one point. Like most illnesses it was treated with penicillin, because there wasn't really another medication at the time. Sergeant Baumann recorded the admittance of a local woman who'd been shot dashing toward the American lines with grenades stuffed in her apron pockets.

At least one technician spoke German, and the chaplain, Morterano, spoke Italian, and some of the higher-ranking enemies didn't need a translator. Etter once operated on an SS sniper who bragged, in good English, about shooting nine Americans in eleven shots. The ambulance driver assigned to evacuate him after the operation returned to report that the sniper had died en route. "He accidentally got a blanket wrapped around his head, or something," the driver said.

By April 14, 1945, the 97th Infantry had advanced so deep into the Ruhr pocket that the medics had to move to keep up. They set up a new clearing station in a chateau in Wahlscheid owned by the Baron La Valette. The "baron's place," as Baumann called it, had a lovely central fountain and an even lovelier Baroque chapel and far less lovely pictures of the baron with Hitler hanging on the walls. The men looted the place as soon as they arrived. When some jewels went missing—the troops would have said they were "liberated"—battalion commanders demanded their return under threat of court-martial. Apparently the guilty parties complied because in exchange for the recovery of his valuables the baron opened his magnificent wine cellar and gave each medical officer, and a few noncoms, a bottle of vintage champagne. My grandfather stowed his in the trunk that held his psychiatric files for a special occasion.

He got a scare that evening when ten soldiers from F Company of the second battalion of the 386th Infantry Regiment came through the clearing station. Five suffered shrapnel wounds. One died. No Duffy, though.

The following afternoon he was relieved from surgical support to treat another mental casualty. This was Private First Class Parsons from E Company of the 386th. Parsons had suffered exhaustion after a three-day blitz that carried the regiment's second battalion through several dozen towns. They'd swept forward against light resistance on April 13 and 14 before enduring a rough night near Bechen. German snipers peppered the position and 88s thundered through the night. As if that weren't enough, rumors swirled that the so-called Werwolf had infiltrated the area—Nazi commandos known for ambushing the Allies on their side of the lines. On April 15 the second battalion jumped off at 0700 hours with E Company on the left flank. They'd hoped to make another quick advance but struggled against heavy rifle fire from the 3rd Paratroopers, and what reports called a "moderate volume" of shelling from those wicked 88s.

Parsons returned to active duty, according to records, and the medical battalion left the baron's place that day, according to Baumann's diary, to keep up with the troops.

THE 97TH INFANTRY broke through the rest of the Ruhr pocket nearly unopposed. The remaining Wehrmacht defenses dissolved when Field Marshal Model, recognizing defeat, released the men of Army Group B from service. (Goebbels soon denounced him as a traitor, and Model shot himself in the forest.) Capitulating soldiers clogged the roads by the thousands; all told, the division took nearly twenty-two thousand prisoners in the Ruhr.

The clearing company scrambled to keep a station close. They left the baron's place for a Nazi school in Bergisch Gladbach, then three days later overtook an opera house in Solingen with a mammoth pipe organ and Steinway concert pianos. There were few casualties now and only one real scare: when Lieutenant Kamine, an administrative officer, misread a map and accidentally led D Company in front of the infantry. "Did we high tail it, you bet," Baumann wrote.

On April 18, 1945, the German powers in Düsseldorf surrendered the city to General Halsey without a fight. That day my grandfather radioed back to headquarters from the opera house that he'd ordered four enlisted men with severe combat fatigue to a rest camp. The heavy fighting was over but the feverish pace of the pocket had caught up with them.

A driver from the quartermaster company named Dworkin recalled evacuating some psychiatric cases to a field hospital right around this time. They might have been these four soldiers my grandfather ordered back, or perhaps another group just like them. As Dworkin drove south along the Rhine his orderlies joked that these mental casualties had gamed the system. They'd accomplished enough on the battlefield to go home with their heads high but removed themselves from whatever dangers lay ahead. The condescending implication was that their maladies were invented. Dworkin wasn't so sure.

"They seemed to be hypnotized, as if in a trance. None of them would talk to us," he recalled. "I personally could sense they had really cracked up mentally."

———

THE CLEARING COMPANY left Solingen on April 21 in a heavy rain. They made their way toward the forests of Bavaria and bivouacked in a field near Elsenfeld. They covered the patients then set up their own pup tents and, according to Baumann, spent the night shivering on the wet ground.

The next evening they arrived at Wunsiedel, near the border of what's now the Czech Republic, and set up a clearing station in a school. There would soon be casualties to receive; the division had joined General George Patton's Third Army for an attack on the receding German forces that everyone hoped would prove decisive. Two days later, during a lull at the station that preceded the action, my grandfather spotted his name in the *Stars and Stripes* military paper at the bottom of a column with a diapered infant on top. His wife had given birth to a son. He uncorked the vintage champagne from the baron's place and drank it down.

His celebration was brief. It quickly transformed into what he later called "considerable anxiety" when he learned the new objective of the second battalion of the 386th Infantry Regiment. Division orders called for supporting Patton's advance into southern Germany and Austria by protecting his left flank. That meant penetrating the border of Czechoslovakia and seizing the city of Cheb, an administrative center and site of a war factory and a large airport.

The infantry was not anticipating a warm welcome. According to intelligence reports the eastward-retreating Germans had guarded the city with a formidable fence of land mines and booby traps and road blocks. The division was sending a platoon of engineers with the second battalion of the 386th just to be sure they could enter Cheb; if they did, their reward would be an entrenched German defense force. Duffy and F Company would play a central role in the mission.

So there was plenty of reason for fear. On the morning of April 25 an F Company squad vehicle was found near the Eger River, which runs toward the Czech border. The truck was burned and the soldiers were missing. Still, the advance on Cheb proceeded as planned. With tanks at their backs and artillery cover ahead, in the face of machine-gun fire and German flak guns, the second battalion of the 386th fought their way into the city. The assault lasted nine hours.

By dark they'd secured the high ground north of Cheb along the river. German 88s and 20-mm shells shrieked throughout the night sky. The next day the 386th met the 387th, which had come up from the south, in the center of the city. After street fighting against German snipers and small pockets of resistance, the Allies controlled their first Czech city.

The medics back at the clearing station in Wunsiedel had their hands full. They treated two engineers whose weapon carrier had been riddled with bullets courtesy of the Werwolf. Captain Etter amputated the leg of a German soldier after another medical officer started the procedure but couldn't finish it. The 386th Infantry Regiment liberated some sixteen hundred Russian slave laborers being housed in a German factory, and about a hundred of them, severely sick or malnourished, were brought to the clearing station for medical attention. My grandfather was put in charge of their care, according to Baumann, with Sergeants Zajac and Andrzejowski acting as interpreters.

Through the commotion he no doubt kept an eye out for any casualties from F Company. Private First Class Mathern came in with gunshot wounds to both legs. Lieutenant Zalenski arrived with a scalp wound. Private First Class Hiskey suffered light wounds of a general nature. As before, no Duffy.

The fighting in Cheb was so severe that even one of the medics in the field couldn't take it. Private First Class Toth was an assistant ambulance driver in C Company, which collected the casualties from the 387th Infantry, manning a vehicle with Private First Class Thomas. Toth was old for an enlisted man. He'd been drafted when he was in his late thirties, according to Thomas, and at night would sit down with a pencil and write letters to his two young daughters. "I think that's what hurt him the most, being away from them," Thomas recalled. Toth was good behind the wheel—he'd been a professional trucker in civilian life—but he did get jumpy under heavy fire. At Cheb the shells came eager and often. One night, during the fight for the city, Thomas returned from the clearing station in Wunsiedel and looked around for his partner. He found Toth sitting in a daze on a wall near an old farm house.

"I said, 'We got to go make another run,'" Thomas recalled. "He said, 'I'm not making another run. I'm going home.' That was the last I saw of him."

WILLIAM MENNINGER HAD sent a representative from the surgeon general's office into an active combat theater in the late spring of 1944 to determine why American soldiers broke down. He'd chosen John Appel, head of mental hygiene for the military's psychiatric service, who arrived in Italy toward the end of the costly battles for Cassino and Anzio. For six weeks Appel had joined the 601st Clearing Company and a few other frontline medical installations set up behind General Mark Clark's advancing Fifth Army. He'd examined several hundred psychiatric cases brought back as the Americans pushed toward Rome. At the time of this mission some military officials still doubted the veracity of mental casualties. Appel had dismissed such skepticism immediately upon his arrival.

"One look at the shrunken apathetic faces of psychiatric patients as they come stumbling into the medical station, sobbing, trembling, referring shudderingly to 'them shells' and to buddies mutilated or dead, is enough to convince most observers," he wrote.

Over the course of his evaluation Appel concluded that military breakdowns occurred in direct relation to the intensity and duration of a soldier's combat service. He estimated the average infantryman could endure about ninety days of fighting before something caused him to crack. Some broke down at the very sound of the artillery. Others lasted until exhaustion weakened their natural psychological defenses. Still others were able to adapt to their strange new world until a shell caught a buddy. These ninety days marked a soldier's "peak of effectiveness," wrote Appel, after which time he became "steadily less valuable." A separate analysis performed during the war confirmed that roughly one in five soldiers broke down within the first three months of combat duty. Decades later, looking back at his service, Appel wrote that the strains of battlefield life "could no more be comprehended by one who had not had it than could the experience of sexual intercourse."

Those who found a way to survive the first ninety days with their faculties intact eventually broke, too. They'd built up an immunity to the terrors of warfare, but as their comrades disappeared, through either death or wounds, they lost the social support that had buoyed them through the hardest times. The prolonged physical and mental strain caught up with them. Seasoned troops became fearful that their time would soon arrive—if only due to the law of averages. They converted this fear into a caution that rendered them useless; sometimes they demoralized the younger replacements in their units. When they broke down they looked no different from those who'd cracked during the very first shell fire. There was a name for this psychological erosion: "old sergeant syndrome." Appel estimated that only about 10 percent of soldiers made it through two hundred aggregate days of combat without succumbing to it.

"Just as a 2.5 ton truck becomes worn out after 14–15,000 miles," he wrote, "it appears that the doughboy becomes worn out."

Two factors above all others moderated a soldier's ability to handle the intensity and duration of his combat service. The first was leadership. Ineffectual line officers made their men vulnerable to mental breakdown. In one infantry regiment documented by Appel, a third of all psychiatric cases came from a company whose commanding officer ducked for cover whenever the firing began. Previous studies from the same theater supported this conclusion. During the Sicilian campaign, in the summer of 1943, one battalion had more than twice the psychiatric casualties as the two others in its same regiment. Roughly 40 percent of soldiers from this unit later said its commanding officers were not the kind worth supporting. Conversely, some leaders were so great their absence caused dismay. Theodore Suratt, psychiatrist for the 44th Infantry, reported that eight men from a single company once broke down on the same day their beloved commanding officer fell wounded. One of these mental casualties had served 114 days until that time without a problem.

The other key factor was a conviction to fight. Some considered motivation—or lack thereof—the main reason the American military had far greater rates of mental casualties than other armies during the war. Psychiatric cases accounted for roughly half of all medical discharges in the U.S. Army but only about 17 percent in the Russian army and around 30 percent in the British. Appel attributed this astonishing disparity to the fact that Russian and British soldiers wanted to avenge the death of their loved ones and restore the honor of their homelands, whereas the American soldier "fights because he has to." (Menninger suspected that low breakdown rates found among German troops were the result of the Third Reich's sophisticated indoctrination program.) Americans often felt they'd done their part and earned the right to go home to loved ones. "We had a way of saying that as many casualties were caused on Guadalcanal by the mail from home as through enemy bullets," wrote one combat psychiatrist after the war.

Upon his return from the combat theater Appel had prepared a report on the reasons for battlefield breakdowns, as well as recommendations for limiting them. He believed the military should establish a clear tour of duty for infantry soldiers (to minimize the intensity and duration of their service), and that replacements should join combat units in groups of at least three (to enhance their social support system). "Under the present policy nobody is removed from combat duty until he has become completely worthless," wrote Appel. "[A]ll he can look forward to is being killed, wounded or completely broken down nervously." The surgeon general's office had forwarded the report to Chief of Staff George Marshall, who appreciated it so much, despite being no friend to the military's psychiatric problem, that he sent it to the commanding officers of all three major theaters of operation: Mark Clark in Italy, Dwight Eisenhower in Europe, and Douglas MacArthur in the Pacific.

In late May of 1945, after much deliberation and internal dissent, the Army approved a tour of 120 aggregate days in combat and a system of group replacements. The military's understanding of psychiatric breakdowns had evolved a great deal since the start of the war: from the initial belief that only weaklings broke, to the recognition that anyone might break, to the realization that many of the broken could be restored. War neuroses didn't come from simple cowardice. Instead, as Menninger wrote in late 1945, they emerged when some unpredictable event on the battlefield upset a precarious balance of severe stress, social support, and individual personality. Of course, by the time the American military reached a consensus and implemented the new psychiatry program, the war in Europe was already won, and many minds already lost.

MY GRANDFATHER EVENTUALLY learned that Duffy had his rifle blown out of his hands during the fighting at Cheb but survived the battle just fine. The two remained friends long after the war. One year the whole family drove out to California to meet the Duffields. My father, just a little kid at the time, remembers that Duffy was mixing his Scotch into a big glass of milk because the doctor had told him not to drink with his ulcers. My aunt and uncle recall these visits as the only times my grandfather really talked about the war. On one occasion Duffy pointed at my uncle and said: "Did I have anything to do with that?" It was the type of bawdy joke my grandmother normally would not have appreciated. Duffy was loud and boisterous, the complete opposite of my grandfather.

"He was from a different planet from us," my uncle once said. "They never would have been friends if it wasn't for the war."

Duffy died long before I came around—pancreatic cancer—and he never had any children. Once, while searching for information about him, I came across a book written by a veteran named Neal Oxenhandler. During the service Oxenhandler had been in F Company of the 386th Infantry Regiment, serving directly under Duffy's command. At the start of the war Oxenhandler had questioned whether or not he could go through with it. "What was worth dying for?" he wrote after a day in which some of his buddies had died. "We had been through a lot together. Maybe they were worth dying for." That same night, while on watch, he shot a German intruder. He stood over the man he'd killed the next morning and felt nothing.

"My friends closed in and there was a rush of solidarity that drove the feeling of emptiness away," Oxenhandler wrote. "After that, I had no more internal debates. I was in the war to stay."

As division psychiatrist, my grandfather understood the psychological importance of soldier camaraderie during combat, but as far as I can tell he never developed much of it himself. After he wrote his memoirs he sat down with my grandmother and aunt one day to discuss them. They spent most of the time trying to tease out details he didn't feel like teasing out. At one point, when my aunt realized that he had nothing to add about the men he served with in Europe, she said to him: "You had no buddies." (It sounded less mean on tape.)

"No wonder you wrote me every day," my grandmother cut in. She started up again with how upset she was that he destroyed the war letters she'd hidden in the attic. "Why did you do that, after forty years?" (This sounded just as mean on tape.)

He didn't respond, and they moved to another topic.

None of the members of the 322nd battalion I tracked down recalled anything significant about my grandfather. Roy Peterman just saw him around the clearing station. Harold Burg, a private first class in D Company, said he'd saluted him but never chatted with him. Joe Meneghelli, a litter bearer in C Company, knew him only as one of the few guys in the battalion shorter than himself. In the battalion roster that accompanied Sergeant Baumann's diary, my grandfather is the only entry whose first name is missing. Evidently no one could remember it.

The closest I came to finding someone of his age, rank, and unit was Warren Miller. I drove out to meet him in Gainesville, Virginia, on an unseasonably warm October day. Miller was about six feet tall and bald, with large glasses; he looked to be in great physical shape for ninety and his memory would have served well at twenty-five. He'd been the intelligence adjutant in the headquarters detachment and the only commissioned officer still alive from the entire battalion, so far as either of us could tell.

"I would go in when they'd bring in prisoners with the ambulance," Miller said as we sat around his kitchen table. "I'd try to interview them to find out what units they were with, what conditions they were living under—this type of thing—to report to the division. I stood right by the side of surgeons who were operating on people."

Six waking hours never went by faster for me. Miller's memory was so sharp that all I had to do was read down my 322nd roster and he'd shoot me an anecdote. (I've limited identifiable details here since the stories are unconfirmed and, in some cases, sensitive.) The lieutenant someone once called "the reason I'm an anti-Semite." The sergeant who suffered in all the ways imaginable for having a first name of Doris. A private with such bad hygiene he was ordered to shower. A cargo truck driver who sat behind the wheel of a six-by-six belting out opera tunes. A white-haired Swedish company captain who raided the infirmary stock for personal use. A warrant officer court-martialed in training camp for going into town one night, stealing a bus, and collecting fares. An excitable Italian ambulance driver who somehow conned his German captor into letting him ride a bicycle back to the American lines. A Mexican who took so much taunting that one night he pulled a knife on the others. An adjutant from Texas who could be "drunk as a skunk" and still look sober and was not afraid of anything. That technician who'd slipped down into the basement of the castle when the shelling began and wouldn't come back up.

One of the best stories he told involved Captain Etter, the surgeon my grandfather had known from medical school. An SS major who entered the clearing station with a bullet in his back had refused to let Etter operate on him because captain was a lesser rank than his own. Etter got red in the face and turned to one of the privates assisting him.

"You've always wanted to probe around for a bullet," he said. "Go ahead!"

The worst memory he had was when a sergeant was brought to the castle after being caught in machine-gun fire.

"I guess I've always lived with it," said Miller. "The chaplain was giving him last rites. And I can remember that guy saying to the chaplain, 'Father, you've gotta pull me through. You've gotta pull me through.' And Etter was looking at the chaplain shaking his head: 'I can't do it.' And the chaplain was trying to console the guy the best he could. Died right there. Something like that really hits you."

I told him it sounded a lot like the officer who pleaded with my grandfather for his life. I wondered if it wasn't the same guy.

"Yeah, he probably was there," said Miller. "I think all the surgeons were working that day."

At one point I pulled out a military head shot of my grandfather but all Miller could recall was seeing him one time, toward the end of the war, talking to a patient in a medical tent near Bamberg, Germany.

"He wasn't very tall, was he?" asked Miller. "Five-six, five-seven?"

And a short psychiatrist who seems to have spent much of the war alone with his thoughts and the cases of madness.

ON APRIL 27, 1945, stationed somewhere in the Pacific, Eli Jaffe read a V-mail note from my grandfather expressing confidence that the end of the war was close at hand. "The supermen here have fared badly, judging from the destruction and devastation of their 'holy soil,' and I can tell you it's done our hearts good to view," he wrote. (The excerpt only survives because Eli copied it into a letter of his own.) The letter had been sent weeks earlier, but it reflected the high spirits of the 97th after the capture of Cheb nonetheless. The next day the medics set up a clearing station in the town of Weiden. The beer there, according to Baumann, was the best of the war; one soldier seconded that opinion by going on a three-day bender. When word arrived of Hitler's suicide, a couple days later, Lieutenant Kamine did his paperwork beneath a photograph signed "to my dear friend" by the führer.

Amid the levity at Weiden the medics got a painful reminder of why they'd been fighting in the first place. An American citizen who'd served in the Serbian military arrived at the clearing station "very thin and undernourished," according to Baumann. Records would later identify this person as Sylvester Kressewitsch. He'd arrived from the Flossenbürg concentration camp.

The Nazis had established Flossenbürg in 1938 with the intention of using prisoners to work the nearby granite quarries. They'd built the camp beside a village of the same name tucked into the crevices of the Oberpfalz Mountains. The SS officers who ran Flossenbürg lived in homes on a hill above the village; the layout was a metaphor, according to camp historian Alicia Nitecki. "In this way, the SS with their slaves at their backs looked down onto a world spreading seemingly endlessly before them, and the villagers looked up to the SS who were to be the models for the future Germany," Nitecki once wrote. The camp was separated from the town by an electrified barbed wire fence.

Though obscured today by the memories of Auschwitz and Dachau, Flossenbürg was the fourth-largest concentration camp on German soil. The camp was originally a place for political prisoners, especially foreign enemies of state, and by the end of the war it held some pretty high-profile ones, among them Kurt Schuschnigg, former chancellor of Austria; Dietrich Bonhoeffer, the German pastor who'd been involved in plots to assassinate Hitler; and, for a brief period, King Leopold of Belgium. It held others, too. At its peak Flossenbürg kept roughly seventeen thousand prisoners on a site built for less than a third of that number.

On April 14, 1945, as an Allied push east seemed imminent, Heinrich Himmler had sent a telegram to the camp commandant that read: "No inmate must fall into the hands of the enemy alive." Two days later the camp's sixteen hundred Jewish inmates had been transferred away. The other prisoners had been rounded up on the morning of April 20, given one piece of bread, and ordered to march—an event later referred to as the March of Death. Anyone unable to keep up was shot and left on the roadside. At certain points mass graves were dug and dozens of weary prisoners were herded into them and shot. Members of the 90th Infantry liberated the camp three days later.

On April 29 a few representatives from the 97th Infantry were chosen to document the camp site for the historical record. Generals Halsey and Hasbrouck went from high command. Colonel Somers, the division surgeon, went to evaluate the survivors; in one picture, taken by dental officer Bill Hill, Somers looks awestruck at a man who is nothing but skin and bones. Ralph Yarborough, the judge advocate and would-be senator, conducted interviews for the record. Father Thompson, the division's Protestant chaplain, and Father Tivenan, the Catholic one, joined a Jewish chaplain to provide a proper burial for the dead. A few enlisted men came along, too; Eisenhower had ordered that a range of troops from all ranks bear witness, according to Yarborough, because he "knew that people would say later that such things had not happened." My grandfather joined the group not as a doctor so much as someone who could, if necessary, speak to the prisoners in Yiddish.

By the time the 97th investigated the camp, only about fifteen hundred inmates remained. Most had been left in the camp's infirmary when the March of Death commenced. The signal corps took photographs and the medics gave treatment. Private First Class Rogers from C Company recalled feeding the survivors milk because their bodies couldn't handle solid food. The division prepared basic reports on life in the camp. Prisoners at Flossenbürg had worked grueling days at the granite works on a diet of only coffee for breakfast and potato soup with sauerkraut midday. Those who got too weak were injected with phenol and piled into carts that traveled along a little track into an underground tunnel that housed the camp's crematorium. The dead were stacked up "like cords of wood" awaiting the fires, wrote Yarborough. "Man, it was full of dead bodies—rooms full of dead bodies," Peterman later said. "It's embedded in your mind."

My grandfather was surprisingly, disappointingly mum about the experience in his memoirs—even by his standards of reticence—but it was embedded in his mind, too. Decades later he brought his family to their local temple for the Jewish high holidays only to find George Lincoln Rockwell and a band of neo-Nazis picketing outside. As soon as my grandfather saw Rockwell dressed as a storm trooper he lost it. My uncle recalls this as the only time he ever saw his father try to physically attack another human being. The police intervened but my grandfather joined some other men who were shouting to Rockwell and company that they'd fought a whole war to get rid of "you bastards." There was something my grandfather said about the camps that my uncle would always remember.

He said, "If you're a sane person living in an insane society, you cannot maintain your own sanity."

THE REST OF the war in Europe proved pleasantly uneventful for the 97th Division. On May 7, 1945, Private First Class Mozzetta of the 387th fired a round at a German sniper in the woods near Klenovice, Czechoslovakia, that's now considered the last shot of the European theater in World War II. The clearing company was stationed in the Czech town of Tachov when the celebration began. Men asked women bold questions and received bold answers. A few lucky boys from the motor pool were washing the trucks down at a lake when some frauleins emerged from out of nowhere and stripped down for a swim. People swarmed the streets and the beer parlors and the scene became "a mad house," Sergeant Baumann recalled.

A few festive days later the division did an about-face and made its way back toward the docks at Le Havre, France, where they'd first arrived a few months earlier. During the next few weeks, as the division traveled west through Europe in stages, my grandfather interviewed some of the soldiers who'd been problematic during the fighting. The evaluations weren't just protocol. Rumor had it, according to Baumann, that the 97th would be hustling to Japan to join the ongoing fight there. Evidently the gossip had swept through the whole Army because Eli Jaffe, still stationed in the Pacific, told his wife about it in a letter dated May 25, 1945.

"I read that Dan's division is coming here," he wrote, "after a furlough in the good old U.S.A."

The furlough lasted a month. Troop ships reached New York Harbor from Europe on June 24, 1945, and the men danced on the deck of the *Brazil* and hung a huge Trident flag over the gangplanks. My grandfather headed straight to Brooklyn to reunite with his wife, who'd been living there with her folks, and meet his two-month-old son. He'd made major in June; General Patton, of all people, had signed the promotion. They spent a week in the Poconos with the Waxmans, their good friends from the training period, drinking and camping and laughing. At one point someone pasted a sign on the door of his room that read: "Anyone who comes in here should have his head examined." The month passed quickly, and when it came time to report again he wasn't ready to say good-bye so he brought the young family with him.

The division reassembled at Fort Bragg, in North Carolina, where they expected to get a few more weeks of jungle warfare training before joining an attack in the Pacific. It was early August. Most of the officers and enlisted men had arrived when news broke of the atomic bomb. The rest got there in time to learn that Emperor Hirohito had agreed to a surrender. No one knew what the Army had in store for them. Some thought they'd just go home. Instead, they learned, they were headed to Japan for occupation duty. On August 17, 1945, my grandfather made the farewell to his wife and infant that he couldn't put off any longer, and boarded a troop train bound for a port on the West Coast. He knew he'd seen the end of war, but if he thought he'd seen the end of its madness, he was very mistaken.

Chapter 10

+≍≍+

Unconsciously Conscious

I found myself in a daze, had the uncanny feeling of being depersonalized, or of being outside myself and looking on at what was going on with me, like one self was watching another self, both being myself.

—Daniel Jaffe, "Memoirs of a Combat Psychiatrist," ca. 1996

Remove the trace of anything Okawa has done from history.

—Okawa Shumei, ca. spring 1946

MY GRANDFATHER WASN'T the only one reluctant to redeploy to Japan. Soldiers started going AWOL before the division left for its point of departure. Men jumped the westbound trains as they slowed through stations. Those who stuck it out were far from content; a special detail scrubbed the sides of some cars after a few soldiers made their protests known in graffiti. General Halsey, division commander, faced a serious morale problem. His men felt the war was over and "had no heart in shipping out again," Halsey recalled. Back in Europe, Eisenhower had personally warned Halsey in a letter that redeployment would be a difficult command task. He advised discharging eligible soldiers the first chance Halsey got, even if it left the division shorthanded. Failure to do so, wrote Ike, could "result in a loss of confidence by the soldier in the Army."

Of course, Halsey couldn't cut everyone loose at once, and as the division neared its date of embarkation, tensions ran high. At Fort Lawton, in Seattle, my grandfather clashed twice with Colonel Herd, who outranked him as a medical officer, in a matter of days. If any soldier had the right to feel disgruntled about his extended service it was Herd, who'd fought in two theaters already and now faced another trip across the ocean. Their first disagreement involved a medic whose short stature led the men to call him "Little Doc." After interviewing Little Doc at Fort Lawton, my grandfather determined he was suffering from clinical depression and recommended his exemption from occupation duty. Herd would be damned to see someone get a free pass. He countermanded the order and confronted my grandfather.

Herd asked "who did I think I was" to grant a psychiatric reprieve, my grandfather recalled. "In my view, I thought that I was the division psychiatrist."

They got into it again the night before the ships set sail. My grandfather took leave to see Seattle without consulting Herd, which meant Herd had to stay in camp for officer duty and was denied a night on the town himself. The confusion seems understandable: my grandfather had always reported directly to Halsey in nonbattle situations, as part of the General Staff, and didn't think he needed clearance from Herd. That wasn't how Herd saw it. He confronted my grandfather once more the following morning, this time visibly incensed.

In late August the ships left for Japan. It was a halting, miserable month at sea. "We longed to be home, were sick of army life, and were bored silly looking out at the endless Pacific," my grandfather later wrote. No one knew who was eligible for separation from the service, and no one knew when they might expect to know. One of the soldiers tried to raise spirits by distributing hand-drawn pictures of nearly naked women beside the word "CHARGE!" As nice as it was to look at nearly naked women, it upset my grandfather, and no doubt many others, to be reminded there was such a thing as nearly naked women.

On September 2, 1945, the ship's newsletter announced that Japanese delegates had signed the articles of surrender, officially ending the war. Two days later the military announced that soldiers with 45 points or more would be excluded from overseas service. During World War II, soldiers earned points for various achievements: one for each month in the service, one for each month overseas, a dozen for each child (up to three), and five for each combat decoration. The news didn't apply to the divisions already dispatched for occupation duty, like the 97th, but it did set a target. My grandfather figured he had about 40 points at the time, but after the fighting in Europe he'd put in for a Bronze Star, an individual decoration for merit, and was still awaiting word. He thought if the citation went through he might be able to leave Japan shortly after he arrived.

As it happened, Colonel Herd was the one who turned right around. When the division reached the port city of Yokohama, on September 24, Herd apparently walked down the gangplank, touched Japanese soil just to say he'd been there, and walked back up. The rest of the division moved to Miizugahara airfield in Kumagaya, about forty miles northwest of Tokyo, where they set up a command post and commenced occupation duties. The task was as thankless as it felt hopeless. "Probably the saddest outfit in all of the U.S. armed forces is the 97th Infantry Division," one Army publication wrote at the time. "Everybody in the division is thoroughly convinced that they'll be in Japan for two years."

My grandfather was just settling into his new life at Kumagaya when he felt himself slipping. The wooden barracks were cold. Large rats raced across the rafters, so large the men used them for target practice. The food was so bad my grandfather needed a shot of Suntory whisky chased with Japanese beer—the occupation boilermaker—just to dull his taste buds enough to eat it. The departure from his family and the uncertainty of his future and the squalor of his new home, each of which would have bothered him on its own, together overwhelmed his composure. He felt dazed and detached, "like one self was watching another self, both being myself." As a psychiatrist, he knew all about the condition called depersonalization, but actually experiencing it was terrifying and strange.

After a few days without any improvement, he worried about losing control. His anxiety increased when he realized there was really nowhere he could turn for help. He was the division psychiatrist, after all. If he couldn't save himself, no one could.

THE OCCUPATION FORCES arrested Okawa Shumei on December 12, 1945. Authorities apprehended him at his home in Aikawa, an outer suburb southwest of Tokyo, and drove him into the city to Sugamo Prison. Knowing they were coming, he'd spent the morning sitting by a fire and watching the Nakatsu River that ran below his hillside property. A low fog covered the river and he enjoyed the way it seemed to mingle with the smoke from the fire. His neighbors had thrown him a big farewell party the night before, as if he were a soldier leaving for service and not a prisoner heading to jail. "Going to Sugamo is like going to battle," Okawa later wrote. "For Japanese, going to battle means being prepared to never come back."

After the Japanese surrender, General Douglas MacArthur guided the country's transition into a demilitarized democratic state. MacArthur had a flair for the symbolic: he set up headquarters in a building across from the Imperial Palace. In recognition of the Potsdam Declaration's call for "stern justice" toward war criminals, MacArthur made wartime premier Tojo Hideki the chief suspect brought into custody. Allied soldiers had arrived at Tojo's home to find he'd shot himself in the chest. The bullet missed his heart, however, and he was stabilized with transfusions of American blood. ("I would not like to be judged in front of a conqueror's court," he reportedly said during the ordeal.) Subsequent arrests ascended the political and social ladder—Marquis Kido Koichi, the former imperial advisor, arrived at Sugamo in a limousine—but stopped short of Emperor Hirohito himself.

Sugamo Prison occupied half a dozen acres of fenced-in land near the Ikebukuro rail station. Furious Allied air raids had destroyed the neighborhood but somehow spared the prison itself. Prostitutes roamed the bombed-out streets and disappeared into alleys with Allied servicemen. Sugamo could house roughly fifteen hundred inmates in six main cell blocks that one American journalist described as a "grim and grey set of square, ugly three-tier buildings." During the war it had been a notoriously wretched home for political prisoners, with blood-stained walls and high-occupancy spiderwebs and what one early post-war prisoner called an "unutterable human odor." By late fall, however, the place had been cleaned and renovated so pleasantly that many had named it Hotel Sugamo.

New prisoners like Okawa first stepped into an examination room where they stripped bare to be dusted from head to toe with DDT powder. Each floor of the prison had two rows of a dozen cells and a grate in the center of the walkway that gave the guards a view of the floors above or below. Each cell had a convertible desk that folded down atop a wash basin, a latrine, and sleeping mats with two blankets and comforters. Inmates took communal baths and shared the exercise yards between the buildings. This made for some unprecedented interactions; men of modest upbringings found themselves beside the empire's military officers, government leaders, and nobility. It wasn't unusual to see one prisoner bowing in obeisance to another.

Despite steeling himself for the battlefield of prison, Okawa Shumei initially found life at Sugamo a nice change of pace. He was upset about leaving his wife, but the maid was there to help her, and he wasn't leaving behind any children. In fact, he enjoyed being surrounded by many dear old friends. Colonel Hashimoto Kingoro was there, his old cohort in the March 1931 coup. So were the diplomats Shiratori Toshio and Matsuoka Yosuke, who'd lectured to his Asianist students at Okawa Juku. And so was his sometimes rival sometimes friend Tojo Hideki. In those early days, Okawa felt his life was even better than it had been at home.

Okawa didn't know much about his fate at that point, and truth be told, neither did the Allied prosecution team. Prisoners assumed the likes of Tojo would be put on trial, but just who would join him was an open question. In December of 1945, the prosecutors had only just started case files on individual suspects. They knew to focus on anyone who'd played a key role in perpetuating Japan's "aggressive warfare policy"—from the start of its advance into Manchuria until the attack on Pearl Harbor. What they lacked was much in the way of "concrete evidence," and many of their leads were little more than soft speculation.

An undated document from this time, prepared in advance of Okawa's arrest, illustrates the limits of American intelligence. The memo correctly noted that Okawa was "the most persistent and persuasive in promoting the 'Asia for Asiatics' theme." It made no mention of his roles in the 1931 coup or the 1932 assassination, however, and mistakenly presumed he played a role in a military revolt that occurred in 1936. Prosecutors also made a big deal of a letter from Okawa they'd found among Tojo's possessions. Though that letter actually marked the end of the Tojo-Okawa friendship, the Allies took it as evidence that the two were on "intimate political terms" during the war. On December 19, 1945, prison authorities transferred Okawa to a first-floor cell typically reserved for lower-ranking prisoners, a further sign they didn't quite know how to classify him.

Part of the problem was that investigators were woefully unprepared for their task. At Okawa's first interrogation session, the interpreter spoke worse Japanese than Okawa spoke English. In several instances Okawa found it more efficient to respond to his American questioners directly. At one point the interpreter betrayed his inexperience by inserting himself into the discussion. Okawa answered a question by saying, "No idea." The interpreter replied, "No idea is not an answer."

"Who the hell are you?" Okawa responded.

"I . . . am the translator. Didn't you know that?"

"When you say, 'No idea is not an answer,' whose words exactly are you translating?"

So by the start of 1946, the situation at Sugamo felt more like the battlefield conditions Okawa Shumei had first expected. He wasn't eating well. He didn't get much rice and his rotten teeth prevented him from eating apples; instead, he traded them to fellow inmate Sasakawa Ryoichi for mandarin oranges and cigarettes. The two men discussed news articles about the impending war crimes trial that were making the prison rounds. Sasakawa concluded the trial would "definitely not be a fair or open one," and Okawa agreed. On January 17, 1946, he told Sasakawa that all he knew for sure was the authorities considered him troublesome and intended to keep him in jail. How long, and to what end, was anyone's guess.

MY GRANDFATHER'S DISSOCIATIVE symptoms persisted for days. He felt, quite literally, beside himself. As if he and his body were two separate entities, each capable of observing the other. As if life were half a realistic dream and half a dreamy reality.

He found his friend Duffy around the division base camps at Kumagaya and told him about the problem. Duffy wasn't a psychiatrist, of course, but it helped to talk things over. They discussed the source of the split. Why one Major Jaffe might be watching another Major Jaffe. As my grandfather spoke about coming to Japan and leaving behind his young family, it dawned on him that he was torn between serving his country and resuming his life. This wasn't an easy conflict to resolve. He'd been willing to defend the United States from the moment news of Pearl Harbor came across his car radio. Then again, he felt he'd done his part, and now he was angry that the military kept him apart from civilian life for reasons that seemed at best arbitrary, and at worst unjust, and above all poorly explained.

He eventually realized he was experiencing some of the very same war neuroses he'd treated in soldiers during combat. "The love-force that had eventually won out in each of them had been the affection for their comrades, strong enough to overcome the hatred and fear that had been tearing their minds apart," he later wrote. He felt that same calming effect after chatting with Duffy, and it was enough to shake the scary feeling for a time.

Still, there wasn't much to distract his mind. He toured the occupied area to see how the troops were holding up, and offered reassurance to soldiers who wanted to go home as badly as he did. Some of the men went into Tokyo to visit the shops in Ginza, but the city smelled of dead fish and old fires, and the stores sold out of kimonos and silk cloth and dolls as soon as they came in stock. Many men found a natural diversion among the geisha girls, though the performances lost their traditional grace, according to one military newspaper at the time, and the experience was "reduced to its lowest common denominator." High command allowed troops to buy six beers a week instead of three, perhaps realizing how intolerable the food really was on its own.

Each month more medical officers mustered out and left their tasks to those who remained. In mid-November, for lack of anyone else to fill the position, my grandfather became division surgeon on top of his psychiatric duties. His first task was to treat the venereal disease running rampant through the infantry units. Soldiers who came in with syphilis received eight days of penicillin from the medical battalion; those with gonorrhea were typically confined to the camp area for two weeks. When the problem lingered, he drove to see the brothels himself. The girls were too attractive; any effort to keep them off-limits was bound to fail. Instead, he took the unusual step of treating the women for their infections, trying to sever the problem at its source.

In December of 1945 headquarters announced that soldiers with 55 points were eligible to leave. That month 87 officers and more than 1,500 enlisted men received their separation orders. My grandfather wasn't among the lucky ones. Meanwhile, the men pestered him for psychiatric discharges—unaware of his own sharp longing for home.

One day around this time, he found out why he'd never heard back about the Bronze Star he'd hoped would put his point total over the top. The news came from his brash old bridge partner, Frazier, the personnel adjutant from the 322nd Medical Battalion. The award had been recommended after the campaign in Europe, but it never reached the desk of General Halsey for consideration. Colonel Herd had seen to that personally. He'd intercepted the citation in retaliation for their disputes over Little Doc and the night out in Seattle. The news was crushing. A short series of small misunderstandings had altered his life—and, more concerning, his mental health—in an excruciating way.

As he thought some more, he recognized a silver lining. If Herd had blocked the citation, it meant Halsey had never actually *denied* the citation. With Herd now out of the picture, he might try again with better luck. Fortune indeed seemed on his side. The new commanding officer of the medics was now-Major Etter, the fellow alumnus from George Washington University's medical school. Etter himself had received a Bronze Star for his tireless efforts back at the castle when the clearing station was filled to capacity with casualties. Etter agreed to put through another Bronze Star recommendation, and my grandfather felt a burst of hope.

He needed only look to his old comrades for optimism. Ainsworth and Gilliatt, both officers from the clearing company, had been decorated for their duties in Europe. Ainsworth had been cited for his efforts at the castle, when he directed arriving patients to their proper destinations. Gilliatt, who'd been Herd's second in command and a capable emergency medic, had been cited for his general work during the advance through the Ruhr pocket. Calibrating his odds against the success of these peers, my grandfather must have felt encouraged. There was nothing they'd done that he hadn't.

Unfortunately, General Halsey no longer had a say. He'd left the division at Yokohama, and a new division commander, General Herman Kramer, had replaced him. That meant the award recommendation had to go through someone unfamiliar with my grandfather's work in the medical battalion—not to mention a bit unimpressed with his unorthodox efforts as division surgeon. Kramer said his service had been "commendable, but not decorable," and the citation was refused. There was little he could do now but wait for his time and hope it came soon.

IN LATE JANUARY of 1946, as Okawa Shumei continued to wonder what was in store for him, General MacArthur announced the charter for the International Military Tribunal for the Far East. With that, chief prosecutor Joseph B. Keenan and his staff began the process of selecting a small handful of top-tier suspects at Sugamo to serve as Class-A defendants at the Tokyo trial. Keenan and company knew exactly what they wanted. First, they'd eliminate anyone who didn't meet the core charge of "crimes against peace" set by the charter. Next, they'd make sure to gather defendants who represented a diversity of leadership positions during the years under investigation, 1928 to 1945. Last, they'd only indict those individuals whose cases were so airtight, in the words of attorney Solis Horwitz, "as to render negligible the chances for acquittal."

For the next few weeks prosecutors made a furious sweep for documentary evidence and corroborating witnesses. That was no easy task: loads of official records had been burned after the surrender, and hundreds of key participants had killed themselves, including prewar prime minister Konoe Fumimaro. Still, Okawa's public past made him particularly vulnerable to the search process. Investigators pulled every book he'd written over the years from the shelves of the imperial library in Tokyo. They unearthed his courtroom testimony from the May 15 Incident and the rest of his official rap sheet. They took sworn statements about his involvement in the Manchurian Incident and his general role as a leading Asianist. By early March of 1946 prosecutors had compiled a picture of Dr. Okawa Shumei as one of the most influential minds behind Japan's imperial rise.

His case entered the hands of a sharp young lawyer from Kentucky named Hugh B. Helm. Over the course of four morning interrogations, which ran to six and a half hours in all, Helm covered Okawa's entire career as an author and activist. The information elicited at these sessions was a testament to Helm's well-crafted approach. He devised a coordinated line of questioning meant to validate the idea that Okawa was a lifelong proponent of Japanese expansion. He showed enough Southern decorum to earn his subject's respect—Helm addressed Okawa as "doctor," and Okawa later called the experience "rather pleasant"—but also enough aggression to fulfill his own agenda.

The result was an official exchange that Helm couldn't have scripted better himself. The two men discussed Okawa's views on global war ("a necessary evil"), Japan's great mission ("the moral organization of humanity"), the Manchurian Incident (he'd known it would occur for "more than three months"), and whether assassination was an acceptable cost of political reformation ("Yes"). Long stretches of interview consisted of Helm reading sinister lines cherry-picked from a book and having Okawa simply confirm that he'd written them.

When Helm received an unanticipated response he simply struck it from the record. On the rare occasion that Okawa showed defiance, Helm steered the conversation back to his desired conclusion. Less prepared for the battlefield than he believed, the tired Okawa often capitulated, as during this March 7 discussion about his infamous prophecy that Japan and America would one day clash in war. The official translated transcript read:

> Helm: In your public speeches and wherever you could make your influence felt, you were trying to gird the Japanese war machine in readiness for this impending crash?
>
> Okawa: Whether I said so or not, those were my ideas.
>
> Helm: Answer my question.
>
> Okawa: I am not a propagandist—
>
> Helm: I did not say so.
>
> Okawa: —so I do not make propaganda, but be that as it may, those were still my thoughts.
>
> Helm: And you did everything in your power to use your influence speaking and writing to gird Japan's war machine against this impending crash, is that so?
>
> Okawa: No, I am not a propagandist.
>
> Helm: I did not say you were. I said you were a leader of the people.
>
> Okawa: Yes.
>
> Helm: Then the answer to my previous question is "yes"?
>
> Okawa: Yes.

For the most part, Okawa was remarkably forthcoming and even oddly acquiescent. An initial reason for his light show of resistance was his failure to recognize just how important Allied prosecutors considered him. Before his first interrogations, Okawa didn't think he could be accused of anything except the Manchurian Incident. When it became clear that Helm considered him a key propagandist for the entire Pacific war, Okawa was shocked—then he was scared. He arrived at the March 9 interview with a book detailing his prewar commercial trading partnership with the United States. The move backfired. What Okawa called an effort to prevent the war, Helm saw as merely an attempt to delay it until Japan achieved its mission of unifying Asia.

Throughout the sessions, the two men often miscommunicated in such a manner. Their perceptions of the war were simply too different. Okawa considered the idea of liberating Asia "from the white man" justifiable, and never denied that position. Helm, on the other hand, saw this same belief as a motive for world conquest. As a result they spoke past each other in an almost comical way at times, both men proceeding as if they'd won the exchange.

> Helm: As a matter of fact the efforts of your life have been devoted to bringing about Pan-Asianism?
>
> Okawa: Yes, and due to the war they became impossible.
>
> Helm: But you also knew that it would be necessary to fight Britain and America someday to carry out your aims.
>
> Okawa: Yes, because I did not believe they would stand aside and let us advance. If they voluntarily emancipated the people [of East Asia] there would be no necessity for war.
>
> Helm: But you knew they would not and you wanted Japan to prepare for war?
>
> Okawa: Yes.

By the time these interrogations were finished, Helm felt certain that Okawa met every marker of a Class-A war criminal. On March 15, 1946, he filed a brief with Arthur Comyns Carr, the prosecution's chief British attorney, describing Okawa as "the brain-trust of military extremists." Five days later he received one last burst of encouragement from an intelligence officer named Lieutenant Colonel T. P. Davis, who'd spent twenty years in Japan before the war. Toward the end of their talk, Davis gave the ultimate endorsement, saying Okawa's lifelong career as a proponent of the great Asianist mission made him even more responsible for the war than Tojo himself.

"I am interested primarily in seeing something done about him," said Davis, "because so many Japanese people point the finger and say, 'You must not let him go free.'"

On the afternoon of March 21, 1946, at a meeting of the executive committee for the prosecution team, Helm submitted his amplified report on suspect Okawa Shumei. The twenty-two-page dossier, based mostly on his interrogations, presented a sound case that Okawa met the criteria for "crimes against peace" as defined by the charter for the Tokyo trial. The totality of this evidence, Helm concluded, suggested that there was no "more sinister figure" in all Japan during this time than Okawa Shumei:

> Long before Tojo and his gang of international outlaws appeared on the scene, Dr. Okawa was busy night and day with his bloody coups and his evil determination for Japan to fulfill its Messianic Mission against an unwilling world.

The executive committee agreed right then to include Okawa in the indictment.

AT THE START of 1946, my grandfather felt that everyone was going home but him. First, there was his brother. Stationed elsewhere in the Pacific, Eli Jaffe was also having trouble accepting postcombat military life. "That demobilization business sure is hell on a man's morale," he wrote to his wife, Wilma, in early November. He met with a psychiatrist at the 4th General Hospital, in Manila, presenting symptoms of depersonalization astonishingly similar to his brother's, as if they were bound by some cosmic genetic cord. In fact, Eli imagined that he had *become* his brother, Dan the psychiatrist, perhaps as a means of advising himself on his deteriorating mental condition.

Still, Eli got worse. On Christmas he sent Wilma an alarming letter filled with existential angst and a sense of doom. "Darling, above all, don't let anything that may befall me . . . impinge itself on you," he wrote. He encouraged her to move on with her life, meet other men, find happiness. At the same time, he wrote to Dan for help.

My grandfather wrote back assuring his brother how common it was for soldiers in their positions to feel uneasy. Then he explained that being a psychiatrist didn't immunize a person from the anguish of uncertainty. What Eli probably hadn't considered was how annoying it was, how indignant it made his brother, to have all these other soldiers begging to be released. They said they couldn't sleep, they couldn't eat, they were anxious. They wanted to go home. Well, *he* wanted to go home, too. By the time these brotherly reassurances arrived, Eli had already received a psychiatric discharge from the service for "chronic anxiety." He was on his way home in a hospital ship called the USS *Hope*.

The men of the 97th Infantry were leaving, too—in droves after the New Year. In January of 1946, roughly 140 officers and 5,100 enlisted men, each with 45 points or more, received their separation orders. In February the division lost another 40 or so officers and roughly 2,100 enlisted men. Twenty-seven Bronze Stars were awarded for the month, including one for Lieutenant Colonel Yarborough, who'd been farther back of the front line than the medics in the clearing station. Soon it was announced that the division itself would be rendered inactive at the end of March. Even that didn't mean everyone would be discharged; many men would be transferred to other units of the occupation forces.

When the 97th Infantry was deactivated on March 31, 1946, my grandfather was among those who stayed behind. Right around that time the dreams that had been plaguing him for weeks got worse. There he was, standing on the docks, watching a ship pull out of a harbor. Sometimes it was a train pulling away from the station, but the basic scenario was the same. It didn't take Freud to figure out what they said about his mental state. "This was a very painful period for me," he later wrote. "Trauma is such a relative thing: the trauma of battle is unspeakable, that of separation is agonizing in a different way." He couldn't have known at the time that these same dreams would persist for years.

In April he joined the staff of the 361st Station Hospital in Tokyo, the occupation's center for neuropsychiatric care. The hospital was on the eastern side of the Sumida River, which fed into Tokyo Bay, across the bridge from what remained of the downtown area. The city had been obliterated by the Allied bombardments of 1945. Some 65 percent of Tokyo homes had been destroyed. Displaced and hungry Japanese soldiers found shelter alongside widows and orphans in railroad stations and abandoned ruins. Block after block of flattened rubble around the Sumida was interrupted by an occasional intact building, as if someone had gone over the city with a great lawn mower but been lazy and missed a few patches. Now and then a body washed up on the banks of the river.

The 361st Station Hospital was one of the few buildings in the area to survive. The grounds had much to offer a nature-loving former Eagle Scout like my grandfather. Outside the officer's club was a tidy Japanese garden with a network of footpaths and a bridge that arched over a little pond. At one end of the garden was a five-tier pagoda, with eaves flipped up at the corners, surrounded by stone lanterns. Inside the pagoda were a number of little wooden boxes holding the remains of people who'd died in the air raids of 1945. A block or two upriver was a cluster of Japanese Cherry trees that usually bloomed in early April.

These pockets of beauty did little to offset the general desolation of my grandfather's situation. Life was a carousel of perfunctory consultations by day and haunting visions by night. The officer's club offered some diversion in the form of a bar and a piano and a wooden dance floor. But aside from Bill Hill, the division dentist from the 97th, my grandfather had very few colleagues left to keep him company. His arrival at the 361st had been the ticket home for the hospital's previous chief of psychiatry—a Baltimore doctor he'd get to know later in life, and who would always thank him for the relief—and he assumed the position wondering if he wasn't the last American psychiatrist left in Japan.

IN LATE MARCH of 1946, awaiting indictment as a Class-A war crimes defendant, Okawa Shumei read Edward Gibbon's *The History of the Decline and Fall of the Roman Empire*. He couldn't sleep and received pills for his insomnia. He had strange and powerful dreams. After one dream featuring General MacArthur, Okawa awoke and felt like English, not Japanese, was his native tongue, and began to speak it more. In another, the Emperor Meiji appeared and told him, with "a voice like a violent thunderclap," to take a hard look at the suffering of Japan. Okawa took the event as a reminder that Sugamo was merely an extension of the war; took it, in other words, as a call to arms.

"There was no doubt in my mind as to the ultimate objective of my enemies—they were trying to completely rewrite Japanese history from the Meiji era onward—and I had to do everything in my power to fight against them," he later wrote.

He'd been paired in a cell with former general Matsui Iwane. Matsui was considered responsible for the horrible rape of Nanking, which took place while the Japanese forces in China were under his command. Nonetheless, Okawa had a great respect for his cell mate, finding him sophisticated and unflappable—a rare breed. For his part, Matsui embraced the Asianist philosophy Okawa had spent a lifetime advancing; his "deepest regret," he once wrote, was failing to realize "a new life for Asia." The men had known each other from the Yamato Society to improve Japanese culture, organized just after Okawa's release from prison in late 1937, and in their Sugamo cell the friendship was rekindled.

Soon Okawa and Matsui were inseparable. They ate together, walked in the prison yard together, passed the time together. Matsui taught Okawa *kanshi,* the Japanese word for Chinese poetry, which Okawa embraced with a furious interest. They prayed together, too. Matsui had a photograph of the Koa Kannon, a statue he'd made of the

Buddhist goddess of mercy associated with Asian revival. He'd molded the idol out of clay from the battlefields of Nanking. They fashioned a little shrine and prayed at seven o'clock every morning and night—prayed so loud they annoyed the other inmates on the cell block, who yelled back at them to keep it down.

In late April the guards split up the party by moving Matsui to another cell. Okawa's odd behavior became even more noticeable. He wore only a Chinese dress and geta, those wooden clogs, everywhere he went. He spoke to himself out loud at night. He shouted at the guards. Two days after Matsui's cell transfer, Okawa flew into a rage and needed a tranquilizer shot to be calmed. His eyesight, which had never been good in the first place, got so bad he couldn't read. Instead, he scrawled nonsensical Japanese, English, and transliterated German phrases into the flyleaves and the margins of his copy of *World History for Historians,* volume 10:

> Kill anyone who mentions Okawa.
> Executed on May 5. Okawa dies.
> Remove the trace of anything Okawa has done from history.

On April 29, 1946, Allied prosecutors announced the Class-A indictments to the public. It was Emperor Hirohito's forty-fifth birthday—another symbolic gesture by MacArthur—and the prisoners gathered at half past eight in the morning to sing the Japanese national anthem. At eleven o'clock the twenty-eight Tokyo trial defendants were revealed. Okawa was the only one among them who'd held neither a military rank nor a government position.

Later that day, while sitting in his cell, Okawa put on a cap and draped a white blanket around his neck. He held a little handbag filled with his things. He stopped fellow prisoner Sasakawa, who was sweeping the walkway, and in a serious tone asked him to open the door. Okawa had decided he was going home. Sasakawa thought it was a prank and told Okawa if he wanted his cell door opened he'd have to ask the guards. Sasakawa continued sweeping, and a moment later, sure enough, he heard Okawa call over a guard and repeat his request.

The other inmates were convinced he'd gone insane. "The last days of Japan's greatest thinker are nothing enviable," Sasakawa wrote in his diary around this time. He was particularly upset that Okawa had squandered a chance to defend the actions of Japan at the Tokyo trial. "[O]nly moments before his chance to stand on this glorious stage, with the whole world in audience, he loses his mind," he wrote. The rumors made their way to the other floors of Sugamo. Kodama Yoshio, who like Sasakawa had escaped indictment but remained imprisoned, was upset by the news.

"It is said that there is only a hair's breadth between genius and madness," Kodama told a fellow prisoner. "Since he is a genius, that hair has presumably snapped."

The American guards weren't so sympathetic. They withheld meals from Okawa for his antics and confined him to his cell for a week. They watched him closely through the grates that separated the floors on the cell block. "The US military apparently believes that Dr. Okawa is feigning madness," Sasakawa wrote.

Sometime in late April of 1946, Okawa met with Ohara Shinichi, the lawyer he wanted to defend him. Ohara had been recommended by Kiyose Ichiro, one of the country's top defense attorneys, who had represented Okawa for the May 15 Incident. (Kiyose was also Tojo's head counsel for the Tokyo trial.) When Ohara arrived at Sugamo and announced his desire to see Okawa, the guard pointed a finger at his head and spun it in a circle, in the casual gesture for insanity.

Okawa appeared wearing geta and what looked like pajamas. He sat down on his side of the metal net that separated inmates from visitors and immediately began to explain why he didn't need a lawyer for the trial that awaited him.

"Mr. Ohara, this trial is political," Okawa said. "It's the same as a medieval religious trial. The citizens of non-Allied nations are guilty just because of who they are. Therefore, I'm doubtful whether or not you can really defend me."

With this preamble out of the way, Okawa nevertheless approved Ohara as his counsel. They discussed the trial for a bit. Okawa worried the court would raise the question of the emperor's responsibility for the war. (Many Japanese shared this fear; in fact, MacArthur's belief that he'd need a million more troops to occupy Japan if the emperor were tried for war crimes was a major reason Hirohito escaped indictment.) Okawa spoke in English, despite Ohara's poor grasp of it, and whenever an American guard walked by he quickly switched to German or French. Once the guard was out of earshot he resumed speaking English again.

"Watching him, I thought he was far from crazy," Ohara later recalled. Then, just as this doubt crept into his mind, Ohara asked why Okawa wasn't speaking Japanese, and received a puzzling reply.

"Today is my English day," Okawa said.

Of all the curious elements of Okawa Shumei's madness, from its perfectly timed onset to its equally punctual disappearance, his suggestion that the Tokyo trial was really an extension of the war is perhaps the most provocative. The idea has led some Japanese to wonder whether Okawa came to the courtroom ready to do whatever it took to get out alive. In his 2006 book on Okawa, the popular writer Sato Masaru argued that the slap heard round the world could be seen as a deliberate form of "intellectual battle" just as easily as a crazed action:

> My understanding is that from the bottom of his heart Okawa was making fun of this court. . . . He wanted to criticize the very foundation of the court, which pretended to be searching for the truth but at its root was a show of force. He felt that turning the court into a tragicomic performance was a more effective strategy than building a rebuttal based on sound legal theories.

Joined by my translator, Chiaki, I met Sato at his pied-à-terre in the Shinjuku ward of Tokyo. He was in his early fifties, with military-short hair, and eyelids half shuttered from the mere three hours of sleep he's famous for getting each night. Sato is a divisive figure, celebrated by some as much as he's scorned by others, considered to be among Japan's most widely read intellectuals—a modern Okawa Shumei, in many ways. A few minutes after we sat down at opposite sides of a wide table beside a wall-to-wall bookshelf, I handed him a copy of my grandfather's report from the Tokyo trial.

"I think your connection with Okawa Shumei through your grandfather is very interesting," he said. "First, I want to talk about my connection—that's the psychological connection."

Sato explained that in 2002, while working in the Russian section of the Japanese foreign ministry, he was arrested for the improper use of government funds. Throughout the legal process, even as he was offered deals to admit guilt, Sato maintained his innocence. He felt he'd been ousted for political reasons; Koizumi Junichiro had recently become Japan's new premier, and the two men didn't see eye to eye. In prison awaiting his trial, Sato felt a spiritual bond with Okawa based on their shared sense of injustice. It occurred to Sato at his arraignment, as it occurred to Okawa at the start of the Tokyo trial, that the entire courtroom scene had the feel of a staged "comedy"—which was exactly what Okawa reportedly called it as he was being dragged away. "At that time I thought of Okawa Shumei," Sato said. "If I'd slapped the head of the person sitting next to me, how everybody in this court would react to that." He thought about writing a book about Okawa someday, and after he left prison, having served 512 days, he did just that.

"In the part where you write about Okawa at the trial, you think his shouting this"—that the court was a comedy—"and slapping Tojo was intentional?" I asked.

"It's difficult to judge," Sato said. "He was unconsciously conscious. I don't think he pretended to be a madman, but it was a very intense situation, and unconsciously he might have thought this was the thing to do."

"So he was probably insane, but some part of him wanted to make this point?"

"He had a disturbed character," said Sato. "It's not a so-called *craziness,* but his character was in an abnormal condition."

In a strange way, one I wasn't totally comfortable admitting, Sato's theory made a bit of sense. After the war, Okawa moved from his peaceful home in suburban Tokyo to a stressful prison environment. Eventually, the intensity of this new life brought him to a point of breakdown. Wasn't that how mental casualties often occurred at the front lines? Maybe the way Okawa had been like a soldier wasn't that he fought against the United States, but that he'd *broken,* too, on his own version of the battlefield. The lost war, the American occupation, the arrest and interrogations, a life's work on Asianism amounting to a soap bubble—it was all a kind of fever dream, an existential catastrophe that ended with Japan being crushed by the West and Okawa's entire vision of the world collapsing before his own weak eyes.

My grandfather's brief dissociative spell in Japan could be seen the same way: the inevitable outcome of a sound mind sent through the wringer of war. He wasn't quite crazy when he recognized his problem—you couldn't be crazy if you knew it; that old catch-22—but he was sort of beyond his own control. A little unconsciously conscious.

With all that in mind, Sato's idea still didn't quite sit right. It completely ignored my grandfather's medical report; or, rather, it gave as much weight to some "psychological connection" with Okawa as it did to my grandfather's acquired expertise. That's what we do with insanity in a way: we can't understand it completely, so we wedge it into the framework of our own experiences, and in doing so we pinch off the sloppy edges that really define it. Perhaps part of what makes madness so fascinating is that the only people who can truly understand it— the mad—can't explain it to the rest of us.

Chapter 11

━━━━━━

Judgment

In the view of the primary diagnosis in this case, it is considered that the patient is unable to distinguish right from wrong, and he is incapable of testifying in his own defense.

> —Major Daniel S. Jaffe, "Examination of Okawa, Shumei,"
> May 11, 1946

It is not an ordinary court. It is a continuation of the war.

> —Okawa Shumei, "Report of the Psychiatric Examination
> on the Mental Condition of Shumei Okawa," filed by
> Dr. Uchimura Yushi, May 11, 1946

O N MAY 4, 1946, one day after he interrupted the Tokyo trial by slapping Tojo Hideki on the head, Okawa Shumei appeared in the courtroom at Ichigaya for the second and final time. Chief Justice William Webb considered the incident in chambers at half past eight in the morning. He approved the request for a competency exam made by Ohara Shinichi, Okawa's lawyer, and Captain Beverly Coleman, the lead defense counsel. The prosecution and the defense would each appoint a psychiatrist to perform the task, and in the event of a split decision the tribunal would name an arbiter. At the start of the day's session, Webb informed the court of the plan and removed Okawa from the dock. Okawa left the courtroom shouting nonsense.

When the session adjourned, shortly before eleven that morning, Okawa joined the other defendants on the bus back to Sugamo Prison. During the ride he announced that he'd reserved a table for lunch at Shinkiraku, a traditional geisha house in Tokyo, and invited everyone to join him. "The Emperor will be there, so why don't you all come along?" he said. When no one responded, Okawa added, as if by way of enticement, "He will pay."

Okawa then informed his fellow defendants that he'd been promoted to major general in the American army, which made him a superior officer to Colonel Robert Hardy, the commandant of Sugamo. "So from now on you take your orders from me in prison," he said.

He was admitted to the psychiatric ward of the 361st Station Hospital later that day. It was a Sunday. By evening a light rain had started to fall. In his hospital room, he made a habit of scattering tobacco ashes everywhere and shouting imperious orders at his nurses. When night came, however, he slept well.

A COUPLE DAYS later, my grandfather arrived at an exam room to find Okawa Shumei waiting for him. Together they made a classic odd-couple sight: the lanky and disheveled fifty-nine-year-old Japanese man with thick glasses, standing half a foot taller than the thirty-one-year-old American in the sharp uniform. Okawa gave him a cheerful greeting, as one might an old friend. Then he launched into the same odd banter he'd held with American reporters at the Tokyo trial. He announced that he no longer needed food to get nourishment. He'd discovered a way to transform the air into sustenance. He talked about his close relationship with Major League Baseball commissioner Happy Chandler, and asked if my grandfather knew him, too. He said he was in a "state of happy intoxication, like a god."

There is definite euphoria, my grandfather noticed, later documenting this and other behaviors in his official report. *He is careless in personal appearance, somewhat untidy.*

Things settled down a bit and my grandfather asked Okawa about his personal history. There was a translator in the room, but no doubt Okawa broke into English now and then, as he'd been doing regularly since his dream about General MacArthur. He discussed his life with clarity and accuracy. How he'd been born in 1886 in a small town in northern Honshu. How he'd been a precocious student, with a particular interest in the classics and religion, but also a bit of a young menace. How he spoke many languages, and held a degree in Indian philosophy and a doctorate in colonial studies.

He's alert and cooperative. He's also talkative and rather tense.

As their conversation continued, Okawa explained that these youthful pursuits had aroused in him a great nationalist spirit, and an urge to share that passion in writing. He said his loyalty to Japan had inspired his involvement in the country's expansion. He admitted his role in the invasion of Manchuria, and his part in the assassination of the prime minister back in 1932, for which he'd received a five-year sentence.

His stream of talk is coherent, and his answers to questions are relevant.

After the brief review of Okawa's life, my grandfather asked about his medical history. Okawa said he'd contracted venereal disease at thirty-three, during his very first sexual experience, but no longer had any genital lesions. He was married without kids. He'd smoked cigarettes most of his life, and gone on sporadic alcohol benders, and used opium now and then. Aside from his father having been a heavy drinker, his family had no history of health trouble. His mother was still alive and well at age eighty-one.

There's no notable distractibility or flight of ideas.

When the conversation shifted from physical health to mental health, Okawa got a little angry. He didn't like having his intelligence questioned. He acknowledged that he'd come into possession of some extraordinary powers, but said that was only because he'd attained such an enlightened knowledge of nature. For instance, he insisted he could kill a man by kissing him. What he did, he explained, was take elements of the air and extract poison from them. He said he'd killed two Chinese in this manner, but would need to kill several hundred more to test and explain the mechanism.

His mood is appropriate to his emotions, but inappropriate to the situation.

Okawa then revealed that he had an even greater power, one capable of killing a million men at a time. He was keeping it secret, however; he said he'd only share it with General MacArthur. Together they could use the power to turn Earth into a paradise where all men were brothers and all religions were one. If MacArthur wouldn't listen he wouldn't try to convince him—chalk it up to God's will—but if he did agree to the plan, then the United States and Japan could join in ruling the world on July 4. First, Okawa said, it was necessary for him to be appointed emperor.

His remarks are frequently facetious.

My grandfather asked whether Okawa was having any hallucinations. "Revelations," Okawa replied, correcting him with a bit of resentment. He said he'd written them down while in prison, then went back to read them, and they made him laugh for two days straight. He said he was certain he'd become the world's leading humorist. My grandfather asked Okawa to say more about the episodes he was having—these revelations. Okawa said when he closed his eyes he had visions that seemed like dreams, but he was not involved. He had no active role. He was merely a bystander.

My grandfather asked why Okawa slapped Tojo in court. Okawa said he wanted to kill Tojo because he loved him, and wanted to protect his family from the humiliation of the trial. He said in fact he *did* kill Tojo. He recognized that Tojo was still alive, but "subjectively and symbolically" he had killed him.

This remark seemed to straddle a hazy line between the profound and the absurd. A moment later, though, Okawa told a weird and remarkable story about something that had happened to him after he was admitted to the hospital. He said Mrs. MacArthur had come to visit him, and that she'd brought ten thousand women to nurse him. He said he'd been deeply moved by this gesture. As my grandfather listened to the tale, he realized that behind the thick glasses, Okawa's eyes had filled with tears.

Is this something he's been coached in, he recalled wondering, *or is this a product of mental disorder?*

THE SAME WEEK my grandfather conducted his exam for the prosecution, a Japanese psychiatrist named Uchimura Yushi conducted his own for the defense. Dr. Uchimura, a medical professor at Tokyo University, recognized many of the same behavioral quirks my grandfather noted. Okawa's attire was slovenly, and he spoke (often in English) with exhilaration, and he shifted from good to ill humor when his mental stability came into question. Uchimura thought Okawa's behavior showed greatly diminished inhibitions but still a trace of restraint; he called it a hypomanic state. The extent of Okawa's deluded grandiosity came across in a list Uchimura prepared of his unusual statements:

"I received the Nobel prize three times. The subjects of my theses I forgot because it's so long since. I have also atomic bombs ready in my head."

"I can walk on water. One simply has to keep the air in one's body a vacuum. Nothing is easier than walking on water like Christ."

"I learned how to make hallucinations from Gandhi when I was about forty. I see and hear Christ and Mohammed calling me from the sky. I would like to go, but if I go, I'll die and I'll not be able to serve my country. That's why I've tied a string to my waist, so that I can't go."

"Yesterday I asked Mrs. MacArthur, 'Mamma, how many times did you enjoy MacArthur last night?' Then she scolded me saying, 'Bad boy, bad boy.'"

"Also, about the food problem, there's nothing to worry since there are 400 million sheep in China. I can go over there and kill them or give them cyanic acid."

Strangely, it was when Okawa started discussing the Tokyo trial that his comments seemed to betray some great latent insight hidden beneath the crazed chatter. "This trial is a kind of tactics," he told

Uchimura. "Suppose one throws a ball and it falls. Then we can see the ball stop. But actually it rolls on for a little while by inertia. In the same way the war is going on yet. It is not an ordinary court. It is a continuation of the war."

Uchimura reacted to what he heard with the same incredulity as my grandfather. When he considered the absurdity of the remarks, and the earnestness with which they were delivered, and the fact of Okawa's well-known intellect, Uchimura couldn't help but wonder if the comments "were not said by way of jokes or on purpose."

MY GRANDFATHER STARTED the physical exam once the mental tests were complete. He was really in his element now—he had specialized in neurology, after all, not psychiatry. He measured Okawa's blood pressure at 150 over 50, then pulled out his stethoscope and placed it against Okawa's chest. The rate sounded normal, but there was a bit of a high-pitched murmur in one place. That was typical of aortic insufficiency; Okawa had a faulty heart.

The first great abnormality presented in the reflex tests. With his patient no doubt sitting off the side of the exam table, my grandfather found the deep tendons in Okawa's left knee and tapped them with his little hammer. The leg gave a kick, but it was weak reaction, a bit delayed. He moved over to the right knee and tapped again. This time nothing happened at all. When my grandfather tapped the Achilles, he saw no response in the foot, either. The reflexes in the upper-body extremities were there, but they were sluggish, too, like the left knee. He asked Okawa to stand up and place his feet together. Okawa swayed a bit—signaling a lack of muscle coordination known as ataxia.

A possible explanation crept into my grandfather's mind.

He moved to an eye exam. He flicked on a little light, held it up to Okawa's face, and observed his pupils as they followed it. They looked a little irregular and didn't react quite how they should have; they failed to contract in the light. The only time they shrank a bit was when Okawa watched my grandfather's finger move from the distance into his near field of vision—a response known to doctors as accommodation. When my grandfather spotted this abnormality, his soft hunch hardened into a sturdy conviction.

He performed a few final tests—took a chest X-ray and an EKG, drew a blood sample, did a spinal tap—and sent them to the hospital lab. Then the test was over and they unceremoniously began the rest of their lives.

ON MAY 11, 1946, my grandfather sat down to type out his report for the Tokyo tribunal on the competency of Okawa Shumei. He had a lot on his mind at the time. There was the usual dread about his interminable service, of course, but on this particular day that probably wasn't the only thing bothering him. It was his thirty-second birthday, the second in a row he'd be spending without his wife and infant son. Little Harry, just thirteen months old, had only known his father in the flesh for a single one. My grandfather's fifth wedding anniversary was approaching, too. His wife had been suffering from a thyroid deficiency and had reached a point where she couldn't take care of the baby alone. She'd written to the Red Cross to see if they might help bring her husband home at long last. My grandfather might actually have considered Okawa's exam a welcome distraction.

Then again, it might have been hard to keep his thoughts from drifting toward home. Home. He still had the notes from Walter Freeman's neurology clinic there. He would keep them forever, even if he didn't need to consult them. He didn't need any notes to remember carrying malarial mosquitoes around St. Elizabeth's Hospital, back in Washington, to treat patients who'd shown the same symptoms Okawa was presenting now. He didn't need notes to recall the limerick he'd learned in medical school:

> *There was a young man from Bombay*
> *Thought syphilis just went away;*
> *And now he has tabes*
> *And sabre-shinned babies*
> *And thinks that he's Queen of the May.*

As my grandfather reviewed the clues of the case one last time, they all seemed to converge on an answer. The venereal disease. The delusions of grandeur, however comical or witty or oddly insightful. The "revelations," as Okawa called them, which by any term meant seeing and hearing things that didn't exist. The sluggish and absent reflexes. The pupils so irregular, so unresponsive to light. The lab results ironed the evidence smooth: positive for the Wassermann and Kahn tests, and a gold curve in the spinal fluid, too. Each clue indicated some aspect of the illness on its own, and together confirmed it as much as medically possible.

He made a heading on the page—"<u>DIAGNOSIS</u>"—and began to type.

Okawa Shumei had syphilis of the brain. In medical terms, my grandfather called it "tertiary syphilis" to explain that it had reached the advanced third stage of the disease; sometimes it was also called "general paresis." Syphilis, contracted and left untreated, often traveled slowly through the body toward the mind, arriving long after any outward signs had vanished from the groin. Once there, it formed little spirochetes, little coiled bacteria that ate away at the brain, leaving behind a degenerative puddle. Without treatment the condition eventually led to death. It didn't matter that twenty-five years or so had passed since Okawa claimed to get the disease. The process often took decades. If the timing of Okawa's insanity was almost impossibly fortuitous, the timeline of his illness was incredibly common.

There were only the whispers of malingering to cause my grandfather any doubt. "I must acknowledge that despite the evidence detailed above, there remains a *possibility* that the findings leading to the diagnosis of paresis had indeed resulted from a hoax," he later wrote. The delusions of grandeur and the ataxia could have been coached. The blood tests, trusty diagnostics for syphilis established by Wassermann and Kahn, could have been falsified. The deep tendon reflexes could, at least theoretically, have been suppressed. Such an extensive cover-up would have required a Japanese expert to burrow into Sugamo unnoticed, teach Okawa to behave in these ways without rousing suspicion, then get word to the lab technicians—all of this perpetrated in an American hospital and an American prison.

Even allowing for this possibility, my grandfather still trusted his own trained mind. What clinched it for him were the pupils that failed to contract in the light and only showed accommodation. This was the so-called Argyll Robertson pupil, named for the nineteenth-century Scottish ophthalmologist who discovered it, known to all neurologists of the day. It was a unique hallmark of general paresis—and presumably one beyond any manual powers of manipulation.

"The primary diagnosis in this case is as follows: Syphilis, tertiary," he wrote. He described the illness a bit then moved to his second task, his opinion of Okawa's fitness to stand trial. It was only by horrible chance that he had any experience with legal competency. The last time had been with his mother. The sweet face he saw whenever he saw madness. Even *she* was back at home now. Everyone was home except him. "In the view of the primary diagnosis in this case, it is considered that the patient is unable to distinguish right from wrong, and he is incapable of testifying in his own defense," he typed. Then he advised prompt treatment with fever therapy, and punched in his name and rank and position as the hospital's chief of neuropsychiatry, and pulled out the sheet to sign.

Three days later he received his long-awaited relief orders. At the urging of the Red Cross, the Army released him on the grounds of hardship at home. He was cleared for air priority to get there quicker. When his plane landed in California he took a train as far as Utah before a railroad strike forced him to find other means of transportation. He was a "casual" again—a soldier traveling without a unit, forced to fend for himself. He hopped a military mail plane heading east. He needed to reach Fort Dix, in New Jersey, his place of discharge. There was one very scary moment on the way, during an electrical storm in Pennsylvania when the pilot flew anyway. In hindsight my grandfather realized how foolish a risk it was, considering how far he'd come. Maybe it was a sign that in those final days of service he'd lost his better judgment, or maybe just a sign that he trusted the man's expertise.

At each delivery stop he sent his wife a Western Union telegram. "Delayed," it read, "but will be home soon."

———

DR. UCHIMURA FROM the defense reached the same conclusion as my grandfather, and the Tokyo trial had its medical consensus that defendant Okawa Shumei wasn't fit to stand trial. Meanwhile, the 361st Station Hospital wasn't fit to provide malarial fever therapy, so on June 4, 1946, the tribunal granted a request to transfer Okawa to Tokyo University Hospital. Justice Webb refused to strike his name from the indictment, however, seeing "no reason to suppose that he will not recover during the progress of the trial."

Okawa arrived at the hospital on June 11 and began therapy that very day. Over the next few weeks, a doctor in the hospital's mental health section inoculated Okawa with malaria until a fever developed. The fever burned off the spirochetes that were attacking Okawa's brain, then was driven away with quinine before doing too much damage to the tissue. At first Okawa didn't respond well. He ate little and grew so weak that doctors worried he might not complete the therapy. He became so excitable they needed sedatives just to keep him calm enough to administer treatment. It was as if his competing sides, the philosophical and the passionate, were once again at war.

By August the treatment was finished but Okawa's mental condition hadn't improved, according to doctors' reports from the period. He became rude and violent. At night he walked the halls of the hospital shouting. He broke windows. Sometimes he entered another room and beat the patient inside. Dr. Uchimura, who was also president of Matsuzawa Hospital for the Insane in a suburb of Tokyo, believed Okawa would respond better to its peaceful environment. Okawa was transferred there with the tribunal's permission on August 27, under heavy sedation.

For the next few months his psychotic symptoms persisted. One reporter, who visited Matsuzawa in late August, wrote that Okawa saw fields of corn, rice, potatoes, and eggplants outside his barred window, and said that every morning a group of farmers gathered beneath it to pay homage to the "greatest living man in the world." His wife visited him one day, too, with the doctor's permission. When she arrived he attacked her, and grabbed her by the hair and tried to choke her. He blamed her for everything that was happening to him.

Meanwhile, his so-called revelations continued in the closely guarded solitary room on the hospital's west wing. A glowing-eyed vision of the prophet Mohammed came to him dressed in a green mantle and white turban. The Emperor Meiji appeared, as did his boyhood idol, Saigo Takamori. The souls of King Edward VII and Woodrow Wilson also made visits, and evidently Okawa felt he could actively converse with them, because he thought his English was getting better as a result.

Toward the end of 1946, his health seemed to get a bit better, too. His head felt clear again. In October he completed a five-hundred-page manuscript attempting to unify all the world's religions; Dr. Uchimura read it, and called it "so beautiful as to deserve admiration." As Okawa began to recover he stated emphatically that his hospitalization was unnecessary, and said his behavioral abnormalities were caused by a "religious ecstasy" he'd entered while reading sutras in his cell at Sugamo Prison. By year's end visitors considered him normal.

"He has improved greatly," wrote one reporter on December 7, 1946, "and when one speaks to him alone, aside from a few instances, it is difficult to believe that this is the insane person who surprised the world."

IN EARLY DECEMBER the prosecution motioned for Okawa to receive a new round of psychiatric exams. Some members of the legal team were having their doubts as to his incompetence. Frank Tavenner, a prosecuting attorney on Okawa's case, reviewed my grandfather's medical report for any suggestions of a fitness to stand trial. When he saw notes like "His stream of talk is coherent, and his answers to questions are relevant," he underlined them in red. Hugh Helm, who'd interrogated Okawa at Sugamo, assured Tavenner that the admissions he received at that time were reliable, based on my grandfather's statement that Okawa's long-term memory was strong.

By the time Chief Justice Webb granted the request to reevaluate Okawa's competency, a new international precedent had been set. Judgment and sentencing against the Nazi war criminals at Nurem-

232 / A CURIOUS MADNESS

berg had been handed down in October of 1946. Webb told the Tokyo tribunal that it might have to follow the actions taken by its counterpart in determining Okawa's fate. He had two specific Nuremberg defendants in mind.

The first was the industrialist and armaments magnate Gustav Krupp. When authorities had initially served Krupp with his indictment, they'd found him far too senile to process it. (He was "incoherent, paralyzed, diapered like a baby, uttering no more than an occasional expletive," according to Nuremberg historian Robert E. Conot.) After further consideration, prosecutors decided not to include Krupp in the tribunal. They retained the charges against him for use in a future trial, however, mental health permitting.

The other was Rudolf Hess. Hitler's former deputy führer had shown signs of legitimate paranoia during his imprisonment and some evidence of amnesia during pretrial interviews. His memory deteriorated after the start of the Nuremberg trial, but the precise diagnosis of his illness seemed to depend on the evaluator's nationality. The Russians, who absolutely despised the Germans, denied all signs of insanity. A British doctor felt Hess wasn't insane "in the strict sense," but that his memory loss would interfere with his ability to mount a defense. American doctors felt the memory loss was being exaggerated and exploited as a defense tactic; Justice Robert H. Jackson, representing the United States at Nuremberg, thought Hess was "in the volunteer class with his amnesia."

So Hess remained on trial and, when the sentences came down, was given life in prison.

To no one's surprise, Dr. Uchimura's second evaluation of Okawa Shumei reached the same conclusion as the first. He believed that Okawa had recovered from general paresis quite well with the help of fever therapy, but that his psychotic symptoms, while less severe than before, hadn't been eliminated. Okawa still occasionally heard a voice—it had "an authority like God's," according to Uchimura's report—that told him to read sutras or study the Koran. In Uchimura's view, even if Okawa had regained the ability to distinguish right from wrong, there was still a chance he would base his legal judgments on this voice instead of his own free will. Okawa therefore still lacked "the various faculties that are needed in standing a trial," in the doctor's estimation. He needed another year of close care. Maybe two.

This time the American doctors disagreed. Lieutenants Herbert Posin and William Schweikert of the 361st Station Hospital acknowledged that Okawa's judgment was slightly impaired and that his hallucinations persisted. His general composure and considerable intelligence impressed them, however. "He speaks with excellent logic on nearly every subject brought out for discussion," they reported. His neurological tests suggested only faint traces of his illness. Okawa's pupils still failed to respond to light, but most of his deep tendon reflexes had returned, and the lab results came back conflicted: positive on the Wassermann but negative on the Kahn. The illness had entered remission, in their opinion, and taken Okawa's incompetence with it.

"We consider that this prisoner possesses the ability to understand the nature of the proceedings against him," concluded Posin and Schweikert. "He possesses the intellectual capacity and judgment necessary to take reasonable steps in the presentation of his own defense."

On April 9, 1947, during a lunch break in the proceedings, Justice Webb mulled over the split medical opinion. The last time around, he'd said the court would appoint a third psychiatrist to break a tie; this time he assigned that task to himself. Though Okawa's case closely resembled that of Rudolf Hess—a disputed competency, a suspicion of malingering—Justice Webb evidently considered it closer to that of Gustav Krupp. After consulting the other justices, Webb announced that the court wasn't satisfied that Okawa had recovered his judgment. Okawa was officially removed from the proceedings, with the caveat that he was eligible to be tried again, upon his recovery, on the same charges or any others.

Ohara Shinichi, Okawa's defense counsel, was caught a little off guard by the decision. When he'd visited Matsuzawa Hospital in late 1946, he'd thought Okawa looked just fine. "Medically he may not have been completely recovered," Ohara later wrote, "but he seemed to be able to make a judgment in terms of the legal context." Okawa himself seemed confused by his removal. He told one visitor, a Buddhist priest from Sugamo named Hanayama Shinsho, that he expected to return to the trial at any time. "His mind seemed to be functioning all right," Hanayama wrote.

Instead, Okawa returned to his room at Matsuzawa Hospital without much of an explanation. He tried to make sense of things by reading the report by Posin and Schweikert, but that only clouded the matter. A family friend who visited Matsuzawa around this time recalled that Okawa kept a copy of this American medical report for his records. When the friend arrived, Okawa read him the report in English, then explained what it said in Japanese. "He told me that he was fine, and wanted to return to the trial, but they wouldn't let him," the friend recalled. "He told me, 'I may have been critical of the trial, but I had every intention of returning.'"

In May of 1947, Ohara Shinichi asked the occupation authorities for permission to move Okawa from Matsuzawa Hospital back into the custody of his wife. Dr. Uchimura believed Okawa would do better with the "quiet, solitude, and peaceful environment" of his serene home in Kanagawa. Rankled by the court's decision, Frank Tavenner from the prosecution team responded that Okawa *had* recovered his senses, or would do so shortly, based on the second American medical report. The only way to ensure he'd go back on trial as soon as he recovered was to keep him in custody. MacArthur's legal division, which had final say on the matter, concurred; the Tokyo tribunal might have removed Okawa from the current proceedings, but it hadn't stripped his status as a "suspected war criminal."

So Okawa was at Matsuzawa to stay. He passed most of his time by translating the Koran into Japanese. He didn't have Arabic, but he collected versions of the holy book in languages he did know: English, German, French, and Chinese. Okawa compared the lines in each, considered their meaning, and piece by piece constructed a translation. Friends saw the books stacked around the hospital room and thought this was Okawa Shumei just being his old self again.

THE MADNESS OF Okawa Shumei influenced the Tokyo trial even in his absentia. During closing arguments, made in 1948, the defense invoked his condition several times in an effort to invalidate the prosecution's entire line of reasoning. Defense attorneys called the information supplied by Okawa about the Manchurian Incident the "contradictory statements of a crazy ideologist." The prosecution, meanwhile, continued to cast doubt on Okawa's insanity—referring to it in their own closing arguments as a "real or pseudo present mental condition."

In November of 1948, roughly two and a half years after it began, the Tokyo trial came to an end. Eight of the eleven justices supported the majority judgment that the Japanese defendants had conspired to wage a war of aggression. The Dutch judge issued a partial dissent on the grounds that Japan's war was a crime but for different reasons. The French judge dissented in full on the grounds that the trial was flawed because it should have involved the emperor.

The Indian judge, Radhabinod Pal, provided the most vigorous dissent against what he called "victor's justice." His book-length opinion ran to 250,000 English words—longer than the majority judgment. Seeing the trial as a sham, like Okawa Shumei before him, Pal called it "formalized vengeance" and argued that every defendant should be acquitted. Among Pal's better points was the fact that Japan's "criminal militaristic clique" could hardly have conspired together, since many didn't even know one another. "The story here has been pushed a little too far, perhaps, to give it a place in the Hitler series," Pal wrote.

In any event, only the majority was read in court. Though Okawa spent the trial on the sidelines, the judgment nonetheless placed him at the center of the conspiracy that justified the fates of the others. The tribunal's ruling on count 1—that Japan had attempted to secure a military, political, and economic domination of East Asia as far back as 1928—named Okawa as the instigator of this aggressive path:

> Already prior to 1928 Okawa, one of the original defendants, who has been discharged from this trial on account of his present mental state, was publicly advocating that Japan should extend her territory on the continent of Asia by the threat or,

if necessary, by use of military force. . . . He predicted that the course he advocated must result in a war between the East and the West, in which Japan would be the champion of the East. He was encouraged and aided in his advocacy of this plan by the Japanese General Staff. The object of this plan as stated was substantially the object of the conspiracy as we have defined it. In our review of the facts we have noticed many subsequent declarations of the conspirators as to the object of the conspiracy. These do not vary in any material respect from this early declaration by Okawa.

. . . The conspiracy was now in being. It remained in being until Japan's defeat in 1945.

What's clear from the judgment is that if Okawa had remained on trial he would have been convicted with the others, and very well might have been hanged. Why such a central figure was never brought back into court always remained a mystery to his defense attorney, Ohara Shinichi. Decades after the trial's conclusion, Ohara wrote a letter to the *Asahi Shimbun* newspaper about his experience as Okawa's counsel. He wondered why Hugh Helm, the prosecutor in charge of Okawa's case, left Japan without pushing for more charges. "Did he stop it because of Okawa's mental illness, or was there another reason?" asked Ohara. "We can't find anything to form a judgment up to this very day."

One theory says that prosecutors hesitated to return Okawa to the trial because they secretly feared putting someone so knowledgeable on the witness stand. Called to testify, Okawa might present uncomfortable examples of America's own history of aggression in East Asia—and in English, too. As he'd done throughout his life when challenging the West, Okawa might point out any number of contradictions embedded in the trial. He might have noted how under the tribunal's own definition of "crimes against humanity," the Americans theoretically could have been guilty of dropping the atomic bombs. Or how the Filipino justice, Delfin Jaranilla, had survived the horrific Japanese-led Bataan

Death March, which in any normal court would have disqualified him. Or how even as Western nations were condemning Japan for imperial expansion, the French, Dutch, and British were trying to regain colonial holds in the Pacific.

Intriguing as that theory is, it doesn't quite align with what transpired in the courtroom at Ichigaya. The very nature of the proceedings restricted the types of arguments the defense could make and the type of evidence it could introduce on its own behalf. When in doubt about a line of reasoning, the tribunal typically sided with the prosecution. Judges routinely dismissed the idea, for instance, that Asianism was a legitimate gripe against Western imperialism. With that the theory falls flat: prosecutors wouldn't have needed to prevent Okawa from making an argument the court wouldn't have allowed him to make. Besides, if prosecutors didn't want Okawa at the trial, they simply wouldn't have indicted him in the first place.

The most likely reason Okawa was released is that by the time the Tokyo trial concluded, people had tired of postwar justice. Initially the occupation officials intended to hold more trials—there were twelve more following Nuremberg's main event, after all—but Japanese war crimes never captured Western attention like Nazi war crimes. When the Tokyo trial was finished, no one had the energy for another. "To be honest, the general public's interest focused not on the proceedings but on the single point of what the verdicts would be," wrote one newspaper in late 1948. Postwar politics had changed, too. By the time the trial came to a close, the United States needed Japan as an ally in the East, to counter Russia's partnership with China. The nineteen Class-A suspects still in custody at Sugamo in December of 1948 were released back into society. Many went on to serve in the postwar Japanese government.

On December 23, 1948, the seven Japanese war criminals given capital punishment went to the gallows outside Sugamo Prison. Okawa Shumei considered their fate from his bed at Matsuzawa Hospital for the Insane. He'd completed his translation of the Koran a couple weeks earlier and now had plenty of time for contemplation. He woke up the next day to see it had rained a bit, and that the sky was still cloudy.

He opened his personal diary and listed his dead comrades by name. "Good or bad, they left their names to world history," he wrote. "Rest in peace with all the contributions you have made as a man."

At three o'clock he was notified of his release. A week later he left the hospital and headed home a free man.

MY GRANDFATHER'S ENTIRE life, from home to battlefield, prepared him for his analysis of Okawa Shumei. So when I initially read in his memoirs that he maintained "the utmost confidence in my clinical acumen and in my diagnosis of paresis," I didn't doubt it. Still, just to be sure, and because I carry an obvious genetic bias, I took his examination report to the only person whose opinion of the case could approach my grandfather's own. Dr. Albert Stunkard arrived in Tokyo in mid-1946, shortly after my grandfather left, and served as a psychiatrist at the 361st Station Hospital as well as at Sugamo Prison. Stunkard visited Okawa at Matsuzawa Hospital on several occasions. He's probably the last American alive to have known him during the Tokyo trial.

Even nearing ninety, Stunkard still commuted every day to his office at the University of Pennsylvania medical school in Philadelphia. I made the short walk there from 30th Street Station along Market Street in a cold drizzle. Stunkard was sitting in an office chair, and for most of our four hours together he rarely rose, preferring instead to cross the room by wheeling the chair with his feet. He wore a blue blazer with brass buttons, khaki pants, and black tennis shoes, and had an impressive crest of white hair for his age. His voice registered maybe three notches above a whisper.

Shortly after I arrived, I showed Stunkard my grandfather's exam, and he wheeled over to a projector machine called a Clearview so he could follow along with his poor vision. For the next forty-five minutes he tracked the page on the machine as I read to him aloud. He was engrossed. If I stopped for a moment, just to jot down a note, he bugged me to keep going. His assistant brought him lunch—a pretzel sandwich and a Pepsi—and he never touched it. Sometimes he finished my sentence before I could, just knowing the old psychiatric jargon.

Stunkard said he thought the evaluation was "pretty correct." If a patient had positive serological tests like the Wassermann and the Kahn, and grandiose ideas like the kiss of death, "that was about all you needed for the diagnosis," he said. He pointed out that general paresis was far more common at that time, so it wouldn't have caught anyone by surprise. (These were the days before penicillin prevented syphilis from reaching its tertiary stage.) As far as he knew, fever therapy treated the problem without causing additional harm to the brain, so Okawa's subsequent recovery could be expected as well. If the damage done to Okawa's brain couldn't be reversed, it would at least have been arrested.

"What's interesting to me is that people afterward thought Okawa was faking his illness," I said.

"I know they did," Stunkard said.

"What do you think about that?" I asked. "Is that not credible?"

"Oh, yeah, I don't think so," he said. "It was classical general paresis, with grandiosity and probably also errors in memory and judgment."

"You don't think someone could fake that?"

"I don't think— He wouldn't have had any idea about how to do that."

Before I left, we chatted a bit about Stunkard's trips to Matsuzawa Hospital. He spoke to Okawa (in German) about religion generally, though Stunkard's primary interest was Buddhism. While in Japan, Stunkard spent some time in a monastery where he meditated from four in the morning until eleven at night. He focused on problems like: What is *mu*? Meaning, in the Buddhist sense of the term, What is nothing? A banner with a thick black circle that represented *mu* hung behind his office door, and I passed it on my way out.

The rain had stopped by the time I headed back to the train station. I saw a circle on a street sign and something came to me. *Mu* was silent, and profound, and yes a little elusive but also present enough to keep you grasping. It was like my grandfather in that way. Even his psychiatric assessment of Okawa Shumei had an element of *mu* to it. There were two distinct sections to the report. There was the clinical evaluation, part of the natural science of medicine, documented point by point with a cold, objective precision. Then there was the competency opinion, part of the human practice of law, derived without much explanation through some murky personal blend of morality and philosophy and emotion. Just how he'd arrived at his competency conclusion was a bit curious. The second American psychiatrists had done what people expected from the Allied side: they'd declared Okawa just sane enough to stand trial, even as the Japanese doctor declared him just insane enough *not* to. They'd lived up to the postwar mentality of *Give them a fair trial, then hang them*. My grandfather had gone a different route. Maybe he'd simply equated clinical madness with incompetence, ipso facto, and reached his opinion that way. Maybe he'd considered Okawa's competency through rational eyes and determined him unfit to stand trial. Or maybe he'd thought back to his mother's own acquittal of murder on the grounds of being mad, and recognized that his very existence was a testament to the belief that insanity was not the same thing as iniquity, and concluded that the sick mind must be treated instead of punished, whatever discomfort that might cause to our ideas of justice. I'm not suggesting that my grandfather exercised compassion on Okawa's behalf, nor do I mean to imply that his competency judgment was even the slightest bit wrong. I'm only acknowledging that there was a step to his decision process that, like so much in his life, will remain forever *mu*.

TOJO HIDEKI'S GRANDDAUGHTER met me at a tea lounge in the lobby of a hotel in Shibuya. The first thing you do when meeting someone in Japan is exchange name cards. Tojo Yuko's name card wasn't quite what I'd expected. It showed a cartoon woman, child, and puppy prancing on a bright and cloudless day in a meadow that extended toward the horizon. "This is an ideal family," she said through my translator, Chiaki. A moment later she opened a book called *Never Talk: The Postwar Life of Tojo Hideki's Family* to a panoramic portrait. The photo was taken October 18, 1941, just after Tojo Hideki moved into the prime minister's residence. She pointed to the little girl beside him.

"I was two years old."

Tojo Yuko was a slight woman with enviable posture and the quiet manner of a librarian. She ordered Darjeeling tea when the waitress came around and complimented my pronunciation of *arigato* while politely ignoring the fact that I drank coffee at a tea lounge in Tokyo. She looked a lot like her grandfather—especially the almond eyes. I wanted to learn what she remembered about the moment Okawa Shumei slapped him during the Tokyo trial.

"I heard a rumor he was too smart to make any kind of statement at the tribunal, and that's why he was sent away to the hospital," she said. "That was the rumor spreading. He was too smart to talk. If he kept talking, it wouldn't work for the U.S. side. They sort of tried to eliminate him."

"When did you hear this rumor?" I asked.

"We started hearing it during the tribunal, and it went on all the way through," she said.

Our drinks arrived. Tojo dumped lots of milk and sugar into hers, which made me feel better when I did the same. "You talked about it even at the time of the tribunal?" I asked.

"Yes, at the time," she said. "Nobody knew whether he was actually ill or just pretending."

That rumor was so flawed it was no better than a conspiracy theory, but I soon discovered that Tojo was quite comfortable with unconventional views toward the war and the Tokyo trial. During our discussion, she suggested that American leaders intentionally failed to prevent Pearl Harbor so the country would have an excuse to enter the war. (That idea, proposed in Robert Stinnett's 2000 book *Day of Deceit*, has been generally doubted by historians.) She insisted that MacArthur himself told Congress in 1951 that Japan had entered the war out of self-defense. (His actual comment—that Japan's reason for war "was largely dictated by security"—is far less conciliatory.) She proposed reversing the outcome of the trial and revising school curricula to reflect Japan's own version of history. She maintained that Japan entered the war to liberate Asia, a position echoing Okawa Shumei's divine mission.

It's not easy to hear someone defend the actions of a nation that started a war. To some people, Tojo Yuko probably came off as a little nutty. (A Tokyo-based journalist once called her "one of the most toxic figures in a growing historical revisionist movement that is again pulling Asia apart.") As we spoke, though, it occurred to me that most of her perspective on the past could be explained by the strong reverence she held toward her family. She published the book about her grandfather because she wanted people to learn the Tojo side of things. She signed a copy for me and stamped it with her grandfather's personal seal, which she evidently carries around. She started an organization that recovers the bones of dead soldiers in the Pacific and returns them to Japan, because if Tojo Hideki were still alive, that's what he would have done.

"Whenever people talked about Tojo Hideki, they talked about how cruel he was, a war criminal," she said. "But my mother told me that my grandfather wasn't like that. He was a respectable person and we should be proud we're born into this family."

For all I knew, Tojo's belief that MacArthur approved the war as self-defense, or that FDR secretly welcomed it, was her unconscious way of coping with the flaws of a person she couldn't help but love. When you stop to think about it, a conspiracy theory is just a way to make sense of a confusing world. Maintaining a sound mind often requires us, for better or worse, to reject inconvenient information. If we accepted every conflicting piece of data we encountered, the chaotic fury of this life would break our minds in no time. Upsetting as it is to see someone deny a fact we consider undeniable, or embrace one we consider unembraceable, I think most of us can admit that, after a certain point, reality is indistinguishable from perspective. Rather than run everything through some objective filter, we latch onto a hunch or an instinct or an appealing notion—not because we're insane, most of us, but because we very sanely want something so elusive from this bewildering existence: answers.

And that, I was starting to believe, was the essence of the obsession with Okawa Shumei and his insanity at the Tokyo trial. It seemed to represent so much of what's wondrous and pitiful and inexplicable about the curious madness that was the Second World War. When people looked at the slap, they saw not just what they wanted to see, they saw what they *needed* to see to endure in its aftermath. The strict scientist convinced of Okawa's insanity saw the triumph of rational observation. The devoted ideological followers saw no need to hide from a belief that wasn't wrong. The deflated patriot saw an embarrassing cover-up to save American face. The inquisitive intellectual saw a limit to how long genius can withstand its own greatness. The skeptic of the West saw a political point made in front of a global audience. The average Japanese saw incredulous timing, just as they doubted their whole country could lose its mind at once. The intelligence agent saw the deceptive nature of the evil enemy. We all saw whatever helped us carry the tragic weight of the world we'd wrought. It felt a little like keeping a picture on your name card, as Tojo Yuko did, of a bright and cloudless day.

Before we parted ways, Tojo and I discussed the slap once more. She laughed about it—laughed in a way she said she wouldn't have been able to during the trial. She thought that since her grandfather was so bald Okawa's hand would have made a loud and clear sound coming down against it. She mentioned the silent, three-second looping animation of the slap that someone compiled from documentary footage of the trial and put up on the Internet.

"People just like to cut this short action portion and watch it repeatedly," she said.

It was there now to be debated in perpetuity, and I suspected it would be.

Chapter 12

✦═══✦

The Ghosts of East and West

Oh, East is East, and West is West, and never the twain shall meet,
Till Earth and Sky stand presently at God's great Judgment Seat;
But there is neither East nor West, Border, nor Breed, nor Birth,
When two strong men stand face to face, tho' they come from the
ends of the earth!

—Rudyard Kipling, "The Ballad of East and West," 1889

THE CIA FOLLOWED Okawa Shumei for years after the Tokyo trial. Many agents never got over the idea that he might have escaped their sense of justice. In the early 1950s, sources told the agency that Okawa was trying to provoke a third world war "in the name of Greater Asia-ism," and that he was orchestrating a military overthrow of the French in Indochina. An agency brief, distributed in February of 1953, said many people still suspected his insanity had been feigned. The word "insanity" itself was put in quotes, as if whoever wrote the memo agreed it probably hadn't existed.

Okawa did have a few active years after the trial, but they weren't nearly as fabulous as American intelligence believed. He toured rural villages across Japan promoting a return to the country's days of agrarian splendor. He spoke to crowds about a bizarre new farming method for growing rice paddies that harnessed the "electrical potential" of the air. Occasionally during these years he criticized the new constitution—he described it as forced on Japan by America, according to yet another CIA source—but in general his goal was to build a quiet new Japan almost literally from the ground up. To regrow the nation from seed. To plow the bad years and plant again.

Now and then, he reflected on that memorable day in court and the madness that followed. His statements rarely aligned. In a postwar autobiography, he admitted to feeling a bit deranged during the trial, but he portrayed the entire experience as a magical occurrence beyond any powers of explanation. The words "syphilis" or "general paresis" or "fever therapy" never made their way into the text. Instead, Okawa wrote that the root cause of his illness was impossible to isolate, and that he couldn't recall anything that accounted for his recovery.

"I have been cured of the psychiatric trouble in a curious way," he wrote.

In the fall of 1952, a newspaper correspondent dropped by Okawa's serene home in suburban Tokyo and asked what he recalled about the slap. Okawa told the reporter he'd become irritated at the farce of the tribunal. "Maybe I went a little out of my mind at that moment," Okawa said. "But I still remember clearly what I did then." He said every psychiatrist who examined him found " 'nothing wrong with his mentality.'" To prove it, Okawa then pulled out the second American psychiatric exam—the one conducted in 1947, after my grandfather left; the one that called him fit to stand trial. The reporter asked why Okawa hadn't returned to the trial if he'd been competent after all. Okawa said he didn't know but that he had a theory: perhaps the prosecutors, fearful that he'd point out "the faults of the Allied nations" on the stand, "treated me as a mad man just to silence me."

In the springtime of 1957, at age seventy, Okawa lost most of his eyesight. Those big iconic glasses that had followed him since youth were of little use. At the end of May he was confined to bed rest after a bout of bronchitis. When he felt the end growing near he reflected on his life and found himself at peace:

During the great turning point of world history, being born in this country where the sun sets and rises, throughout the seventy-some years of my life, the sadness, delight, sorrow, and pleasure, these thousands and ten thousands of emotional tides, heaved endlessly on the surface of the ocean of my heart, but in the depths of my heart I was always at ease.

On December 24, 1957, at twenty to noon, that heart gave out.

IMMEDIATELY AFTER THE war my grandfather worked part-time at a veterans' mental health clinic, treating former soldiers suffering post-combat trauma, while studying psychoanalysis with the help of the GI Bill. The family settled down in Washington. By the early 1950s it had become a party of five. His training complete, my grandfather ran a private analytical practice from his home, seeing patients in a wing of the house converted into an office, complete with its own private side entrance. Over time he published papers in leading journals, gave talks at international meetings, served a faculty position at a D.C. medical school—became the doctor his father had wanted him to be.

The height of his career came in the early 1960s, when he served two years as president of the Washington Psychoanalytic Society. His tenure coincided with the Kennedy administration, and during this period his family often spotted a black sedan parked on their street. The children surmised, on the basis of the car and the imposing security figures surrounding it, that my grandfather counted among his regular patients someone of great importance in Washington. They always asked who it was. They were never told.

His mother lived a long life but couldn't escape the wicked reach of her illness. Sometimes she survived completely on her own. Sometimes my grandfather or one of his siblings took her into their home. Sometimes she got too sick again and they sent her to another hospital or an institution. She was still having episodes on occasion when she finally died in 1969. When I came along, many years later, I was given

a name made from the first letter of her own, but I was never told anything about her troubled life.

Long after his kids became adults, when it was time to move to a
smaller home, my grandfather destroyed all his letters from the war.
Later on, that decision complicated his ability to write his memoirs of
being a combat psychiatrist. My aunt worked with him for a while to
improve the manuscript. They held a series of recorded interviews to
inject more emotional life, more details, into certain sections. Those
chats devolved into a futile vocal merry-go-round: my aunt would pose
a question, my grandfather would answer it the same reserved way he'd
written it, my grandmother (who was also present) would insert her
own two cents, and they'd move on. At one point he stopped respond-
ing at all, and they realized he was staring out the window, trying to
identify a bird. I don't think his heart was really in it.

Except for the section on Okawa Shumei. He clearly wanted to
share his side of that story. He wrote in the memoirs that obviously
Okawa would lie about his sickness, since few people would be eager to
admit they'd contracted syphilis. In the fall of 1996, he pitched a brief
summary of his exam to the editor of the *New England Journal of Medicine,* and evidently he wrote to the *Journal of the American Medical Association,* too. Nothing ever came of these efforts.

"In my mind there had never been any doubt," he wrote.

The Alzheimer's that defined his final few years also robbed him
of any last-ditch attempt to publish his side, or to divulge whatever
impenetrable secrets those war letters contained. He died in October
of 2007. All anyone could talk about at the funeral was how ironic it
was that a man who lived the life of the mind had lost his senses at the
end. At the headstone unveiling, the following fall, the rabbi placed a
little rock on top of the stone in the Jewish tradition. He said the rock
kept the ghost of the deceased from escaping, kept the soul nearby and
at peace. He said a scientific man like Daniel Jaffe wouldn't have cared
much for all this talk about ghosts, but he went ahead and put the rock
there anyway, then we all did the same.

DURING ONE OF my many research trips to Washington, my father and I went into the den that is a shrine to my grandfather and took down the samurai sword my grandfather had brought home from the Japanese occupation. Together we arranged some pictures of the scabbard, and the hilt, and the blade. We uploaded them onto my computer so I could send them to a well-regarded appraiser of Japanese swords. He'd agreed to look at the pictures for me and tell me about the one we displayed at the top of the room.

After we put the sword away I could sense that my father didn't want the task to end there. He has a certain way of getting stiff and sheepish and nervous right before broaching a serious subject, and I knew enough to ask what was on his mind.

"Well, we know more about Grandpa's mom than we ever wanted to," he said. "Can you at least tell me he was right about the exam?"

There it was. The question I'd been avoiding out in the open. I knew in that moment I'd hurt my father a little, the very fact that I'd questioned his own father's wisdom. There was a picture of my grandfather in uniform right beside the sword. His official separation from the military came on May 27, 1946. He made the short trip from Fort Dix, in New Jersey, to Brooklyn, and rejoined his wife and thirteen-month-old son. As the story goes, the little guy refused to accept this new figure in his life. "He's not my father," the boy said, then he pointed to a framed picture of my grandfather in his military uniform.

"*That's* my father."

The scene serves as an enduring metaphor for everything the family doesn't know about Daniel Jaffe, and never will. He was a looming figure, exalted and revered, but his silence made him almost a cameo in his own life—a character whose brevity on the stage forced us to mediate our relationships with him through our own imaginations. Since we lacked enough information for nuance we rarely supplied any: a brilliant word here made him brilliant, a sharp insight there made him insightful. Rather than dilute this brilliant insight with questions, we let the silence distill it into something timeless and perfect.

His refusal to discuss his life gave us a license to invent his legend. Take the patient of great importance in Washington—the one who showed up to the house in the black sedan with the security personnel during the Kennedy administration. His children still hold court on just who it was. The exchanges typically go something like this:

"I think it was the president. Why else would there have been Secret Service?"

"We don't know it was Secret Service."

"Maybe it was the First Lady."

"Maybe it was Marilyn."

"I would have recognized Marilyn."

"But you're sure it was a woman?"

"I'm almost positive it was a woman."

"Maybe it was RFK."

"I'm pretty sure it was [names a senator]'s wife."

"Why would a senator's wife have two Secret Service agents?"

"They might have been bodyguards."

"Why would a senator's wife have two bodyguards?"

The debate will remain irresolvable, because after my grandfather died, my father and my uncle burned his patient records at his request. To their credit, before that day came, they tried one last time to wrestle the gossip from the vault of his voice. *That* story typically goes like this:

"Pop, we know there was a famous person who came to the house."

"There waaaaas?"

"Yes, we saw the Secret Service. We know you saw someone."

"I diiiiiid?"

"You really didn't see anyone famous?"

Then my grandfather would open his eyes wide and press his lips into a wry smile and shake his head.

My uncle once told me that burning those records without peeking through them was "the most honorable thing we ever did." For a long time I figured he meant the best way to honor a man who destroyed the records of his own life was to burn those of other lives he wanted to protect. After a while, though, I wondered if they had refrained from looking for another reason, one they maybe failed to realize. Perhaps they burned those records not to protect the confidentiality of his patients, or the sanctity of his final requests, but to uphold the image the family had created in its collective mind. Not out of some irrational fear that he was looking down on them from a distant place, but out of some very understandable fear that they might find something that would force them to change what they believed. That maybe my grandfather *hadn't* seen some great patient during those Washington days. That maybe he *wasn't* the steady anchor for a wobbly family past. That maybe he was, shudder to think it, an average man. Just like the Japanese saw what they needed to see in Okawa Shumei, our family saw what we needed to see in Daniel Jaffe. We could look at that sword forever and see everything in its right place, even after my appraiser wrote back to explain that the binding looked a bit too new for a traditional samurai sword, and that the *habaki*—the metal collar at the base of the blade—struck him as unusual, too, and that the blade itself seemed rather flat, and that a lot of Japanese had been making fake swords to sell to Allied soldiers during the occupation, and he hated to say it but my grandfather had probably bought one.

"Of course he was right," I told my father, and I knew he felt relaxed again, because I did, too.

OKAWA SHUMEI'S GRAVE site in Meguro, home to half his remains, was nearly as curious to me as the man himself. The burial plot consisted of a modest parcel of real estate marked with a little monument. It was situated just below a Japanese Cherry tree, the beloved national symbol, and it faced the plot for Kita Ikki, Okawa's old prewar reactionary comrade. That seemed like a most favorable placement considering that Okawa was a war crimes suspect and Kita had been executed by the state for his role in an uprising. The tree was in bloom, and pink petals fluttered onto the graves, like gentle posthumous kisses, as Okawa and Kita conspired together into eternity. An old groundskeeper named Ohashi led Chiaki and me to the plots and explained that interest in the two men had waned after the war but had recently picked up again.

"Now I see young people coming here," Ohashi said. "Society has changed quite a bit."

The shifting mind-set toward Okawa Shumei reminded me of

something I'd noticed several times in the course of studying his fateful incident at the Tokyo trial: insanity, too, seemed to change over time. Immigrant Jews were once mad simply because they were Jewish, then they were more or less normal people adapting to a strange new environment. The lobotomist Walter Freeman was a fearless savior of the insane, then his technique began to seem reckless and a bit insane in its own right. American soldiers cracked up in combat because they possessed weak minds, then they broke because everyone broke if strained hard enough. Okawa's own mental health existed behind some kaleidoscopic curtain of personal belief and redacted recollection and medical opinion. The very history of madness felt like an endless coil of perception.

As the cherry blossoms showered us, I thought about my grandfather, and how much he looked forward to spring in Washington, when the city's own Japanese Cherry trees burst into little pink life. He might not have agreed with the idea of madness as something subjective, flexible, a bit captive to context. That could imply mental illness wasn't real, when he'd known since childhood how very real it was. What I couldn't figure out, what I wished I could go back and ask him, was the threshold for *when* it became real. What if you could stop time at that precise moment before Okawa Shumei's blood turned the Wassermann test positive? Was his madness real then? Had it been real between Esther Jaffe's first and second breakdowns and simply eluded detection? Or had it been real, then unreal, then real again? I wondered if these conflicting sides of insanity—the slippery social definitions and the steady clinical ones—weren't a little irreconcilable. I wasn't ready to suggest that madness escaped all rational inquiry, but it seemed very nearly out of reason's reach.

My strongest memory of my grandfather, one I recall sharing with people after his funeral, was the time he took me as an adolescent to see the opera *Faust* at the Kennedy Center. Not a moment after the final curtain fell, he burst into the aisle and hustled toward the stage. I followed, wondering if we were trying to get a better view of the curtain call, but when the actors returned to the stage we kept moving. As the audience rose to applaud we cut across the very front row—cut toward the exit at the side of the theater. I recall stepping over a woman in an elaborate gown who flashed me a look of disgust so sharp it still hurts me in a physical way. When we got outside and into the car I asked why we'd made such a quick escape; he replied, without a hint of embarrassment, "To beat the traffic."

I've always thought that story captured his character: cerebral to the point of obsession, so brainy as to render emotion a little meddlesome. That didn't mean he lacked a softer side—he wouldn't go to the opera at all if that were the case—but it did mean he could mute it with almost preternatural ease. Perhaps he went to great lengths to impose rationality on the world precisely because he knew how irrational it became when you didn't. Life was far more manageable when you beat the opera crowd out of the parking lot, or destroyed the letters that detailed your breakdown in Japan, or stayed silent on the traumas of your childhood, or generally distilled everything around you into dispassionate pieces. When you accepted that in the East and West of heart and mind, sometimes the twain should never meet.

Behind Okawa's little monument was a rack holding tall, flat stakes called *sotoba,* which marked the number of years since he'd died. The wind picked up and they clattered around in the rack. I put a stone on Okawa's grave, as I'd once done for my grandfather's own, so his ghost could rest, too. Strange how much I thought of the two men as a unit. They'd been in the same room for maybe only an hour or two of their entire lives. I had become far more curious about their encounter than either of them had ever been, and suddenly felt like the referee of a contest being played entirely in my own head. I could keep score, but victory and defeat would come from the same source, and there'd be nothing real about either one. Probably best for my own sanity if these twain didn't meet for a while. As we walked back down the hill, the rattling of the death stakes got quieter, and quieter, and then so quiet I forgot they were there.

Acknowledgments

W HEN YOU WRITE a book about one man who never spoke
and another who spoke a foreign language, you end up with
a lot of people to thank. The only rightful place to begin is with the
three children of Daniel Jaffe—my uncle, Harry Jaffe; my aunt, Evelyn
Schreiber; and my father, Mark Jaffe—who have been wonderfully
supportive every step of the way. They may not love every word I wrote
in this history, but they always respected that I had to write it. An enormous debt is owed to my great-aunts, Sylvia Abrams and Wilma Jaffe.
Without their vivid memories and dusty documents, and their ready
willingness to share them, this book probably wouldn't exist.

My second round of thanks must go to the many veterans and
families of veterans who so generously gave their time or documents
or both, either in person or over the phone or by mail, to facilitate my
research. They are, in alphabetical order, Harold Burg, Carol Davis,
Richard Davis, Clara Hasbrouck, William Hill Jr., Stan Huff, John
Kelly, Raymond Lee, Norman Mathis, Joe Meneghelli, Warren Miller,
Roy and Jean Peterman, Bertram Schaffner (with a special nod to Carol
Schaffner), Ken and Yvonne Thomas, Lucianna Twitchell, Sylvia Waxman (with a special thanks to Mike Waxman), Frank Williams Jr. (with
a special thanks to Bonnie and Santos Delgado for their fine hospital-
ity), and Ann Yarborough. Jon Halsey—the grandson of General Milton Halsey, who commanded the 97th Infantry in battle—deserves an
extended mention for providing access to a treasure trove of material
on the division.

Warren Poland, Richard Waugaman, and Elaine Cotlove, my grandfather's colleagues, offered some thoughtful descriptions on his abilities as a professional and his character in general. Bruce Hirschauer, a historian of the 97th Infantry, gave me a very helpful orientation on the division in the project's early days. Una Gozelski had some very helpful memories about her father, Dr. James Vavasour, who cared for Esther Jaffe at Louden Hall before the war. Rebecca Schwartz Greene was generous enough to sit down and discuss her 1977 dissertation on psychiatry during World War II, which remains the most robust scholarly analysis of the subject.

My understanding of occupied Japan would not have been complete without the help of Bill Barrette, who's studied Sugamo Prison extensively, and Jack Mallory, who served at the 361st Station Hospital. I'm also forever in the debt of Albert Stunkard for being kind enough to review my grandfather's examination of Okawa with me and to share the memories of his service at both Sugamo and the 361st during the occupation.

A great many people contributed their time to help me understand the life and work of Okawa Shumei. I'm grateful to them all. In the United States, I got help from Cemil Aydin, Eri Hotta, and Yuma Totani. In Japan, this sphere of assistance extended to Sven Saaler and Christopher Szpilman (in English), and Awaya Kentaro, Ishida Takeshi, Kato Kenshiro, Matsumoto Ken'ichi, Okawa Kenmei, Otsuka Takehiro, Sato Masaru, Sato Shoichi, Tojo Yuko, Usuki Akira, and Yamamoto Tetsuro (partly or entirely with a translator). Any errors I made about Asianism or Okawa are my own, but any insights I made go to their credit.

The staff members who helped my research at various libraries and archives and documentary repositories are too numerous to thank one by one, but a few deserve particular recognition. I'll always be grateful to Cecilia Brown and Elizabeth Ladner at the Frank S. Tavenner Collection in the University of Virginia Law Library, Ken Cobb at the New York City Municipal Archives, Sanders Marble at the U.S. Army's Office of Medical History, Gary McMillan at the American Psychiatric Association, and Diane Richardson at the Oskar Diethelm Library on the History of Psychiatry. Jay Barksdale, who runs the Wertheim Study in the New York Public Library, was most generous in extending my time there again and again (and again).

The Japan Foundation Center for Global Partnership and the Social Science Research Council generously awarded me an Abe Fellowship for Journalists, which enabled my long research trip to Japan. I could not have secured that spot without the advice of the great Japan scholar Gerald Curtis of Columbia University. John Glusman, author of the wonderful *Conduct Under Fire,* gave me some very useful early advice on writing a book involving both Japan and the military service of a relative. The Hertog Fellowship at the Columbia University MFA program provided me with the very valuable research services of Alex Cunningham for several months. I was fortunate to find two smart and reliable translators: Chiaki Kitada in Japan and Geoff Waring in New York.

A word of gratitude is in order for Colin Harrison, Jim Hornfischer, and Kelsey Smith, the professional hands that guided this project from conception to completion. Another for Sam Freedman, who will get an acknowledgment in my books as long as I'm writing them. And another for Jeneen, the only girl I know whose eyes light up at the mention of archival research; I'm very lucky that her support never wavered, because whether I said so or not, it was always needed.

Sources and Notes

F INDING STANDARD BIBLIOGRAPHIES poor guides, I believe an annotated description of my sources, broken down by chapter, will give readers the greatest insight into the research and reporting conducted for particular sections of the book. This approach results in some repetition among chapter summaries but makes up for that in overall clarity and transparency.

Generally speaking, sources are only cited in full on their first appearance. The individual citations that follow each chapter summary are mostly limited to quotations, dates and figures, and unique facts. In the case of quotes, these citations reference the final three words of the statement. Any edits to quoted material have been noted in the individual citations. Unless otherwise noted, all archival material was acquired personally by the author.

For consistency with the main text, Japanese diacritical marks have been removed, but names have been kept in the traditional style of surname followed by given name. Exceptions occur with Japanese authors who use the Western name style by choice.

The amount of work Okawa Shumei published in his lifetime would take another lifetime (and a small fortune) to translate. I've had selected portions of this massive oeuvre translated. Unless noted as my own author translations, all translated quotations appear as published in the cited works.

My personal scenes in Japan all occurred in April or May of 2012 as part of an Abe Fellowship for Journalists, sponsored by the Japan Foundation Center for Global Partnership and the Social Science Research Council. Conversations during these scenes that occurred in English have been noted in the text; all the others were translated on the spot, with a few edits made after the fact, in consultation with the interpreter, for clarity. The scenes did not all take place in the order they appear.

Abbreviations

CR/KCC   Competency records, Kings County Clerk's Office, Brooklyn, New York

IPS   International Prosecution Section

JWC   *Japan Weekly Chronicle* (an English-language publication)

JWP   Joseph Wortis Papers in the Oskar Diethelm Library at Weill Medical College of Cornell University, New York, New York

M1683   Numerical case files relating to particular incidents and suspected war criminals, International Prosecution Section, 1945–47, in the National Archives at College Park, Maryland

M1690   Numerical evidentiary documents assembled by the prosecution for use as evidence before the International Military Tribunal for the Far East, 1945–47, in the National Archives at College Park, Maryland

MHP   Milton Halsey Papers, private collection

NACP   The National Archives at College Park, Maryland

NP-WWII   *Neuropsychiatry in World War II* (2 vols.; Washington: Office of the Surgeon General, Dept. of the Army, 1966–1973)

NYCMA   New York City Municipal Archives, New York, New York

NYT   *New York Times*

ODL   Oskar Diethelm Library at Weill Medical College of Cornell University, New York, New York

PA   Sven Saaler and Christopher W. A. Szpilman, eds., *Pan-Asianism: A Documentary History* (2 vols.; Lanham, Md.: Rowman & Littlefield, 2011)

PPFT   Personal papers of Frank S. Tavenner Jr., Arthur J. Morris Law Library, University of Virginia School of Law, Charlottesville, Virginia

RG 112   Records of the Office of the Surgeon General (Army) in the National Archives at College Park, Maryland

RG 263   Records of the Central Intelligence Agency in the National Archives at College Park, Maryland

RG 319   Records of the Army Staff in the National Archives at College Park, Maryland

RG 331   Records of Allied Operational and Occupation Headquarters, World War II, in the National Archives at College Park, Maryland

RG 407 Records of the Adjutant General's Office in the National Archives at College Park, Maryland

SR/KCC Surrogate records, Kings County Clerk's Office, Brooklyn, New York

TSP Thomas W. Salmon Papers in the Oskar Diethelm Library at Weill Medical College of Cornell University, New York, New York

TWCT R. John Pritchard and Sonia Magbanua Zaide, eds., *The Tokyo War Crimes Trial* (22 vols.; New York: Garland, 1981)

UKNA The National Archives, Surrey, United Kingdom

VHPC Veterans History Project Collection at the American Folklife Center, Library of Congress, Washington, D.C.

WBP Walter E. Barton Papers at the American Psychiatric Association, Washington, D.C.

WFJWP Walter Freeman and James Watts papers, 1918–1988, at University Archives, George Washington University, Washington, D.C.

Chapter 1: The Slap Heard Round the World

The vast majority of my research on Okawa Shumei came from primary documents housed in the National Archives at College Park, Maryland, collected and translated into English by the Allied occupation in Japan after the war. Key archived files were found in three main record groups: Records of the Central Intelligence Agency (RG 263), Records of the Army Staff (RG 319), and Records of Allied Operational and Occupation Headquarters, World War II (RG 331). The NACP microfilm department holds documents collected for the Tokyo trial by the prosecution (M1690) as well as case files on the defendants (M1683).

I have translated in full a very revealing personal essay written by Okawa describing his several prison terms, his indictment for war crimes, and his behavior at the Tokyo trial: Okawa Shumei, "Ichigaya no Rakuten Shujin" ("The Optimist Prisoner of Ichigaya"), *Bungei Shunju* 32 (1954). This account was part of Okawa's postwar autobiography *Anraku no mon* (Tokyo: Izumo Shobo, 1951). I also drew heavily from a Japanese biography by Otsuka Takehiro, *Okawa Shumei* (Tokyo: Chuo Koronsha, 1995), translated into English in full.

There are only a handful of English-language works on Okawa Shumei. They include Cemil Aydin, "The Politics of Civilizational Identities: Asia, West and Islam in the Pan-Asianist Thought of Okawa Shumei" (PhD diss., Harvard University, 2002); Christopher Szpilman, "The Dream of One Asia:

Okawa Shumei and Japanese Pan-Asianism," *The Japanese Empire in East Asia and Its Postwar Legacy,* edited by Harald Fuess (München, Germany: Iudicium, 1998); Mary Estes Lieberman, "Okawa Shumei and Japan's 'Divine Mission,'" (PhD diss., University of California–Berkeley, 1956); and Takeuchi Yoshimi, "Profile of Asian Minded Man X: Okawa Shumei," *Developing Economies* 7 (1969), 367–79. Aydin's work later formed the basis of a book, *The Politics of Anti-Westernism in Asia: Visions of World Order in Pan-Islamic and Pan-Asian Thought* (New York: Columbia University Press, 2007); while this work was consulted, all citations in the entire notes section come from the dissertation.

Key descriptions of Okawa's courtroom behavior were found in contemporary news reports (often via wire services). Additional details were found in key works published by trial correspondents—notably, Arnold C. Brackman, *The Other Nuremberg: The Untold Story of the Tokyo War Crimes Trials* (New York: Morrow, 1987), and Mark Gayn, *Japan Diary* (Rutland, Vt.: Tuttle, 1981 [1948]). Video footage of Okawa's slap appeared in Masaki Kobayashi's 1983 documentary *Tokyo saiban* (*Tokyo Trial*), which was later released with an English narration.

For the Tokyo trial itself, *The Tokyo War Crimes Trial*, edited by R. John Pritchard and Sonia Magbanua Zaide (New York: Garland, 1981), offered a transcript of the proceedings. Other primary documentation was found among the personal papers of Frank S. Tavenner Jr., a member of the prosecution team for the Tokyo trial, housed along with official trial records at the University of Virginia Law Library.

Contextual knowledge of the trial emerged from several secondary sources. The best objective summary is a lengthy article by participating attorney Solis Horwitz: "The Tokyo Trial," *International Conciliation* 28 (1950), 473–584. The best book-length work is Richard H. Minear, *Victors' Justice: The Tokyo War Crimes Trial* (Princeton, N.J.: Princeton University Press, 1971). John Dower, *Embracing Defeat: Japan in the Wake of World War II* (New York: Norton, 1999), is the leading general source on the occupation. Yuma Totani, *The Tokyo War Crimes Trial: The Pursuit of Justice in the Wake of World War II* (Cambridge, Mass.: Harvard University Asia Center; distributed by Harvard University Press, 2008), supplemented.

The primary source on Daniel Jaffe's life before the war was his unpublished, unfinished 137-page memoir titled "Memoirs of a Combat Psychiatrist," written circa 1996. A series of lengthy interviews about that manuscript, conducted by Evelyn Schreiber, his daughter, and given alongside Caroline Jaffe, his wife, augmented this work. Additional details on various aspects of his life emerged in the pages of *Grandfather Remembers* (New York: Harper & Row, 1986), a fill-in-the-blank–style personal history book he prepared for the author in 1994. Personal stories were collected, and when possible confirmed, by surviving relatives and veterans and colleagues.

1   light blue: Otsuka, *Okawa Shumei*, 186–87. An AP wire photo of the entire pris-
    oner dock best captured Okawa's contrasting appearance at the arraignment:
    "Japan's Accused War Criminals Arraigned Before Allied Court in Tokyo,"
    NYT, May 9, 1946.
2   "criminal militaristic clique": Pritchard and Zaide, *The Tokyo War Crimes Trial,*
    1:1 (Indictment).
2   "in the indictment": Hugh Helm, memo to Frank S. Tavenner, August 28, 1946,
    M1683, Roll 37, NACP.
2   "heart of it": Hugh Helm, interrogation of T. P. Davis, March 20, 1946, M1683,
    Roll 37, NACP.
2   prepare the venue: Details about the courtroom come from Brackman, *The Other
    Nuremberg,* 89.
3   "in all history": David Nelson Sutton, "The Trial of Tojo: The Most Important
    Trial in All History?" *Journal of the American Bar Association* 36 (1950): 93.
3   "cunning grin": "Co-defendant Slaps Tojo," *New York Sun,* May 3, 1946. Other
    news reports consulted for this section include "Jap Removed from War Crimes
    Trial," *Washington Post,* May 4, 1946; "Tojo and War Aides Arraigned," *Stars
    and Stripes,* May 4, 1946, Pacific edition; and "Tojo Gets Slap on Pate from Co-
    defendant," *New York Herald Tribune,* May 4, 1946.
3   fifteen-minute recess: *TWCT* 1:47 (Transcript).
3   "of the comedy!": Otsuka, *Okawa Shumei*, 186–87, author translation.
4   anteroom . . . behavior: Additional news reports consulted for this sequence
    include "Happy Jap Slaps Tojo's Bald Pate; Eyes U.S. Career," *Los Angeles Times,*
    May 4, 1946, and "Court Orders Psychiatrists to Study Okawa," *New York Herald
    Tribune,* May 5, 1946.
4   "Brooklyn Man": "Tojo's Slapper to Be Examined," *New York Sun,* May 4, 1946.
5   thirty-five thousand miles: H. Stanley Huff, *Unforgettable Journey: A World War II
    Memoir* (Fort Wayne, Ind.: Bridgeford Press, 2001), 203.
5   fewer than a hundred: The chief of psychiatry for the military during World War
    II recalled 91 division psychiatrists of record. William Menninger, *Psychiatry in
    a Troubled World: Yesterday's War and Today's Challenge* (New York: Macmillan,
    1948), 237.
7   "startled the court": E.g., "Tokyo Trial in Recess," *NYT,* May 5, 1946, and "Jap
    Slapper of Tojo to Have Head Examined," *Chicago Daily Tribune,* May 5, 1946.
    Also see "War Crimes: Road Show," *Time,* May 20, 1946, and "Shumei Okawa's
    Big Moment," *Washington Post,* May 15, 1946.
7   "jerry-built shack": Okawa Shumei, "Gateway," Box 165a, RG 319, NACP.
7   "decidedly unattractive": Herbert Posin and William C. Schweikert, "Psychiatric
    Examination of Japanese Prisoner of War," March 13, 1947, Box 1424, RG 331,
    NACP.
7   Kant and Plato: Szpilman, "One Asia," 61; Aydin, "Politics," 112.
8   "life-and-death struggle": Okawa Shumei, *A History of Anglo-American Aggres-
    sion in East Asia,* trans. Yoshio Ogawa with P. B. Clarke (Tokyo: Daitoa Shup-
    pan Kabushiki Kaisha, 1944). See the chapter 8 summary for more on this work,
    originally a radio broadcast from December 1941.
8   "intellectual malcontent": Brief bio of Dr. Okawa Shumei, Box 96, RG 263,
    NACP.
8   "Goebbels of Japan": David Bergamini, *Japan's Imperial Conspiracy* (2 vols.; New
    York: Morrow, 1971), 313.
8   "Oriental Don Quixote": Gayn, *Japan Diary,* 209.
8   "nervous and passionate": Uchimura Yushi, "Report of the psychiatric examina-
    tion on the mental condition of Shumei Okawa," May 11, 1946, Box 1424, RG
    331, NACP.

8 Jekyll and Hyde: "Dr. Okawa Believed Sound in Mind," Box 165a, RG 319, NACP.

9 "his own defense": Daniel S. Jaffe, "Examination of Okawa, Shumei," May 11, 1946, Box 1424, RG 331, NACP. See the chapter 11 summary for an explanation about the multiple versions of this record.

9 "ideological instigator": "Japs Question Amnesty Atop Tojo Hanging," *Washington Post*, December 25, 1948.

9 "to go free": "Man Who Slapped Tojo Is Released from Asylum," *NYT*, December 31, 1948.

9 informal scorecard: Brackman, *The Other Nuremberg*, 188.

12 *Time* magazine reporter: "David Bergamini Dies; Wrote About Hirohito," *NYT*, September 4, 1983.

12 hoax: Bergamini, *Japan's Imperial Conspiracy,* 2:1057–60.

15 "insanity was feigned": 201 file on Okawa Shumei, Box 96, RG 263, NACP.

16 "staging an act": "Jap Removed from War Crimes Trial," *Washington Post*, May 4, 1946.

16 "dangerous playhouse": Usuki Akira, *Okawa Shumei: Isuramu to tenno no hazama de* (Tokyo Seidosha, 2010), selected passages translated for the author.

16 "deceived": Brackman, *The Other Nuremberg*, 103.

16 "with my mind": "Why I Hit Tojo on the Head," *Tokyo Nichi Nichi Shimbun*, September 11, 1952, Box 165a, RG 319, NACP.

Chapter 2: A Young Philosopher-Patriot

My account of Okawa Shumei's early life drew heavily from Otsuka Takehiro's biography, cited above, as well as an interview with the author. Additional details came from translations of Harada Kokichi, *Okawa Shumei Hakushi no shogai* (Yamagata-ken Sakata-shi: Okawa Shumei Kenshokai, 1982), and Shinsuke Kudo, "Okawa Shumei's Formative Years: Religion and Socialism," *Junior Research Journal* 15 (2008): 27–48, with the title translated by the author. Select details and quotations were drawn from Okawa's diary, kept with diligence throughout his lifetime: *Okawa Shumei nikki* (Tokyo: Iwasaki Gakujutsu Shuppansha, 1986). The aforementioned English-language secondary sources again served as guides: Aydin, Szpilman, Lieberman, and Takeuchi.

An understanding of Saigo Takamori emerged mostly from Mark Ravina, *Last Samurai: The Life and Battles of Saigo Takamori* (Hoboken, N.J.: Wiley, 2004), and correspondence with the author. Charles L. Yates, *Saigo Takamori: The Man Behind the Myth* (London, New York: Kegan Paul International; New York: Distributed by Columbia University Press, 1995), supplemented.

My research on Meiji era Japan required dozens of secondary sources. Of these a few bear specific mention. James L. McClain, *Japan: A Modern History* (New York: Norton, 2002), was a wonderfully readable and comprehensive account. Chitoshi Yanaga, *Japan Since Perry* (Hamden, Conn.: Archon Books, 1966 [1949]), was older but equally approachable. Richard Storry, *Japan and the Decline of the West in Asia, 1894–1943* (New York: St. Martin's Press, 1979), served as a strong complement. Frederick R. Dickinson, *War and National Reinvention: Japan in the Great War, 1914–1919* (Cambridge, Mass., and London: Harvard University Asia Center, 1999), and Robert A. Scalapino, *Democracy and the Party Movement in Prewar Japan* (Berkeley and Los Angeles: University of California Press, 1953), were essential guides to understanding the basics of Japan's prewar national polity. Nakae Chomin, *A Discourse by Three Drunkards on Government*, translated by Nobuko Tsukui (New York: Weatherhill, 1984), offered a famous and fascinating contemporary window into this period.

Quotations from Sir Henry Cotton's *New India* came from the 1907 edition of this classic work (London: Kegan Paul, Trench, Trübner, & Co., Ltd.). Okakura Tenshin, *The Ideals of the East* (London: J. Murray, 1905), was originally published in English. The best guide to Okakura's philosophy was F. G. Notehelfer, "On Idealism and Realism in the Thought of Okakura Tenshin," *Journal of Japanese Studies* 16 (1990): 309–55, followed closely by Christopher Benfey's enjoyable popular work, *The Great Wave: Gilded Age Misfits, Japanese Eccentrics, and the Opening of Old Japan* (New York: Random House, 2003). *Okakura Tenshin and Pan-Asianism: Shadows of the Past*, edited by Brij Tankha (Folkestone, UK: Global Oriental, 2009), and Prasenjit Duara, "The Discourse of Civilization and Pan-Asianism," *Journal of World History* 12 (2001): 99–130, supplemented.

19   Arabian horse: Otsuka, *Okawa Shumei*, 19–20.
20   moral advice: *Okawa Shumei nikki*, August 17, 1936, 153–54.
20   *Revere heaven, love man*: This slogan is an abbreviated version of the complete injunction read by Okawa Shumei in school; however, interviews with Okawa's former students (e.g., Kato Kenshiro) made clear that this four-character synopsis remained dear to Okawa for many decades.
21   "What is life?": *Okawa Shumei nikki*, January 12, 1904, 52, author translation.
22   "from the West": McClain, *Japan*, 179.
23   brandy: Nakae, *Three Drunkards*, 49.
24   "of the masses": McClain, *Japan*, 263.
24   "change the system": Otsuka, *Okawa Shumei*, 36–40, author translation. Other quotes in this paragraph from the same source.
25   Kurino Incident: Ibid., 44.
25   "The Giraffe": Ibid., 46.
25   "to save myself": Ibid.
26   "search" . . . "path": Ibid., 50.
26   German documents: Lieberman, "Okawa Shumei," 2–3.
26   *Meiji no hokori*: McClain, *Japan*, 316.
26   "spirit of Japan": Minutes of the Third Trial, IPS Doc. 1908b, Roll 271, M1690, NACP.
27   "and Western ideals": Notehelfer, "Okakura Tenshin," 337.
27   *The Ideals of the East*: All quotes in this paragraph are from the 1905 edition of this book, cited above.
28   "of English prejudice": Cotton, *New India*, vi.
28   "saddened, and angered": Okawa Shumei, *Various Problems of Reviving Asia*, IPS Doc. 689, Roll 90, M1690, NACP. In the introduction to this book, Okawa

recalls at length the significance of discovering Cotton's work. Recollective quotes in the following paragraph come from the same source.

29 cremation . . . mourning: Harada, *Okawa Shumei,* 14.
29 "revival of Asia": Aydin, "Politics," 64.

Chapter 3: The House on Lyme Avenue

"Memoirs of a Combat Psychiatrist" and *Grandfather Remembers,* both cited above, served as the recollective and documentary foundation for Daniel Jaffe's childhood. Additional details came from an unpublished and unfinished eighty-six-page memoir written in 2000 by his brother, Eli Jaffe, titled "The Jaffe Family." Interviews with living relatives provided secondhand confirmation whenever possible.

A few documentary sources provided unique insight into Daniel Jaffe's youth. Vital records for Kings County, New York (better known as the borough of Brooklyn), were found in the Local History and Genealogy room of the New York Public Library, as was the 1930 Census. The library's map division holds an atlas of Brooklyn from 1929 (New York: E. Belcher Hyde Map Co., 1929) that revealed useful property information. A photograph of the house on Lyme Avenue was found in the 1930s tax photos at the New York City Municipal Archives. Official transcripts were obtained from the registrar offices of New York University (unidentified number) and the George Washington University Department of Medicine (No. 62053).

Several archived sources illuminated Esther Jaffe's mental illness. The indictment records of the Kings County Criminal Court, housed at the New York City Municipal Archives, in the city's Department of Records and Information Services, detail the tragic events of 1910; these were acquired with the help of that staff. Surrogate court records (File No. 1641), housed at the Kings County Clerk's Office, run from early 1936 through 1938, with reference to some earlier years. Competency ruling records (Docket No. 46083), housed at the same office, run from mid-1938 through early 1943. Contemporary newspapers supplemented.

The bulk of my research on the fascinating history of psychiatric illness and immigration in early-twentieth-century America was done at the Oskar Diethelm Library at Weill Medical College of Cornell University in New York City, a hidden gem of primary documents on the history of psychiatry. Particularly helpful were the Thomas Salmon Papers and the library's collection of contemporary medical journals. Salmon's chapter "Mental Hygiene," in Milton J. Rosenau, *Preventive Medicine and Hygiene* (New York and London: D. Appleton, 1917), was a useful contemporary window. Ian Robert Dowbiggin, *Keeping America Sane: Psychiatry and Eugenics in the United States and Canada 1880–1940* (Ithaca, N.Y.: Cornell University Press, 2003), was a helpful introduction to Salmon in particular and this era in general. Barbara Sicherman, "The Quest for Mental Health in America, 1880–1917" (PhD diss., Columbia University, 1967), provided context.

The two books with the greatest influence on young Daniel Jaffe were Paul de Kruif, *Microbe Hunters* (New York, Harcourt, Brace, 1926), and Karl Menninger, *The Human Mind* (New York: Literary Guild of America, 1930). The personal essay mentioning his mother was Daniel S. Jaffe, "On Words and Music: A Personal Commentary," *Psychoanalytic Quarterly* 52 (1983): 590–93.

37   Pale of Settlement: This section draws from Samuel Joseph, *Jewish Immigration to the United States: From 1881 to 1910* (New York: Columbia University, 1914), and Simon Kuznets, "Immigration of Russian Jews to the United States: Background and Structure," in *Perspectives in American History* 9 (1975): 35–126.

37   "air was charged": Pauline Wengeroff, *Rememberings: The World of a Russian-Jewish Woman in the Nineteenth Century*, trans. Henny Wenkart (Potomac: University Press of Maryland, 2000), 224.

38   artificial flowers: The *NYT* documented this trend in a number of articles from the 1890s, including "Sweaters to Be Tried," October 23, 1892; "Artificial Flower Makers to Organize," May 18, 1894; "Cheap Pay for Shirts," May 26, 1895; and "A New Industry," December 5, 1897.

38   August 25, 1906: Marriage certificate no. 7398, Kings County vital records.

39   Arthur: John F. Clarke, district attorney, indictment of Esther Jaffe, September 13, 1910, NYCMA.

39   "a mental overthrow": "Mother Hurls Her Baby to Death While Insane," *Brooklyn Daily Eagle*, September 13, 1910. Additional details came from "Threw Baby from Window," *NYT*, September 14, 1910.

39   Officer Trumpfeller: Kings County Criminal Court, docket, September 1910, NYCMA.

39   "very much disturbed": Roy to Clark[e], September 24, 1910, NYCMA.

39   "and in unison": O'Reilly to Clarke, September 30, 1910, NYCMA. Other details in this paragraph, including the red sweater, come from this source.

40   not guilty: Kings County Criminal Court, verdict, October 4, 1910, NYCMA.

40   "previous children": Birth record, Elihu Jaffe (No. 11444), February 14, 1913, City of New York Department of Health. Despite an extensive search of vital records and family belongings, my grandfather's own birth certificate has never been located.

41   "bag of shit": Eli Jaffe, "The Jaffe Family," 12.

41   "ordinary boy would": De Kruif, *Microbe Hunters*, 58.

42   Abraham Edelstein: All names in this paragraph from the 1930 Census.

42   twenty-thousand-square-foot: "Real Estate at Auction," *NYT*, May 18, 1930.

42   Alfred Smith: "Gov. Smith Visits His Son," *NYT*, September 20, 1926.

42   $85 a month: This rent, from the 1930 Census, is roughly equivalent to $1,100 today.

43   13.5 percent: Thomas Salmon, "The Diagnosis of Insanity in Immigrants," *Public Health Service Report* (1906), Box 5, TSP, ODL.

43   Salmon's findings: Thomas Salmon, "The Relation of Immigration to the Prevalence of Insanity," *American Journal of Insanity* 64 (1907), ODL.

44   "in future generations": William Williams, "Immigration and Insanity" (1912), Box 1, TSP, ODL.

44   "of the race": Salmon, "Mental Hygiene," 337.

44 "much-feared menace": Aaron Rosanoff, "Some Neglected Phases of Immigration in Relation to Insanity," *American Journal of Insanity* 72 (1915): 45.

45 "in my youth": Jaffe, "Memoirs," 4.

45 "accidents of life": Menninger, *The Human Mind*, 22.

46 twenty-two: The naturalization record for Harry Jaffe, filed with the U.S. District Court in Brooklyn on July 29, 1904, indicates that he arrived November 14, 1898.

46 indicted Maslow: *NYT* reported regular updates about the case. See "Monopoly Bid Laid to Linen Suppliers," April 7, 1955; "Linen Trust Suit Upheld by Court," May 24, 1957; and "Linen Suppliers Fined $319,000 in Trade Monopoly in This Area," December 1, 1961. Maslow's fine came to $10,000; as of 1961 his business grossed $20 million a year ("Associated Laundries," October 5, 1961).

47 "my father's ambition": Jaffe, *Grandfather Remembers*, 19.

47 *chordae tendineae*: Jaffe, "On Words and Music," 592. All published quotes in this section come from this article.

49 "dementia praecox-catatonic type": James F. Vavasour, sworn statement, April 29, 1938, CR/KCC. Quotes and details in this paragraph are all from this source.

50 Louden Hall: My understanding of the Louden Hall campus and history emerged from descriptions and pictures found in *Amityville*, published by the Amityville Historical Society (Charleston, S.C.: Arcadia, 2006), and Dean F. Failey et al, *Edward Lange's Long Island* (Setauket, N.Y.: Society for the Preservation of Long Island Antiquities, 1979).

50 "legally sane": "Albert Fish Loses Plea," *NYT,* January 9, 1935. Background on Vavasour's service as a psychiatric witness emerged from additional contemporary news articles.

50 wept for hours: James F. Vavasour, sworn statement, April 29, 1938, CR/KCC.

51 $43,000: Balance sheets, Victory Barber Towel Supply, December 31, 1935, SR/KCC.

51 *Les Misérables:* Eli Jaffe, "The Jaffe Family," 5.

51 January 26, 1936: Death certificate, Harry Jaffe, No. 2296, Kings County vital records.

51 Maslow sale price: Supplemental file, July 27, 1936; Harry M. Peyser, statement of the special guardian, August 4, 1936, SR/KCC.

52 $100,000: Account of proceedings, Schedule E-1, July 11, 1938; final decree and summary statement, September 22, 1938, SR/KCC.

52 intense resentment: James F. Vavasour, affidavit, July 7, 1936, SR/KCC.

52 "paranoid delusional system": James F. Vavasour, sworn statement, April 29, 1938, CR/KCC.

52 shaky hand: Esther Jaffe, renunciation, February 21, 1936, SR/KCC.

Chapter 4: Heavenly Mission

My baseline understanding of Okawa's life from 1914 to 1925 came from Otsuka, cited above, with Harada, Szpilman ("One Asia"), Aydin, and Lieberman supplementing. Aforementioned Tokyo trial documents housed at the National Archives (M1690) contain substantial translations of every important book Okawa published from 1922.

This chapter owes an enormous debt to the primary documentation translated in *Pan-Asianism: A Documentary History*, edited by Sven Saaler and

268 / Sources and Notes

Christopher Szpilman (2 vols; Lanham, Md.: Rowman & Littlefield, 2011). Eri Hotta, *Pan-Asianism and Japan's War, 1931–1945* (New York: Palgrave Macmillan, 2007), was an invaluable secondary source on Asianism. My understanding of that philosophy also benefited from multiple discussions and correspondence with Aydin, Saaler, Szpilman, and Hotta.

Facts about Okawa's activities with Indian dissidents came from primary documents found in the United Kingdom National Archives. The most helpful was David Petrie's memo "The Pan-Asiatic Movement" (FO 371/4242); additional reports by Agent P (FO 115/2236 and FO 371/3067) supplemented. The British Library may be the only place in the world with a partial translation of Okawa's 1916 book *The Nationalist Movement in India*. All material from Britain was collected by a research assistant.

Wonderful secondary sources covering this period include Takeshi Nakajima, *Bose of Nakamuraya: An Indian Revolutionary in Japan*, translated by Prem Motwani (New Delhi: Promilla & Co., Publishers, in association with Bibliophile South Asia, 2009); Tapan K. Mukherjee, *Taraknath Das: Life and Letters of a Revolutionary in Exile* (Calcutta: National Council of Education, Bengal, Jadavpur University, 1998); and Yukiko Sumi Barnett, "India in Asia: Okawa Shumei's Pan-Asian Thought and His Idea of India in Early Twentieth-Century Japan," *Journal of the Oxford University History Society* 1 (2004): 1–23. Michel P. Richard, *Without Passport: The Life and Work of Paul Richard* (New York: Peter Lang, 1987), supplemented.

Okawa's activist groups, particularly Yuzonsha and Kochisha (often mistakenly transliterated as Gyochisha), emerged from several aforementioned sources and two invaluable English-language works by Christopher W. A. Szpilman: an essay, "Kita Ikki and the Politics of Coercion," *Modern Asian Studies* 36 (2002): 467–90, and a book chapter, "Between Pan-Asianism and Nationalism: Mitsukawa Kametaro and His Campaign to Reform Japan and Liberate Asia," in *Pan-Asianism in Modern Japanese History: Colonialism, Regionalism and Borders*, edited by Sven Saaler and J. Victor Koschmann (London, New York: Routledge, 2007). Two works by George M. Wilson provided additional details about Kita Ikki: *Radical Nationalist in Japan: Kita Ikki, 1883–1937* (Cambridge, Mass.: Harvard University Press, 1969) and "Kita Ikki, Okawa Shumei, and the Yuzonsha: A Study in the Genesis of Showa Nationalism," *Papers on Japan* 2 (1963): 139–81. A Columbia University master's thesis by William P. Schultz ("Okawa Shumei: The Philosophy of an Ultranationalist," 1962) provides a substantial translation of Okawa's 1926 book, *Japan and the Way of the Japanese*, which explains the ideals of Kochisha.

General context for prewar Japanese nationalism emerged from a number of excellent secondary sources: McClain and Yanaga, cited above, as well as Richard Storry, *The Double Patriots: A Study of Japanese Nationalism* (Boston:

Houghton Mifflin, 1957), and Delmer M. Brown, *Nationalism in Japan* (Berkeley: University of California Press, 1955). Ben-Ami Shillony, *Revolt in Japan: The Young Officers and the February 26, 1936 Incident* (Princeton, N.J.: Princeton University Press, 1973), supplemented. "The Brocade Banner: The Story of Japanese Nationalism," a declassified document prepared by the U.S. Army in the immediate aftermath of the occupation, offered a thorough and contemporary, if subjective, view (via RG 331, NACP).

The best English source on the 1919 racial equality clause was Shimazu Naoko, *Japan, Race and Equality: The Racial Equality Proposal of 1919* (London, New York: Routledge, 1998). On the 1924 immigration act that crown went to Izumi Hirobe, *Japanese Pride, American Prejudice: Modifying the Exclusion Clause of the 1924 Immigration Act* (Stanford, Calif.: Stanford University Press, 2001). Additional details came from Raymond Leslie Buell, "The Development of Anti-Japanese Agitation in the United States," in *Political Science Quarterly* 37 (1922): 605–38; and Tosh Minohara, "The Road to Exclusion: The 1920 California Alien Land Law and U.S.–Japan Relations," *Kobe University Law Review* 30 (1996): 39–73.

53   "yellow": Otsuka, *Okawa Shumei*, 69, author translation.
53   *Ajiashugi*: Okawa uses the term as early as 1913.
54   autumn of 1915: Nakajima, *Bose*, 67.
54   Union Jack: Barnett, "India in Asia," 7.
54   basket of fruit: Nakajima, *Bose*, 105–6. Unless otherwise noted, all details in this paragraph and the next come from this source.
55   "under Western control": Barnett, "India in Asia," 9.
55   "underneath the lamp": Nakajima, *Bose*, 106.
56   "in the world": Abbreviated translation, Okawa Shumei, *The Nationalist Movement in India, Its Present Condition and Origin* (London: India Office, 1917), 1, British Library, United Kingdom.
56   "leading spirit": Petrie, "The Pan-Asiatic Movement," 7, 11, UKNA.
56   "unity a reality": Otsuka, *Okawa Shumei*, 88, author translation.
56   headquarters in Aoyama: Petrie, "The Pan-Asiatic Movement," 11, UKNA.
57   naval department: Mukherjee, *Taraknath Das*, 105.
57   "liberator of Asia": *PA* 1:291.
57   Genyosha: Background on this society emerged from E. H. Norman, "The Genyosha: A Study in the Origins of Japanese Imperialism," *Pacific Affairs* 17 (1944): 261–84.
57   Matsumotoro . . . Seiyoken: Petrie, "The Pan-Asiatic Movement," 11, 26, UKNA.
57   "great mission": "Japan's Mission," *Chicago Tribune*, May 9, 1915.
58   "in their brilliancy": Petrie, "The Pan-Asiatic Movement," 38, UKNA.
58   "of their 'mission'": Ibid., 39, UKNA.
58   108 square feet: Ibid., 35, UKNA.
59   "ridiculous fantasy": "No 'Yellow Peril,'" *NYT*, February 18, 1904, via *PA* 1:13.
59   Asian Monroe Doctrine: See Aydin, "The Politics of Civilizational Identities," 33; Petrie, "The Pan-Asiatic Movement," 14, UKNA; *PA* 1:11.
60   "of Pan-Asiatic ideals": *PA* 1:16.

60   Kodera Kenkichi: Sven Saaler, "The Construction of Regionalism in Modern Japan: Kodera Kenkichi and His 'Treatise on Greater Asianism,'" *Modern Asian Studies* 41 (2007): 1261–94.

60   "East to fulfill": Rabindranath Tagore, *The Message of India to Japan* (New York: Macmillan, 1916), 29.

61   Rice Riots: Research on this event drew from McClain, *Japan*, 325–27.

61   Mitsukawa Kametaro: Insight into Mitsukawa's character drew mostly from Szpilman, "Between Pan-Asianism and Nationalism."

62   "and the chrysanthemums": Storry, *Double Patriots*, 39.

62   August 8, 1919: Wilson, *Radical Nationalist*, 97.

62   *Tenkou*: This and other details about Okawa's recruitment trip are from Wilson, *Radical Nationalist*, 97, and Otsuka, *Okawa Shumei*, 108–10.

63   *The Outline of a Plan for the Reconstruction of Japan*: Details and quotes from this work are from a translation of the document in *Pan-Asianism*, vol. 1, chap. 27.

64   *Mein Kampf*: Maruyama Masao, *Thought and Behavior in Modern Japanese Politics* (London, New York: Oxford University Press, 1969), 28.

64   1921 . . . zealot: Szpilman, "Kita Ikki," 481.

64   ¥300: Wilson, *Radical Nationalist*, 99.

64   "free the universe": "Brocade Banner," 13–14, Box 307, RG 331, NACP, capitalization edited for clarity.

64   Mao-o, Susano-o: Lieberman, "Okawa Shumei," 21.

64   Westernization: Background on this period drew heavily from McClain, *Japan*, 345–56.

65   *Asia in Revival*: IPS Doc. 689, Roll 90, M1690, NACP; all quotations of this text came from this source except the title translation, which was taken from chap. 4 in vol. 2 of *Pan-Asianism*.

65   "the Japanese nationalists": Unidentified bio of Okawa Shumei, undated, Box 165a, RG 319, NACP.

66   Yuzonsha activities: Szpilman, "Between Pan-Asianism," 89; Herbert P. Bix, *Hirohito and the Making of Modern Japan* (New York: HarperCollins, 2000), 95–99.

66   1923: Harada, *Okawa Shumei*, 67.

66   redbrick: Ito Takeo, *Life Along the South Manchurian Railway: The Memoirs of Ito Takeo*, trans. Joshua A. Fogel (New York: East Gate Books, 1988), 44.

67   Daigakuryo: Minutes of the Third Trial, IPS Doc. 1908b, Roll 271, M1690, NACP.

67   "the Japanese Spirit": Otsuka, *Okawa Shumei*, 116; quote from Okawa Shumei, "An Inquiry into the Japanese Spirit," IPS Doc. 697, Roll 92, M1690, NACP.

68   "rare" earnestness: Szpilman, "Between Pan-Asianism," 260, note 35.

68   Sekiya . . . Araki . . . Watanabe: "Brocade Banner," 14, Box 307, RG 331, NACP; some capitalization edited for clarity.

68   February of 1925: Matsumoto Ken'ichi, *Okawa Shumei* (Tokyo: Iwanami Shoten, 2004); select portions translated for the author.

68   February 11, 1925: In fact, the group had existed for about ten months by the time of its formal inauguration.

68   "energy and attention": Otsuka, *Okawa Shumei*, 126, author translation.

69   seven lofty principles: My understanding of these tenets emerged from Minutes of the Third Trial, IPS Doc. 1908b, Roll 271, M1690, NACP; Schultz; and Otsuka, *Okawa Shumei*, 128–37.

70   *Asia, Europe, and Japan*: Okawa, "Asia, Europe, and Japan," IPS Doc. 684, Roll 88, M1690, NACP. For consistency, all quotes of this work came from *A History of Anglo-American Aggression in East Asia* (1944), cited above. The quote about "antagonism, struggle and unification" is a retrospective description of Okawa's intentions with the original work.

71   "relieving the congestion": Buell, "Anti-Japanese Agitation," 623.
71   "pay the consequences": Yanaga, *Japan Since Perry*, 435–36.
71   "of the Empire": Shimazu, *Japan, Race and Equality*, 22.
71   Hirohito later called: Ibid., 181.
72   "of the world": Okawa Shumei, "Asia, Europe, and Japan," IPS Doc. 684, Roll 88, M1690, NACP.
72   146 Japanese newcomers: Yanaga, *Japan Since Perry*, 442–43.
72   "grave consequences": Hirobe, *Japanese Pride*, 8–9.
72   "action of America": Ibid., 32.
73   "a Happy War": Ibid., 54.
73   "1925 to 1945": Hugh Helm to Arthur Comyns Carr, brief on Okawa Shumei, March 15, 1946, Roll 37, M1683, NACP.

Chapter 5: Loose Ends

Key sources on Daniel Jaffe's life between 1936 and the start of the war were "Memoirs of a Combat Psychiatrist" and *Grandfather Remembers,* cited above, as well as interviews with various friends and family members. His medical school transcript, cited above, established a basic timeline. Kings County Court surrogate and competency records, also cited above, described Esther Jaffe's ongoing battle with mental illness and Daniel Jaffe's role as her legal committee. His medical school notes, in the possession of the family, illuminated his professional education.

The sections on mental health disorders and treatments during this period emerged from close readings of various documents found at the Diethelm Library, cited above, particularly the papers of Joseph Wortis. The Walter Freeman and James Watts papers, 1918–1988, are housed at the University Archives of the George Washington University in Washington, D.C. Two invaluable secondary sources for the period were Jack El-Hai's biography of Freeman, *The Lobotomist: A Maverick Medical Genius and His Tragic Quest to Rid the World of Mental Illness* (Hoboken, N.J.: Wiley, 2005), and Edward Shorter, *A History of Psychiatry: From the Era of the Asylum to the Age of Prozac* (New York: Wiley, 1997). Manfred Sakel, *Schizophrenia* (New York: Philosophical Library, 1958), gave useful and unique insight into that terrible illness.

My understanding of neurosyphilis and the development of malaria therapy came from the following texts: Julius Wagner-Jauregg, "The History of Malaria Treatment of General Paralysis," translated by Walter L. Bruetsch, in *American Journal of Psychiatry* 102 (1946): 577–82, in the Diethelm Library; a chapter on Jauregg in Walter Freeman, *The Psychiatrist* (New York: Grune & Stratton, 1968); Edward M. Brown, "Why Wagner-Jauregg Won the Nobel Prize for Discovering Malaria Therapy for General Paresis of the Insane," in *History of Psychiatry* 11 (2000): 371–82; and Magda Whitrow, "Wagner-Jauregg and Fever Therapy," in *Medical History* 34 (1990): 294–310.

Details about the selection of Army psychiatrists were found in the Records of the Office of the Surgeon General (Army) (RG 112) at the National Archives, primarily Boxes 1333 (RITCHIE material file) and 1335 (Neuropsychiatry NRC file).

My meeting with Wilma Jaffe occurred in May of 2010, though we spoke and exchanged correspondence numerous times between 2009 and 2013 with regard to Dan and Eli Jaffe. Eli's memoir, *Oklahoma Odyssey*, was published by a vanity press in 1993. Those interested in the Oklahoma "Red" trials will love Shirley A. Wiegand and Wayne Wiegand's great history, *Books on Trial: Red Scare in the Heartland* (Norman: University of Oklahoma Press, 2007). Family documents obtained through the Freedom of Information Act were released by the Federal Bureau of Investigation and the Department of the Army.

77 "loose ends": Jaffe, *Grandfather Remembers*, 24.
78 Smithsonian: James Watts oral history, January 25, 1979, Folder 20, Box 41, WFJWP.
78 goatee and eyeglasses: El-Hai, *Lobotomist*, 7.
78 "agitated depression": Freeman Autobiography, 14-3, Folder 2, Box 9, WFJWP.
79 "if it doesn't": Walter Freeman, "The Development of Neurology at GWU, 1924–54," 9, Folder 21, Box 8, WFJWP. My description of Freeman's teaching style draws heavily from this document.
79 "be so described": Freeman and Watts, "Prefrontal Lobotomy in the Treatment of Mental Disorders," *Southern Medical Journal* 30 (1937): 21, Box 11, WFJWP.
79 "last resort": Freeman, "Psychosurgery: 1936–1946," 5, Folder 1, Box 10, WFJWP.
80 arsenal of treatments: G. de M. Rudolf, "Experimental Treatments of Schizophrenia," *Journal of Mental Science* 77 (1931): 767–91.
80 60 percent: F. E. James, "Insulin Treatment in Psychiatry," *History of Psychiatry* 3 (1992): 221–35.
80 frenzy of debate: Details and quotes from "Southern Doctors," *Time*, November 30, 1936, WFJWP.
80 "central interest": Jaffe, "Memoirs," 4.
81 "in modern neurology": Freeman, *Neuropathology*, 181, Box 19, WFJWP.
81 "to high heaven": Freeman Autobiography, 9-6, Folder 2, Box 9, WFJWP.
82 "even austere": Freeman, *The Psychiatrist*, 20.
82 June of 1917: Wagner-Jauregg, "The History of Malaria Treatment," 580.
82 "ten ton truck": Freeman Autobiography, 9-6, Folder 2, Box 9, WFJWP.
82 50 percent: Whitrow, "Wagner-Jauregg," 308–10.
83 "Christian Science practitioner": James F. Vavasour, sworn statement, April 29, 1938, CR/KCC.
84 "in the schizophrenics": James Watts oral history, January 25, 1979, Folder 20, Box 41, FWP, WFJWP.
84 first physician: El-Hai, *Lobotomist*, 132.
84 mid-August: " 'Shock' for Dementia Praecox to Be Tried at St. Elizabeth's," *Washington Post*, August 10, 1937.
84 began insulin treatment: James F. Vavasour, sworn statement, April 29, 1938, CR/KCC.
84 "Pasteur of psychiatry": File on Dr. Manfred Sakel, Box 37, JWP, ODL.
84 "restless," "tranquil": Shorter, *A History of Psychiatry*, 209.

85 "be held out": "Dementia Praecox Curbed by Insulin," *NYT*, January 13, 1937, Box 5, JWP, ODL.

85 typical treatment course: Details in this section draw from contemporary descriptions and photographs found in Boxes 19 and 37 of JWP, ODL.

85 "the right path": File on Dr. Manfred Sakel, Box 37, JWP, ODL.

85 "describe them accurately": *Bulletin of the New York Academy of Medicine* 13 (1937), 97–109, JWP, ODL.

86 1,039 schizophrenia patients: Annual Report, 1937–38, New York State Department of Mental Hygiene, ODL.

86 "were to awake": "Insulin Is Used to Cure Insanity," *Philadelphia Evening Bulletin*, February 20, 1937, JWP, ODL.

86 strangle herself: James F. Vavasour, sworn statement, April 29, 1938, CR/KCC.

86 "probability be permanent": Daniel Jaffe, petition for committee, May 3, 1938, CR/KCC.

87 early June: Demand for jury trial, July 1, 1938, CR/KCC.

87 "considerable astuteness": F. Campbell Good, Report of the Special Guardian, June 27, 1938, CR/KCC.

87 "form of psychosis": James F. Vavasour, sworn statement, April 29, 1938, CR/KCC.

87 June 20, 1938: Jury's verdict, July 1, 1938, CR/KCC.

88 ice cream: Final decree and summary statement, December 31, 1940, CR/KCC.

88 "to going home": Letter, Louden to Gallagher, in final decree and summary statement, December 31, 1940, CR/KCC. This John Louden was a relative of the original founder of Louden Hall, who died in 1933 (*NYT*, August 9, 1933).

88 $65 a month: Petition, affidavit, and order, November 9, 1938, CR/KCC.

91 subacute bacterial endocarditis: Walter Freeman and Daniel Jaffe, "Occlusion of the Superior Cerebellar Artery: Report of a Case with Necropsy," *Archives of Neurology and Psychiatry* 46 (1941): 115–26.

92 "William Randolph Hearst": "Turning the Mind Inside Out," *Saturday Evening Post*, May 24, 1941, Box 20, WFJWP.

93 Rosemary Kennedy: El-Hai, *Lobotomist*, 173.

93 rating of IV: List of reserve officers, March 5, 1941, National Research Council, Committee on Neuropsychiatry, Box 1333, RG112, NACP.

93 March 12, 1941: Circular Letter No. 19, "Neuropsychiatric examination of applicants for voluntary enlistment and selectees for induction," Box 1335, RG 112, NACP.

93 "another world war": Jaffe, "Memoirs," 5.

Chapter 6: Showa Restoration

The prosecution's documents from the Tokyo trial, cited above (M1690), served as the primary material for the thoughts and actions of Okawa Shumei from 1925 to 1941. The most important of these was IPS Doc. 1908b, or the Minutes of the Third Trial from the May 15 Incident, during which Okawa summarized his entire life in great detail for the court. Other integral primary sources, cited above, included the trial transcript edited by Pritchard and Zaide (*TWCT*), the personal papers of Frank Tavenner, the Records of the Army Staff (RG 319), and the Records of Allied Operational and Occupation Headquarters, World War II (RG 331). Otsuka's biography once again provided a sound research platform, and Matsumoto Ken'ichi's biography, also cited above, contributed details about Okawa's personal life.

The Tokyo trial documents provided most of the details on the coups and incidents of 1931 and 1932—especially IPS Doc. 1908b; affidavits submitted by Tokugawa Yoshichika, Shimizu Konosuke, Koiso Kuniaki, and Ugaki Kazushige; "Notebook of Major X" (IPS Doc. 2124); the diaries of Tokugawa (IPS Doc. 2638); and the Saionji-Harada memoirs (via RG 331). For the Manchurian Incident, the description of Okawa's speaking tour (IPS Doc. 1918) was invaluable. For the May 15 Incident, the civilian trial records (IPS Doc. 2226) and contemporary issues of the English-language *Japan Weekly Chronicle* provided critical details. Okawa's trial is covered by several primary documents held in M1690. Okawa writes about his arrest in *Bungei Shunju,* cited above; some details and quotations from this experience were taken from a similar essay called "Gateway to Ease and Comfort" (via RG 319).

General background on this period emerged through a number of secondary sources cited above, including McClain, Yanaga, Dickinson, Scalapino, Brown, and Storry (*Double Patriots*). James B. Crowley, *Japan's Quest for Autonomy: National Security and Foreign Policy, 1930–1938* (Princeton, N.J.: Princeton University Press, 1966), is essential to any prewar study. Robert Butow, *Tojo and the Coming of War* (Princeton, N.J.: Princeton University Press), centering on Tojo, is also among the best academic works on this era. Hotta, cited above, gave insight into the use of Asianist rhetoric by Japanese officials, as did Sven Saaler, "Pan-Asianism in Modern Japanese History," in *Pan-Asianism in Modern Japanese History,* also cited above. The diary of U.S. ambassador Joseph Grew, *Ten Years in Japan* (New York: Simon & Schuster, 1994), offered valuable contemporary insight.

My understanding of Japan's relationship with Manchuria, in particular, was supplemented by several secondary texts. Louise Young, *Japan's Total Empire: Manchuria and the Culture of Wartime Empire* (Berkeley: University of California Press, 1998), was an essential work on the subject. *The Japanese Informal Empire in China, 1895–1937,* edited by Peter Duus, Ramon H. Myers, and Mark R. Peattie (Princeton, N.J.: Princeton University Press, 1989), was a very useful compilation, especially the chapter by Myers, "Japanese Imperialism in Manchuria: The South Manchuria Railway Company, 1906–1933." Akira Iriye, "Chang Hseuh-liang and the Japanese," *Journal of Asian Studies* 20 (1960): 33–43, and Herbert Bix, "Japanese Imperialism and the Manchurian Economy, 1900–1931," *China Quarterly* 51 (1972): 425–43, provided context. Ito Takeo's memoir of the South Manchurian Railway, cited above, offered a rare contemporary window.

Takehiko Yoshihashi, *Conspiracy at Mukden: The Rise of the Japanese Military* (New Haven and London: Yale University Press, 1963), and Seki Hiroharu,

"The Manchurian Incident, 1931," translated by Marius B. Jansen, in *Japan Erupts: The London Naval Conference and the Manchurian Incident, 1928–1932,* edited by James William Morley (New York: Columbia University Press, 1984), were the most helpful scholarly reconstructions of the Manchurian Incident.

95 horseback ride: Matsumoto, *Okawa Shumei,* 254.
95 to back China: Crowley, *Japan's Quest,* 81.
96 "lifeline": E.g., Ito, *Life Along the South Manchurian Railway,* 11. The term is pervasive during the period.
96 seven hundred miles: Myers, "Japanese Imperialism," 109.
96 ten thousand troops: Young, *Total Empire,* 30.
96 law doctorate: Otsuka, *Okawa Shumei,* 97.
96 "at least self-sufficient": Minutes of the Third Trial, IPS Doc. 1908b, Roll 271, M1690, NACP.
97 tried everything: Okawa's letter to the foreign ministry is described in "Japanese Police for China," IPS Doc. 1070, Roll 164, M1690, NACP; his meetings with Chang in Minutes of the Third Trial, IPS Doc. 1908b, Roll 271, M1690, NACP.
97 "be left alone": Minutes of the Third Trial, IPS Doc. 1908b, Roll 271, M1690, NACP.
98 "renovate the country": *TWCT* 1:1963 (Transcript).
98 cherry blossom symbol: Butow, *Tojo,* 33.
98 forty-nine politicians: "Tokyo Scandal Case," *JWC,* October 15, 1931.
98 minuscule margin: Hotta, in *Pan-Asianism,* 260–61, says the London treaty fell short of Japan fleet preference by 0.025 percent.
99 "accomplish its ambition": Okawa, *Anglo-American Aggression,* 54–55.
99 five or six: *TWCT* 2:2159 (Transcript).
99 early 1930: Okawa Shumei, "Words and Actions in the Japanese Way," IPS Doc. 695, Roll 91, M1690, NACP.
99 Tokugawa Yoshichika: Background on Tokugawa came from E.J.H. Corner, *The Marquis: A Tale of Syonan-to* (Singapore: Heinemann Educational Books, 1981).
99 Hashimoto . . . Shigeto: Background on these figures came from a January 1946 article in *Chuo Koron* (IPS Doc. 575, Roll 45, M1690); "Notebook of Major X" (IPS Doc. 2124, Roll 291, M1690); Walter I. McKenzie, "Japanese Military and Economic Aggression in Manchuria, Summary of Proof," 10, Box 25, PPFT; Crowley, *Japan's Quest,* 98–99; and Yoshihashi, *Conspiracy,* 97–101.
99 favored haunt: Jiji press, undated article, Box 165a, RG 319, NACP; *TWCT* 1:1402–12 (Transcript); and Matsumoto, *Okawa Shumei,* 254–56.
100 "these dangerous spells": Okawa Kane, affidavit, December 17, 1946, Box 1424, RG 331, NACP.
100 "should be crushed": Minutes of the Third Trial, IPS Doc. 1908b, Roll 271, M1690, NACP.
100 February 7, 1931: Details and quotations in this section are from "Notebook of Major X," IPS Doc. 2124, Roll 291, M1690, NACP. Background on Major Tanaka from "Interrogation of Tanaka Kiyoshi," IPS Doc. 1107, Roll 166, M1690, NACP.
101 "around the army": Minutes of the Third Trial, IPS Doc. 1908b, Roll 271, M1690, NACP.
101 February 11: Quotes in this section are from Saionji-Harada Memoirs, chap. 17 (October 1931), Boxes 845–46, RG 331, NACP.
102 "at party politics": Minutes of the Third Trial, IPS Doc. 1908b, Roll 271, M1690, NACP.

102   acquire the bombs: *Chuo Koron* (January 1946), IPS Doc. 575, Roll 45, M1690, NACP.

102   "like Dr. Okawa": Quotes in this and the ensuing paragraph come from "Notebook of Major X," IPS Doc. 2124, Roll 291, M1690, NACP.

103   "the Showa Restoration": *TWCT* 1:1610–13 (Transcript). The punctuation of this letter has been edited slightly for readability.

103   showed up unannounced: Koiso Kuniaki, notes, IPS Doc. 2965, Roll 361, M1690, NACP.

104   March 19: Details and quotes of this meeting are from "Diaries of Marquis Tokugawa Yoshichika," IPS Docs. 2638–46, Roll 343, M1690, NACP.

104   Young Men's Hall: Seki, "The Manchurian Incident," 175.

104   "diplomacy had passed": Otsuka, *Okawa Shumei*, 151, author translation.

105   Manchurian problem: Okawa's role in the Manchurian Incident, IPS Doc. 1918, Roll 272, M1690, NACP. Unless noted, all details about his speaking tour come from this source.

105   Oshima talk: Mitsukawa Kametaro, "A Trip to Oshima with Mr. Okawa," IPS Doc. 686, Roll 89, M1690, NACP; Hugh Helm, interrogation, March 5, 1946, Box 165a, RG 319, NACP.

106   forty-two yellow packages: McClain, *Japan*, 405.

106   10:40 train: Seki, "The Manchurian Incident," 228.

106   political cartoon: Butow, *Tojo*, 38.

107   "direct, national policies": Ben Dorfman, "The Manchurian 'Incident' of 1931," *Harper's* 169 (1934): 449–62.

107   "some bellicose Chinese": "Warlike Incidents," *JWC*, September 24, 1931.

107   full cooperation: See IPS Doc. 1908b, Roll 271, and IPS Doc. 1918, Roll 272, M1690, NACP.

108   "civilian brain": "The Japanese Criminals," *NYT*, April 30, 1946.

108   "the real danger": Saionji-Harada Memoirs, chap. 13 (October 2, 1931), Boxes 845–46, RG 331, NACP.

109   "of important problems": Minutes of the Third Trial, IPS Doc. 1908b, Roll 271, M1690, NACP.

109   early November: Saionji-Harada Memoirs, chap. 45-C (June 23, 1932), Boxes 845–46, RG 331, NACP.

109   "of the world": Butow, *Tojo*, 79.

109   Koga . . . Nakamura: These visits are detailed in Records of Trials of Civilians of 5-15 Incident," IPS Doc. 2226, Roll 303, M1690, NACP.

109   "of the Orient": *JWC*, August 3, 1933.

110   "of the action": Records of Trials of Civilians of 5-15 Incident, IPS Doc. 2226, Roll 303, M1690, NACP.

110   May 15, 1932: Several articles, *JWC*, August 3, 1933.

110   "the true Japan": Mori Shozo, "Twenty Years in a Whirlwind," IPS Doc. 845, Roll 128, M1690, NACP.

111   "at my home": Saionji-Harada Memoirs, chap. 45-C (June 23, 1932), Boxes 845–46, RG 331, NACP.

111   "of nationalist intrigue": "Brocade Banner," 38, Box 307, RG 331, NACP. The names of the documents at Okawa's home include "The Kwantung Army Control and Operations Bureau," "A Plan for the Construction of a New Japan," "The Political Party Problem," and "The Manchurian and Mongolian Problem and a Quick Realization of the Showa Restoration."

112   nine pinky fingers: "Brocade Banner," 47, Box 307, RG 331, NACP.

112   publicly praised: *JWC*, August 3, 1933; Maruyama, *Thought and Behavior in Modern Japanese Politics*, 67.

112   "dared to use": Tsuyoshi Hida, "Reflections on the May 15 Case," in *Contemporary Japan* (December 1933).

112 September of 1933: Okawa's first trial is detailed in IPS Doc. 2226, Roll 303, M1690, NACP. All details and quotes in this paragraph and the next come from this source.
112 "of noble character": Notes on Okawa's trial, IPS Docs. 1918a–c, Roll 272, M1690, NACP.
113 prosecution appealed: Otsuka, *Okawa Shumei*, 160.
113 "or subdue them": Okawa, "Japanese History Reader," IPS Doc. 690, Roll 91, M1690, NACP.
113 "life in hell": Okawa, "Gateway," Box 165a, RG 319, NACP. Edited slightly for readability.
113 "on loftier foundations": Okawa, "A History of Modern European Colonization," IPS Doc. 688, Roll 90, M1690, NACP.
113 "moral pains": Okawa, "Gateway," Box 165a, RG 319, NACP.
114 "are *too* severe": Okawa, *Bungei Shunju*, author translation.
114 July of 1937: Marquis Tokugawa, diary, 1937, IPS Doc. 2582, Roll 337, M1690, NACP.
114 "of dark memory": Okawa, "Gateway," Box 165a, RG 319, NACP.
114 "reconstruction of Asia": Roger H. Brown, "Nagai Ryutaro: 'Holy War for the Reconstruction of Asia,'" in *PA* 2:155–59.
115 debated whether Fascism: For the pro-Fascism position, see Yoshino Sakuzo, "Fascism in Japan," *Contemporary Japan* 1 (1932); for the other side, see *JWC*, June 2, 1932.
115 Yamato Society: Details from "Diaries of Marquis Tokugawa Yoshichika," IPS Docs. 2638–46, Roll 343, M1690, NACP.
115 "very best terms": Hugh B. Helm, interrogation, March 11, 1946, Box 165a, RG 319, NACP.
115 persuaded an admiral: Szpilman, "One Asia," 55.
115 "absolutely no good": Saionji-Harada Memoirs, chap. 262 (February 9, 1938), Boxes 845–46, RG 331, NACP.
115 ¥150,000: E. H. Norman, preliminary interrogation, December 26, 1945, Box 96, RG 263, NACP.
116 sleeping quarters: Kato Kenshiro, author interview, April 21, 2012, Sakata, Japan.
116 Pan-Asian societies: Aydin, "Politics," 152–60; Grew, *Ten Years*, 106.
116 "of the world": Okawa, "2,600 Years of Japanese History," IPS Doc. 692, Roll 91, M1690, NACP.
117 "really fooling themselves": Grew, *Ten Years*, 84.
117 "Mission in Asia": *JWC*, October 21, 1937.
117 through force: James W. Morley, ed., *The Fateful Choice: Japan's Advance into Southeast Asia, 1939–1941* (New York: Columbia University Press, 1980), 303.
118 "inherently evil notions": Hotta, *Pan-Asianism*, 192.
119 little bells: Butow, *Tojo*, 407.
119 "of the East": Hotta, *Pan-Asianism*, 185–86.

Chapter 7: The Making of a Combat Psychiatrist

Daniel Jaffe's military service through early 1945 emerged largely from "Memoirs of a Combat Psychiatrist," cited above. Additional information was gathered through dozens of interviews with relatives, surviving soldiers, and relatives of surviving soldiers. A captioned photograph album in the family's possession clarified much of the timeline. Wilma Jaffe, widow to Eli Jaffe, generously granted permission to review her husband's personal papers, which include his wartime letters to his brother. Jon Halsey, grandson of General Milton B. Halsey of the 97th Infantry, kindly permitted a review of the general's military papers.

Primary documentation on military psychiatry is housed in the Records of the Office of the Surgeon General (RG 112) in the National Archives at College Park. Two other archives contributed key material: the Thomas Salmon Papers in Diethelm Library, cited above, illuminated psychiatry during World War I; the Walter E. Barton Papers, at the American Psychiatric Association in Washington, D.C., provided details about Valley Forge General Hospital, as well as psychiatric work in stateside hospitals in general. Documents on individual divisions from World War II are kept in the Records of the Adjutant General's Office (RG 407) in the National Archives at College Park.

The best place to begin a study of psychiatry in World War II is a doctoral dissertation by Rebecca Schwartz Greene, "The Role of the Psychiatrist in World War II" (Columbia University, 1977). This work was followed closely in importance by the two-volume *Neuropsychiatry in World War II* prepared by the U.S. government well after the war (Washington, D.C.: Office of the Surgeon General, Department of the Army, 1966–73). Edward A. Strecker and Kenneth E. Appel, *Psychiatry in Modern Warfare* (New York: Macmillan, 1945), was a helpful contemporary source. William C. Menninger, *Psychiatry in a Troubled World,* cited above, offered valuable insight from the head of the U.S. military psychiatry program.

Strangely, very few popular histories of this subject have been written—particularly book-length histories. The strongest was Ben Shephard, *A War of Nerves: Soldiers and Psychiatrists in the Twentieth Century* (Cambridge, Mass.: Harvard University Press, 2001). Albert E. Cowdrey, *Fighting for Life: American Military Medicine in World War II* (New York: Free Press; Toronto: Maxwell Macmillan Canada; New York: Maxwell Macmillan International, 1994), was also helpful.

There were a number of valuable shorter secondary sources: Nathan G. Hale, *The Rise and Crisis of Psychoanalysis in the United States: Freud and the Americans, 1917–1985* (New York: Oxford University Press, 1995); Gerald N. Grob, "World War II and American Psychiatry," *Psychohistory Review* 19 (1990): 41–69; Paul Wanke, "American Military Psychiatry and Its Role among Ground Forces in World War II," *Journal of Military History* 63 (1999), 127–46; and an unpublished 2009 research paper, Rebecca Jo Plant, "Combat Exhaustion and Democratic Manhood: American Psychoanalysts and Military Psychiatry during World War II," generously provided by its author.

The sections covering the Washington conference represent a composite of information gathered through the Surgeon General Records; Colonel William Menninger's address to the new division psychiatrists was acquired from the Menninger Collection of the Kansas State Historical Society, with the help of that staff.

My interviews with Bertram Schaffner occurred at his apartment in New York City in the fall of 2009; his family generously made additional material about his life and service available.

123 four physical wounds: Menninger, *Psychiatry,* 11.

123 "of modern war": 1917 material, Box 2, TSP, ODL.

124 eighteen cases: Thomas W. Salmon and Norman Fenton, eds., *The Medical Department of the United States Army in the World War* (Washington, D.C.: U.S. Government Printing Office, 1921–29), Vol. X: Neuropsychiatry, 311, ODL.

124 "love him most": "Shell-Shocked," *Atlantic Monthly* (1921): 738–49.

124 "sound of artillery": Salmon, "War Neuroses ('Shell Shock')," *Military Surgeon* 41 (1917): 18, ODL.

125 65 to 85 percent: See Salmon, "War Neuroses"; Edward A. Strecker, "Experiences in the Immediate Treatment of War Neuroses," *American Journal of Insanity* 76 (1919): 45–69; and Salmon, "Psychiatric Lessons from the War," *Transactions of the American Neurological Association* 45 (1919): 151–53.

125 "the battle line": Salmon, "War Neuroses," 19, ODL.

125 "so breaks down": Greene, "The Role of the Psychiatrist," 1:11.

126 685 pages: Wanke, "American Military Psychiatry," 130.

126 billion dollars: Greene, "The Role of the Psychiatrist," 1:89–90.

126 twelve hundred psychiatrists: *NP-WWII* 1:42.

127 "over by history": Jaffe, "Memoirs," 7.

127 180 acres: Valley Forge General Hospital, Box 101304, WBP.

127 March 12: Annual reports, 1943–45, Valley Forge General Hospital, Box 100, RG 112, NACP.

128 980 neuropsychiatric admissions: Annual reports, 1943–45, Valley Forge General Hospital, Box 100, RG 112, NACP.

128 142 former soldiers: Dallas Pratt, "Persistence of Symptoms in the Psychoneurotic Ex-Soldier," *Journal of Nervous and Mental Disease* 101 (1945): 322–29, Box 101304, WBP. Pratt doesn't name Valley Forge Hospital in his paper but records show that he was ward officer there from October 1942 through 1943, so it couldn't have been another.

129 two hundred minutes: Greene, "The Role of the Psychiatrist," 1:168.

130 "are merely guessing": Ibid., 1:123–24.

130 "careful psychiatric examination": Eleanor Roosevelt, My Day, October 6, 1942.

130 "somewhere in Brooklyn": Gordon Hain, memo, March 14, 1943, Box 1333, RG 112, NACP.

130 "misfits": Memo no. W600-30-43, March 25, 1943, Box 1301, RG 112, NACP.

130 Tulsa's 1943 football team: Elliot D. Cooke, *All But Me and Thee: Psychiatry at the Foxhole Level* (Washington, D.C.: Infantry Journal Press, 1946), 71.

131 "present too low": The investigation, dated September 21, 1943, is found in Box 1305, RG 112, NACP.

131 "down in combat": Marvin Plesset, "Psychoneurotics in Combat," *American Journal of Psychiatry* 103 (1946): 87–90, ODL.

131 15 to 25 percent: Several sources suggest psychiatric cases fell into this range, but the most authoritative is NP Consultants Annual Report of 1944, Box 498, RG 112, NACP, covering July 1943 to July 1944.

131 60 neuropsychiatric cases: Summary on NP problem, October 1943, Box 1301, RG 112, NACP.

131 115,000 men: Roy Halloran to Chief of Staff G-2, August 11, 1943, Box 1314, RG 112, NACP. For the entire war, 12 percent of all men who showed up at induction stations (roughly 1,846,000) were rejected for psychiatric reasons.

132 "weed out everybody": NP Consultants Annual Report of 1944, Box 498, RG 112, NACP.

132 General policy: WD Circular 293, November 11, 1943, "Enlisted Men—Utilization of Manpower Based on Physical Capacity." See NP Consultants Annual Report of 1944, Box 498, RG 112, NACP, and *NP-WWII* 1:381.

132 "of mobile warfare": Memo, May 14, 1942, HD:730 (Neuropsychiatry), Commitment Policy, Box 1295, RG 112, NACP.

132 "division in combat": H. T. Wickert to Halloran, June 30, 1943, HD:730 (Neuropsychiatry), Correspondence Roy D. Halloran, Box 1297, RG 112, NACP.

133 "are needed most": Conference on NP Consultants, October 25, 1943, Box 1296, RG 112, NACP.

133 three-day orientation: See NP Consultants Annual Report of 1944, Box 498, and memo, November 17, 1943, HD:730 (Neuropsychiatry), History of NP Services in ETO, Box 1340, RG 112, NACP. *NP-WWII* 1:408–10 gets the date wrong but has useful details. The full program schedule is found in Box 1296, RG 112, NACP.

134 "and [a] magic touch": Leo Rangell, "In Memoriam, William C. Menninger," *Journal of the American Psychoanalytic Association* 15 (1967): 923.

134 Nazi stamps: Menninger to Frederick Hanson, August 8, 1944, Box 1343, RG 112, NACP.

134 "Call me Bill": John W. Appel, "Fighting Fear," *American Heritage* 50 (1999): 22–30.

134 opening address: All quotes from Menninger, "The Divisional Psychiatrist," Collected Papers of William C. Menninger, 1943–1946, Box WCM-MS-6, Menninger Collection, Kansas State Historical Society Manuscript Division. The speech is dated December 11, 1943, but the official reports indicate very clearly that the conference took place December 13–15, which makes sense since that was a Monday through Wednesday.

138 Appel's prevention program: See J. M. Caldwell, "Organization and Administration of Neuropsychiatry in the Office of the Surgeon General, 1942–1947," *Military Surgeon* 107 (1950): 19–25.

138 "anything in between": Malcolm J. Farrell and John W. Appel, "Current Trends in Military Neuropsychiatry," *American Journal of Psychiatry* 101 (1944): 19.

138 "will to live": Wanke, "American Military Psychiatry," 141.

138 58 percent: Halloran to Chief of Staff G-2, August 11, 1943, Box 1314, RG 112, NACP.

139 "restricted" copy: All details and quotes about this work come from Roy R. Grinker and John P. Spiegel, "War Neuroses in North Africa: The Tunisian Campaign, January–May 1943," prepared and distributed for the Air Surgeon, Army Air Forces, by Josiah Macy Jr. Foundation, 1943. The 72 percent return rate is found on page 234.

140 "of 'startle' states": Hale, *The Rise and Crisis,* 189.

140 "low and calm": Cowdrey, *Fighting for Life,* 140.

140 August 1942: Frederick Hanson, August 10, 1942, Box 1332, RG 112, NACP.

141 60 . . . 89 percent: Hanson to Halloran, June 29, 1943, Box 1343, RG 112, NACP.

141 "disquieting reports": Menninger to division NPs, January 24, 1944, Box 1301, RG 112, NACP. For examples, see Box 1340, RG 112.

141 "nut pickers," "red-blooded": *NP-WWII* 1:409.

142 "we must save": Menninger, "The Divisional Psychiatrist," Collected Papers of William C. Menninger, 1943–1946, Box WCM-MS-6, Menninger Collection, Kansas State Historical Society Manuscript Division.

142 "not discharge them!!": Menninger to division NPs, January 24, 1944, Box 1301, RG 112, NACP.
142 "of his effectiveness": Kirk to division surgeons, undated (draft), Box 1340, RG 112, NACP.
142 "or a brother": Jaffe, "Memoirs," 20.
142 "to get out": Greene, "The Role of the Psychiatrist," 2:294.
143 "pain and sickness": Menninger, "Public Relations," Box 1320, RG 112, NACP.
143 "or you don't": Cooke, *All But Me and Thee*, 146.
143 prefer to evacuate: Thompson, report, October 6, 1943, Box 1332, RG 112, NACP.
143 Patton "slapping" incidents: These events draw heavily from Ladislas Farago, *Patton: Ordeal and Triumph* (New York: Ivan Obolensky, 1964), 319–50. All details and quotes are from that source unless otherwise noted. Plant, "Combat Exhaustion," was a guide to contemporary news articles. In addition to those cited below, "War's Underside," *Time*, November 29, 1943, provided context.
143 "means of escaping": Patton order re: NP cases, August 5, 1943, Box 1339, RG 112, NACP.
144 "soft": Letters, *Time*, December 20, 1943.
144 "unpardonable": "Court Martial Demanded," *NYT*, November 26, 1943.
145 "fanatical as ever": Jaffe, "Memoirs," 25.
146 "under a bushel": Eli Jaffe to Wilma Jaffe, August 22, 1944.
146 January 7, 1945: All quotes and details from this section come from the following sources: Daniel Jaffe circular, "Psychiatric Orientation for Division Medical Officers," October 9, 1944; report on morale, Daniel Jaffe, December 15, 1944, Box 1307; and Jaffe to Menninger, January 7, 1945, Box 1300, RG 112, NACP. Also see R. Robert Cohen, "Factors in Adjustment to Army Life: A Plan for Preventive Psychiatry by Mass Psychotherapy," *War Medicine* 5 (1944): 83–91, Box 1334, and TB Med 12, "Lecture Outlines for Officers on Personnel Adjustment Problems," February 22, 1944, Box 1325, RG 112, NACP.
149 three thousand soldiers: Halsey, notes on 97th Infantry Division, October 28, 1947, MHP.
149 "you go too": Jaffe, "Memoirs," 24.
149 50-cent bounty: "No Soldiers Get Rat Bounty So Far in Trip," *Atlantic Daily*, February 26, 1945, MHP.
150 "sheer Chinese torture": Jaffe, "Memoirs," 27.

Chapter 8: A War for Asian Liberation

All previously cited archival material on the Tokyo trial housed in the National Archives at College Park provided primary details about Okawa's life during the Greater East Asia War. Details about Okawa Juku emerged through the aforementioned material as well as interviews with two graduates of the program, Yamamoto Tetsuro and Kato Kenshiro, with Harada (cited above) supplementing.

Otsuka was once again the key biographical source on Okawa, supplemented by Szpilman ("One Asia") and Aydin. McClain and Butow, cited above, were key sources on the period; Hotta again provided context for Asianism during the war. John W. Dower, *War Without Mercy: Race and Power in the Pacific War* (New York: Pantheon, 1986), was an indispensable study of

East–West racial tension. Details and dates about the battles in the Pacific were verified in the chronology provided in James F. Dunnigan and Albert A. Nofi, *The Pacific War Encyclopedia,* 2 vols. (New York: Facts on File, 1998).

Okawa's December 1941 radio broadcasts were translated into English and published in 1944 as *A History of Anglo-American Aggression in East Asia,* cited above. All quotes came from this version, located on microfilm at the Asian Reading Room of the Library of Congress. A translation of the original Japanese version (IPS Doc. 3236, M1690, NACP) supplemented this document by providing dates of the broadcasts.

151 6.6 million radios: McClain, *Japan,* 467.
153 he well knew: Okawa admits to knowing the tracks in Mukden were blown up by the Kwantung Army in postwar interrogations (see Helm, amplified report, March 21, 1946, Roll 37, M1683, NACP). In his publications, on the other hand, he blames the Chinese for the incident, in keeping with the official Japanese position.
154 very next month: Otsuka, *Okawa Shumei,* 176.
154 "On War": Ibid., 174, author translation. Other details about Okawa's ambivalence from select translations of Matsumoto, *Okawa Shumei,* cited above.
154 traveled to Nanking: These trips are documented in Helm, interrogation, March 11, 1946, Box 165a, RG 319, and Tokugawa, diary, 1938, IPS Doc. 2639 (supplement), Roll 343, M1690, NACP.
155 Pan-Pacific Trading and Navigation Company: Details of this strange affair came from Otsuka, *Okawa Shumei,* 164–70, as well as documents presented by former Okawa student Yamamoto Tetsuro during an interview. Much of that material was independently confirmed by records in the Franklin D. Roosevelt Presidential Library in Hyde Park, New York (memo, President's Secretary's Files–Departmental File–Navy: July–October 1940).
155 July of 1940: Okawa's falling-out with Tojo is documented in IPS Doc. 2902, Roll 351, M1690 (quotations from the July 21 letter come from this source); Helm interrogation, March 9, 1946, Box 165a, RG 319; and CIS, notes on Okawa, May 16, 1946, Roll 37, M1683, NACP.
156 sleeping poorly: Okawa Kane, affidavit, December 17, 1946, Box 1424, RG 331, NACP.
156 *monpe*: McClain, *Japan,* 507.
156 Gandhi, Nehru letters: Aydin, "Politics," 160–61.
157 "He persecuted me": Helm, interrogation, March 11, 1946, Box 165a, RG 319, NACP.
157 thirty shows: Broadcast list, undated, Box 165a, RG 319, NACP.
157 "will end well": Okawa, "The Creation of Greater East Asia Culture," *Sunrise* (1943), Box 165a, RG 319, NACP.
157 *Greater East Asia*: IPS Doc. 685, Roll 88, M1690, NACP.
157 "to other Asiatics": Dower, *War Without Mercy,* 6.
158 "truly Asian vision": Storry, *Japan,* 8.
158 Okawa Juku: Most details about the academy in this section come from three primary sources in Box 96, RG 263, NACP: a preliminary interrogation of Okawa on December 26, 1945, another on January 3, 1946, an interrogation of Kasuya Takeo in January 1946, and a postwar document about the school from 1951.
159 0530: Harada, *Okawa Shumei,* 132.

159 "the right direction": Okawa, "The Founders of Asia" (1941), IPS Doc. 694, Roll 91, M1690, NACP.
159 "of Asian independence": Kato Kenshiro, author interview, April 21, 2012, Sakata, Japan.
160 Iwakuro Hideo: See Stephen C. Mercado, *The Shadow Warriors of Nakano: A History of the Imperial Japanese Army's Elite Intelligence School* (Washington, D.C.: Brassey's, 2002).
161 fall 1944 talk: Details about this event come from IPS Doc. 2945, Roll 355, M1690, and a discussion of this document in Okawa's case file (M1683). The document itself is a censored *Mainichi Shimbun* article written during the Tokyo trial, after Okawa's courtroom outburst, by a reporter who witnessed the talk in Sakata in 1944 but never wrote about it. Given the time lapse, readers might consider the quoted lines an approximation of Okawa's words.
162 start to slip: Okawa Kane, affidavit, December 17, 1946, Box 1424, RG 331, NACP.
162 heavy bombing: See McClain, *Japan*, 505–10. The extent of the initial destruction is also covered in D. Fedman and C. Karacas, "A Cartographic Fade to Black: Mapping the Destruction of Urban Japan During World War II," *Journal of Historical Geography* 38 (July 2012), 306–28.
163 May 24: Interrogation of Kasuya Takeo, January 17, 1946, Box 96, RG 263, NACP.
163 "a soap bubble": Szpilman, "One Asia," 60.

Chapter 9: Breakdown

"Memoirs of a Combat Psychiatrist," cited above, described much of my grandfather's war, but many details of his service were re-created with the help of several key primary sources. Most important were a diary kept by August J. Baumann and the battalion history recorded by Richard Etter (compiled in 1973 using contemporary documents), acquired from Roy Peterman. The personal papers of Eli Jaffe and the Milton Halsey papers, cited above, provided additional details.

Additional records on the 97th Infantry were found in the Records of the Adjutant General's Office (RG 407) in the National Archives, cited above. *The Trident Heritage: A Brief History of the 97th Infantry Division and 97th U.S. Army Reserve Command* (Fort George G. Meade, Md.: The Department, 1996) is the official division history. Scenes recounting the actions of the 386th Regiment drew heavily from four detailed firsthand accounts of the war from the Veterans History Project Collection at the American Folklife Center, Library of Congress: Richard Fredrick Durig (AFC/2001/001/11189), John C. Thiessen (AFC/2001/001/5078), Clarence E. Taylor (AFC/2001/001/19488), and Clarence Wilson Scofield (AFC/2001/001/47876).

Additional details about this period were gathered from a number of interviews of veterans from the 97th Infantry in general, and the 322nd Medical Battalion in particular, with many generously providing access to unpublished documents. My meeting with Roy J. Peterman occurred August 10, 2010, and with Warren Miller on October 11, 2010. (Sadly, Peterman died in 2012.) In a few cases, when potentially touchy personal details could not be confirmed, I've withheld identifying or source information; in general, I referred to the soldiers by last name since I could not confirm all first names and they called each other by last name anyway.

The Surgeon General Records at the National Archives at College Park, cited above (RG 112), provided details about the practice of combat psychiatry on the battlefield, as well as insight into why soldiers broke down. Special mention should go to John W. Appel's seminal report, "Prevention of Manpower Loss from Psychiatric Disorders," found in Box 1310. Norman Q. Brill and Gilbert W. Beebe, "A Follow-up Study of War Neuroses" (Washington, D.C.: U.S. Government Printing Office, 1956), is a great summary of psychiatry during the war. Albert J. Glass, "Psychiatry at the Division Level," in Frederick Hanson, "Combat Psychiatry" (Washington, D.C.: U.S. Government Printing Office, 1949), is an essential official overview by a combat psychiatrist; Eli Ginzberg, John L. Herma, and Sol W. Ginsburg, *Psychiatry and Military Manpower Policy* (New York: King's Crown Press, 1953), is a valuable compilation of accounts from others who served at the front. Greene, Shephard, Hale, Grob, *NP-WWII*, Menninger (*Psychiatry*), and Appel ("Fighting Fear"), cited above, were once again critical secondary sources.

Numerous journal articles informed my understanding of combat psychiatry and soldier breakdowns. A few bear specific mention: Eli Ginzberg, "Logistics of the Neuropsychiatric Problem of the Army," *American Journal of Psychiatry* 102 (1946): 728–31; William C. Menninger, "Modern Concepts of War Neuroses," *Bulletin of the New York Academy of Medicine* 22 (1946): 7–22; Philip S. Wagner, "Psychiatric Activities during the Normandy Offensive, June 20–August 20, 1944," *Psychiatry* 9 (1946): 341–64; Roy L. Swank and Walter E. Marchand, "Combat Neuroses: Development of Combat Exhaustion," *Archives of Neurology and Psychiatry* 55 (1946): 475–508; Theodore P. Suratt, "Combat Psychiatry in an Infantry Division," *Psychiatric Quarterly* 22 (1948): 536–47; David G. Mandelbaum, "Psychiatry in Military Society" (Parts I and II), *Human Organization* 13 (1954); and Hans Pols, "War Neurosis, Adjustment Problems in Veterans, and an Ill Nation: The Disciplinary Project of American Psychiatry During and After World War II," *Osiris* 22 (2007): 72–92.

Alicia Nitecki is the best historian on the Flossenbürg concentration camp; her books *Jakub's World: A Boy's Story of Loss and Survival in the Holocaust* (Albany: State University of New York Press, 2005) and *Recovered Land* (Amherst: University of Massachusetts Press, 1995) provided wonderful details, and correspondence with the author was helpful as well. A number of veterans or their surviving families provided additional materials on Flossenbürg (including a photograph). Patrick Cox, *Ralph W. Yarborough, the People's Senator* (Austin: University of Texas Press, 2001), a biography of the division's judge advocate, and "A Personal Memory of Flossenbürg" (January 14, 1989) by Leslie A. Thompson, the division chaplain, were especially helpful.

167 March 27, 1945: Hist. Year 1945, Box 11591, RG 407, NACP.
168 fourteen thousand soldiers: History—97th Inf. Div., 1945, Box 11565, RG 407, NACP.
168 tracers: Jaffe, "Memoirs," 28.
169 "Ruhr pocket": See Derek Zumbro, *Battle for the Ruhr: The German Army's Final Defeat in the West* (Lawrence: University Press of Kansas, 2006), for an exhaustive history of this campaign.
169 "Pittsburgh of Germany": Ira Bernard Dworkin, *A G.I. Remembers: The 97th Infantry Division* (Chicago: Adams Press, 1985), 26.
169 325,000 trapped troops: Zumbro, *Ruhr,* 260.
169 "best field marshal": Ibid., 348.
170 seventy-five hundred troops: G-2 Periodic Reports, April 6, 1945, MHP.
170 "the Germans had": Warren Miller, author interview, October 11, 2010, Gainesville, Virginia.
170 1100 hours: *The Trident Heritage,* 15.
170 "to be known": Jaffe, "Memoirs," 28.
170 "a little shell-shocked": Roy Peterman, author interview, August 10, 2010, Oakland, Maryland.
174 Private Johnson: The events surrounding this breakdown were reconstructed using a number of primary sources—chiefly 397-INF 7 (386)-1.0: Casualty Report, March 27, 1945–May 12, 1945, Box 11587, and 397-INF (386)-0.1: Histories of the regiment, Box 11584, RG 407, NACP; and Richard Fredrick Durig, diary, VHPC.
175 "in civilian life": Jaffe, "Memoirs," 29.
175 Case records: Details about the NP cases in this section come from Seventh Army Reports, Box 1339, and 5th Army Case Histories, Box 1343, RG 112, NACP.
176 "in all cases": Menninger, "Modern Concepts," 21.
176 forty-some: One official document puts the combat duty at 31 official days (397-0: AGF Fact Sheet 97th Inf. Div., February 25, 1943–March 31, 1946, Box 11565, RG 407, NACP); General Halsey recorded it at 43 days (MHP). The calendar dates March 27 to May 7 are closer to the latter.
177 Duffy in command: Roster of officers, January 3, 1945, MHP.
177 "optimum plane": Hanson to Appel, September 28, 1944, combat psychiatry correspondence 1943–45, Box 1343, RG 112, NACP.
178 5 to 10 percent: Mandelbaum, "Psychiatry," 9.
178 60 percent: See Mandelbaum, "Psychiatry," 9, and Grob, "World War II," 58; also NP Excerpts from ETO, Box 1338; combat psychiatry correspondence 1943–45, Box 1343; and NP Consultants Division Annual Report of 1945, Box 498, RG 112, NACP.
178 twenty-three psychiatric cases: Ginzberg, "Logistics," 729.
178 D-day: Statistics in this paragraph from Ginzberg, "Logistics," 729–30, and Wagner, "Normandy," 362.
178 "to become fixed": NP Consultants Division Annual Report of 1945, Box 498, RG 112, NACP.
179 "relationship to 'insanity'": Stephen W. Ranson, "Psychiatric Treatment in Forward Areas in World War II," Box 1332, RG 112, NACP.
179 blast concussions: Swank and Marchand, "Combat Neuroses," 245–46.
179 "that of self-preservation": Jaffe, "Memoirs," 18.

180 eleven months: Brill and Beebe, "A Follow-up Study of War Neuroses," 257.
180 "and definitely established": NP Consultants Division Annual Report of 1945, Box 498, RG 112, NACP. The 15 to 20 percent recurrence rate comes from this source, too.
180 "passage of time": Menninger, "Modern Concepts," 16.
180 "the toughest battles": Sherman Hasbrouck, "Reflections on the 97th Infantry Division," June 18, 1988, 5, MHP.
181 "could hardly move": Baumann, diary, April 5–14, 1945, entry. Edited slightly for punctuation.
182 "'me back home'": Jaffe, "Memoirs," 30.
183 ten soldiers: 397-INF 7 (386)-1.0, Casualty Report, March 27, 1945–May 12, 1945, Box 11587, RG 407, NACP.
183 "moderate volume": G-2 Periodic Report, April 15, 1945, 397-3.2: April 15–17, 1945, G3 files, Box 11571, RG 407, NACP.
184 Model shot himself: Model's final hours are recounted in great detail by Zumbro, *Ruhr*, 373–79.
184 twenty-two thousand prisoners: History—97th Inf. Div., 1945, Box 11565, RG 407, NACP.
184 "you bet": Baumann, diary, April 18, 1945, entry.
184 rest camp: 397-1.1: G-1 Journal, March 27–May 10, 1945, Box 11565, RG 407, NACP.
184 "cracked up mentally": Dworkin, *A G.I. Remembers*, 31.
185 "considerable anxiety": Jaffe, "Memoirs," 32.
185 seizing the city of Cheb: Details on the battle for Cheb, and F Company's central role, come from after-action reports in the Commanding General Journal, April 23–May 8, 1945 (MHP), and Box 11565, RG 407 (NACP); Durig, diary (VHPC); and *The Trident Heritage*, 17–19.
186 sixteen hundred Russian: Durig, diary, VHPC.
187 "saw of him": Ken Thomas, author phone interview, July 18, 2010, edited slightly for clarity.
187 "convince most observers": Appel, "Prevention of Manpower Loss from Psychiatric Disorders," Box 1310, RG 112, NACP. Unless otherwise noted, all quotes in the ensuing paragraph are from this source, too.
188 one in five: NP Excerpts from ETO, March 1945, Box 1338, RG 112, NACP.
188 "of sexual intercourse": Appel, "Fighting Fear," 22–30.
188 "old sergeant syndrome": Combat Psychiatry correspondence, 1943–45, Box 1343, RG 112, NACP. The phrase was apparently coined by division psychiatrist Raymond Sobel of the 34th Infantry.
188 "becomes worn out": Appel, "Prevention of Manpower Loss from Psychiatric Disorders," Box 1310, RG 112, NACP.
188 40 percent: NP Consultants Division Annual Report of 1945, Box 498, RG 112, NACP.
189 114 days: Suratt, "Combat Psychiatry," 542.
189 conviction to fight: Percentages for Russian and British breakdowns come from Hale, 204; Menninger's ideas on Germany's indoctrination program are from Greene, "The Role of the Psychiatrist," 2:420.
189 "through enemy bullets": Ginzberg, *Psychiatry*, 33.
189 May of 1945: For the effects of Appel's report, see Appel and Beebe, "Preventive Psychiatry," *Journal of the American Medical Association* 131 (1946): 1469–75, and Greene, "The Role of the Psychiatrist," 2:440.
191 "war to stay": Neal Oxenhandler, *Looking for Heroes in Postwar France* (Dartmouth College, published by University Press of New England: Hanover and London, 1996), 19–20.

193 "good to view": Eli Jaffe to Wilma Jaffe, April 27, 1945.
193 "my dear friend": Baumann, diary, April 28, 1945, entry.
193 Sylvester Kressewitsch: Flossenbürg material, Box 11566, RG 407, NACP.
194 "the future Germany": Nitecki, *Jakub's World,* 54.
194 "the enemy alive": Ibid., 75.
194 March of Death: Flossenbürg material, Box 11566, RG 407, NACP.
195 "had not happened": Nitecki, *Jakub's World*, 95.
195 "cords of wood": Cox, *Yarborough,* 85.
196 "good old U.S.A.": Eli Jaffe to Wilma Jaffe, May 25, 1945.
196 97th homecoming: Details are from *New York Herald Tribune* (June 25, 1945) and "The Trident Daily News" (ship newsletter), MHP.
197 "his head examined": Jaffe, "Memoirs," 39.

Chapter 10: Unconsciously Conscious

The sections in this chapter on my grandfather are based almost entirely on sources cited above. The chief personal source was "Memoirs of a Combat Psychiatrist." The main archival sources were the surgeon general records (RG 112, NACP) and the 97th Infantry records (RG 407, NACP), supplemented by the papers of General Milton Halsey. Additional details on the 361st Station Hospital emerged from numerous exchanges from 2010 to 2012 with Jack Mallory, who served as a dentist at the hospital during the occupation, as well as photographs and documents generously provided by the family of dental commander Bill Hill.

The sections on Okawa Shumei are based on a number of sources mentioned above, too. Once again the chief secondary source was Otsuka's biography, and the chief personal source was Okawa's prison memoir (*Bungei Shunju,* 1954). Documentary material centered on the case file prepared by the Allied prosecution during the Tokyo trial (M1683, NACP), as well as the interrogations of Okawa during his imprisonment (via RG 319, NACP). A great deal of additional documentation from this period was found in the Tavenner Papers. Butow, Brackman, Minear, and Horwitz, all cited above, provided context.

Okawa's recollections of prison life at Sugamo were supplemented by several diaries kept by other inmates or prison attendants: Sasakawa Ryoichi, *Sugamo Diary* (London: C. Hurst & Co. Ltd., 2010); Kodama Yoshio, *Sugamo Diary,* translated by Taro Fukuda (Tokyo, 1960); and Hanayama Shinsho, *The Way of Deliverance: Three Years with the Condemned Japanese War Criminals* (New York: Charles Scribner's Sons, 1950). Harada Kokichi, *Okawa Shumei,* also cited above, supplied details of the pretrial meeting between Okawa and Ohara, his attorney, in the spring of 1946.

Bill Barrette, who has studied life at Sugamo as much as any American, wrote about it in "Art and Exchange at Sugamo Prison, 1945–52: Visual Communication in American-occupied Japan" (JPRI Occasional Paper No. 33, 2004). He also generously shared a number of photographs and unpublished prison manuscripts with the author—most notably, James Sasaki, "The Life of War Criminals at Sugamo Prison," written in 1949.

Sato Masaru is the author of dozens of books and articles. His work on Okawa Shumei is *Nichi-Bei kaisen no shinjitsu: Okawa Shumei cho "Bei-Ei Toa shinryakushi" o yomitoku* (Tokyo: Shogakkan, 2006).

199   "shipping out again": Halsey, notes on 97th Inf. Div., October 28, 1947, MHP.
200   "in the Army": Eisenhower to Halsey, April 10, 1945, MHP.
200   "Little Doc": The story of Little Doc comes from Jaffe, "Memoirs," 49–51. I was unable to identify the soldier's true name.
200   "the endless Pacific": Jaffe, "Memoirs," 40.
201   45 points: "Men with 45 Points Won't Go Overseas," *St. Petersburg Times,* September 5, 1945.
201   "for two years": Unidentified news clip quoted in Jaffe, "Memoirs," 45.
201   "both being myself": Jaffe, "Memoirs," 43.
202   December 12, 1945: Daily report, December 13, 1945, Box 994, RG 331, NACP.
202   home in Aikawa: Despite a postwar statement made by Okawa that he lived in Tokyo at the time of his arrest, several sources make clear that he moved to his final home in Kanagawa before the end of the war. In "Gateway to Ease and Comfort" (Box 165a, RG 319, NACP), Okawa describes being at his Kanagawa home when the occupation authorities took him to Sugamo Prison. Okawa may have simply confused the timeline when placed on the spot during his interrogation, since he did live in Tokyo for most of the war.
202   "never come back": Okawa, *Bungei Shunju,* 151, author translation.
202   Tojo suicide: See Butow, *Tojo,* 452–62; quote from "His Suicide Foiled," *NYT,* September 12, 1945.
202   Kido limousine: Brackman, *Other Nuremberg,* 51.
203   "ugly three-tier buildings": Ibid., 86.
203   Hotel Sugamo: Butow, *Tojo,* 471.
204   "concrete evidence": John Darsey, memo, December 9, 1945, Folder 3, Box 1, PPFT.
204   undated document: The document is found with other prosecution material in Box 165a, RG 319, NACP; all quotes from this source.
204   first-floor cell: Sasakawa, *Sugamo Diary,* 13.
204   "are you translating?": Okawa, *Bungei Shunju,* 153, author translation.
205   "or open one": Sasakawa, *Sugamo Diary,* 35–36.
205   "their minds apart": Jaffe, "Memoirs," 44.
206   "lowest common denominator": Unidentified news clip, quoted in Jaffe, "Memoirs," 47.
206   six beers: Daily bulletin, September 20, 1945–February 28, 1946, Box 11565, RG 407, NACP.
206   VD treatments: Daily bulletin, September 20, 1945–February 28, 1946, Box 11565, RG 407, NACP.
206   1,500 enlisted men: 97th Infantry Division monthly narrative historical report, December 1945, Box 11565, RG 407, NACP.
206   Bronze Star: For Etter, see "Medicine and the War," *Journal of the American Medical Association* 131 (1946): 223. For Ainsworth and Gilliatt, Historical Unit Medical Detachments (HUMEDS), 322nd Medical Battalion, RG 112, NACP.
208   "chances for acquittal": Horwitz, "The Tokyo Trial," 496.
208   Hugh B. Helm: *Who's Who in American Law,* 1st ed. (Chicago: Marquis Who's Who, 1977), 235.

208   four morning interrogations: All quotes and details from these interrogations, conducted every other day from March 5 through March 11, 1946, come from the official transcripts (Box 165a, RG 319, NACP).

210   "of military extremists": Helm to Comyns Carr, brief on Okawa Shumei, March 15, 1946, Roll 37, M1683, NACP.

211   "'him go free'": Helm, interview of T. P. Davis, March 20, 1946, Roll 37, M1683, NACP.

211   "an unwilling world": Helm, amplified report, March 21, 1946, Roll 37, M1683, NACP.

211   Eli depersonalization: These experiences are tracked in two letters from Eli Jaffe to Wilma Jaffe (November 3 and December 25, 1945; January 22, 1946), as well as Eli Jaffe, "Memoir," 35–37.

212   January of 1946: History—97th Inf. Div., January 1, 1931–March 31, 1946, Box 11565, RG 407, NACP.

212   Yarborough Bronze Star: Awards, Box 11566, RG 407, NACP.

213   "a different way": Jaffe, "Memoirs," 52, edited slightly for clarity and punctuation.

213   65 percent: Dower, *Embracing Defeat*, 45–48.

214   Gibbon's *The History*: Uchimura Yushi, "Report of the Psychiatric Examination on the Mental Condition of Shumei Okawa," May 11, 1946, Box 1424, RG 331, NACP.

214   "a violent thunderclap": Okawa, *Bungei Shunju*, 154, author translation. Following quote from the same source.

214   "deepest regret": Hanayama, *The Way of Deliverance*, 256.

215   seven o'clock: Okawa Shumei, "Gateway," Box 165a, RG 319, NACP.

215   *History for Historians*: Okawa's copy of this book was viewed at the Hikarigaoka Library in Sakata, Japan; however, the author's translations of Okawa's scribbled notes come from Sato Masaru, *Okawa Shumei*, 86.

216   "loses his mind": Sasakawa, *Sugamo Diary*, 92–93.

216   "presumably snapped": Kodama, *Sugamo Diary*, 87.

216   "is feigning madness": Sasakawa, *Sugamo Diary*, 95.

216   "trial is political": This and all ensuing quotes from this conversation come from Harada, *Okawa Shumei*, 158–60, author translation.

217   "sound legal theories": Sato Masaru, *Okawa Shumei*, 97–98, author translation.

217   widely read intellectuals: For more on Sato's influence, see Gavan McCormack, "Ideas, Identity and Ideology in Contemporary Japan: The Sato Masaru Phenomenon," *Asia-Pacific Journal*, November 1, 2010.

Chapter 11: Judgment

My grandfather's examination of Okawa Shumei was found in the Records of Allied Operational and Occupation Headquarters, World War II (RG 331). Many copies were signed by Benneth L. Snider, who took over as chief psychiatrist at the 361st Station Hospital after my grandfather's departure. On May 21, 1946, prosecutors made a request for Major Jaffe to re-sign all four copies of the exam after a slight amendment to its official salutation, evidently unaware that he'd already left Japan; Snider signed in his stead. The original copy, signed by Major Jaffe, was found in Okawa's case file (M1683). Additional details from this encounter drew from "Memoirs of a Combat Psychiatrist."

Primary details of Okawa's treatment and hospitalization from May of 1946 through the end of the year came from several record groups at NACP, cited above. Some of Okawa's progress during late 1946 and 1947 was learned through his second psychiatric examination (via RG 331). Thoughts on Okawa's health at the time, including from Okawa himself, came from the biographies by Otsuka and Harada, cited above, as well as a January 2011 email correspondence (via a relative) with family friend Ishida Takeshi, who visited him in Matsuzawa during the trial. My meeting with Albert Stunkard occurred in April of 2011 in Philadelphia. A few details emerged from a select reading of Okawa's diary, *Okawa Shumei nikki,* cited above.

The Allied prosecution's view of Okawa emerged from these sources as well as the Tavenner Papers. Official motions related to the examination were found in the official trial transcript (published in *TWCT,* cited above). Details about the cases of Rudolf Hess and Gustav Krupp came from the official Nuremberg transcript (Box 21, PPFT), as well as a number of secondary sources, including Robert E. Conot, *Justice at Nuremberg* (New York: Harper & Row, 1983), and John R. Rees, *The Case of Rudolf Hess: A Problem in Diagnosis and Forensic Psychiatry* (New York: Norton, 1948).

My understanding of Okawa's larger place in the Tokyo trial, particularly the judgment, came from a select reading of the judgment (*TWCT,* vol. 20); my understanding of "victor's justice" and the procedural quirks of the trial came from Dower (*Embracing Defeat*) and Minear, cited above, as well as a select reading of Justice Pal's dissenting opinion (*TWCT,* vol. 21). Once again, Brackman and Totani supplemented. Details on Okawa's release came from contemporary news articles.

221 half past eight: Paper No. 48, Box 1424, RG 331, NACP; also see *TWCT* 1:62–65 (Transcript).
222 "me in prison": Kodama, *Sugamo Diary,* 93.
222 scattering tobacco ashes: Uchimura, "Report of the Psychiatric Examination on the Mental Condition of Shumei Okawa," May 11, 1946, Box 1424, RG 331, NACP.
222 "like a god": With one exception, noted below, all details and quotes in this scene come from Jaffe, "Examination of Okawa, Shumei," May 11, 1946, Box 1424, RG 331, NACP. The general flow of their exchange isn't precisely documented but was inferred from the report. For my grandfather's mental notes, italics have been used instead of direct quotes since the exact wording of his thoughts at that moment can't be determined. That said, the italicized statements are more or less direct quotes from the report. The concluding thought ("of mental disorder") comes from Jaffe, "Memoirs," 57, which suggests that my grandfather considered the possibility of malingering at the time of the exam; again, however, this thought is italicized because its precise wording at the time is uncertain.
225 Uchimura examination: All quotes and details in this scene come from Uchimura, "Report of the Psychiatric Examination on the Mental Condition of Shumei Okawa," May 11, 1946, Box 1424, RG 331, NACP.

227   *of the May*: Jaffe, "Memoirs," 65.
228   "from a hoax": Jaffe, "Memoirs," 62, slightly edited for italics.
229   Argyll Robertson pupil: J.M.S. Pearce, "The Argyll Robertson Pupil," *Journal of Neurology, Neurosurgery & Psychiatry* 75 (2004): 1345.
229   "be home soon": Jaffe, "Memoirs," 67.
230   "of the trial": *TWCT* 1:377 (Transcript).
230   "in the world": Jiji Press article, August 30, [1947], Box 165a, RG 319, NACP.
231   green mantle, white turban: Posin and Schweikert, "Psychiatric Examination of Japanese Prisoner of War," March 13, 1947, Box 1424, RG 331, NACP.
231   Meiji, Saigo: Uchimura, "Report of a Psychiatric Examination of Okawa, Shumei," February 23, 1947, Box 1424, RG 331, NACP.
231   "to deserve admiration": Ibid.
231   "religious ecstasy": Ibid.
231   "surprised the world": Unidentified document, December 7, 1946, Box 3, Folder 7, PPFT.
231   underlined them in red: 361st Hospital report on Okawa, Folder 3, Box 2, PPFT.
232   "an occasional expletive": Conot, *Nuremberg*, 76–77.
232   "the strict sense": Rees, *Hess*, 217.
232   "with his amnesia": Ibid., 161.
233   "standing a trial": Uchimura, "Report of a Psychiatric Examination of Okawa, Shumei," February 23, 1947, Box 1424, RG 331, NACP.
233   Posin and Schweikert: See "Psychiatric Examination of Japanese Prisoner of War," March 13, 1947, Box 1424, RG 331, NACP. All quotes from this source.
233   April 9, 1947: *TWCT* 8:19637.
234   "the legal context": Harada, *Okawa Shumei*, 158–59, author translation.
234   "functioning all right": Hanayama, *The Way of Deliverance*, 34.
234   "'intention of returning'": Ishida Takeshi, author email interview, January 2011, author translation.
234   "and peaceful environment": "Transfer of Okawa, Shumei," April 30, 1947, Box 1424, RG 331, NACP.
234   "suspected war criminal": "Petition for the Release of Okawa, Shumei," June 11, 1947, Box 1424, RG 331, NACP.
235   "a crazy ideologist": *TWCT* 17:42558–9 (Transcript).
235   "mental condition": *TWCT* 16:39118 (Transcript).
235   250,000 English words: Ushimura Kei, "Pal's 'Dissentient Judgment' Reconsidered: Some Notes on Postwar Japan's Response to the Opinion," *Japan Review* 19 (2007): 217.
235   "the Hitler series": Minear, *Victors' Justice*, 133.
236   "defeat in 1945": *TWCT* 20:49763–64 (Judgment).
236   "this very day": Harada, *Okawa Shumei*, 158–59, author translation.
236   Delfin Jaranilla: Dower, *Embracing Defeat*, 464.
237   routinely dismissed: Ibid., 468.
237   "verdicts would be": Ibid., 450.
237   cloudy: *Okawa Shumei nikki*, December 24, 1948, entry, 499.
238   "diagnosis of paresis": Jaffe, "Memoirs," 62.
241   Stinnett's theory: See David Kahn, "Did Roosevelt Know?" *New York Review of Books*, November 9, 2000.
241   "dictated by security": Edward T. Imparato, compiler, *General MacArthur: Speeches and Reports, 1908–1964* (Paducah, Ky.: Turner, 2000).
242   "pulling Asia apart": David McNeill, "Family Ties: The Tojo Legacy," *Japan Focus*, November 10, 2005.

Chapter 12: The Ghosts of East and West

Most of my understanding about Okawa's postwar life emerged from the CIA records (RG 263) and the Army records (RG 319) in the National Archives, cited above. The biographies of Otsuka and Harada once again provided important context and additional details.

Daniel Jaffe's postwar life drew from interviews with his colleagues and relatives—chiefly, his three children—as well as his memoirs.

245 "of the earth!": Rudyard Kipling, *The Writings in Prose and Verse of Rudyard Kipling,* 36 vols. (New York: Charles Scribner's Sons, 1897–1937), 11:61.

245 "of Greater Asia-ism": Okawa Shumei, various notes, Report KK, February 7, 1950, Box 96, RG 263, NACP.

245 February of 1953: Okawa Shumei, various notes, Report No. FJJ-90, February 27, 1953, Box 96, RG 263, NACP.

245 farming method: National Salvation Movement, agent report, February 3, 1955, Box 165a, RG 319, NACP.

246 criticized the new constitution: Okawa Shumei, various notes, *Asahi Shimbun,* June 16, 1953, Box 96, RG 263, NACP.

246 "a curious way": Okawa Shumei, "Gateway," Box 165a, RG 319, NACP.

246 fall of 1952: All details and quotes from this encounter are from "Why I Hit Tojo on the Head," *Tokyo Nichi Nichi Shimbun,* September 11, 1952, Box 165a, RG 319, NACP.

247 "always at ease": Otsuka, *Okawa Shumei,* 191–96, author translation.

248 "been any doubt": Daniel Jaffe to the editor of the *New England Journal of Medicine,* October 22, 1996.

248 October of 2007: "D.C. Psychoanalyst Daniel Solomon Jaffe," *Washington Post,* November 6, 2007.

Index

Nakamura Yoshio, 109–12
Nakano spy school, 160
Nanking, Japanese atrocities at, 3, 154–55, 156, 214–15
narcosynthesis, 139–40
narcotherapy, 177
National Archives, Archives II, 13–16
Nationalist Movement in India, The (Okawa Shumei), 55
Navy, Japanese, 68, 98
Navy, U.S., 71, 145
Nazis, 76, 193
  neo-, 195
  at Nuremberg, 1–3, 9, 137, 231–32, 237
Nehru, Jawaharlal, 156, 159
neuropsychiatrists, military, *see* division psychiatrists
neurosyphilis, *see* general paresis
New England Journal of Medicine, 16
New India, 28
New Order in East Asia, 117–19, 151, 157
New York, N.Y., prevalence of mental illness in, 43–44
New York Sun, 4
New York Times, 85, 108
New York University, 49
NHK (radio broadcast), 119, 152
Nichiren, 63
97th Infantry Division, 5–6, 123, 163, 176, 193–96
  in combat, 169–70, 180–83
  deactivation of, 212
  deployment to Europe of, 149–50
  D. Jaffe in, 133–34, 141–42, 144–50
  Pacific redeployment of, 196–97, 201
  training period for, 133–34, 141–42, 144–46
Nippon (Japan), 69, 99
Nitecki, Alicia, 194
Nobel Prize for Medicine, 82–83
Nogi Maresuke, 26, 29
Normandy, D-Day invasion at, 178
Nuremberg trial, Tokyo trial compared to, 1–3, 9, 137, 231–32, 237

October military coup plot, 108–9, 110–11, 112, 166
Ohara Shinichi, 216–17, 221, 233–34, 236
Ohashi (groundskeeper), 251
Ohashi, Madam, 99–100
Okakura Tenshin, 27–28

Okawa Juku academy (University of Okawa), 31, 115–16, 118, 154, 158–60, 163, 166, 203
Okawa Kaneko, 68, 100, 116, 156, 160, 162, 203, 230, 234
Okawa Kenmei, 30–35
Okawa Shuken, 19–21, 29, 32, 53, 223
Okawa Shumei:
  appearance of, 5, 7, 20, 25, 56, 101, 104–5
  birth of, 19, 223
  current mind-set toward, 251–52
  death of, 15, 99
  dualistic and paradoxical nature of, 8, 19–20, 23, 24, 29, 35, 61, 74–75, 100, 164–66
  education of, 23–26
  emerging doubts and disillusionment of, 154–56, 160, 161–62, 163, 199, 219
  ethical system of, 31–32, 69, 112, 166
  evolving Asianism of, 27–29, 53–58, 60–62, 64–71, 73–76, 208, 210–11, 219, 241, 245, 246
  family heritage of, 19–21, 30–35, 60–61
  grave sites of, 32, 251, 253
  growing celebrity of, 115–16, 154, 161
  as influential in Japanese aggression, 119, 121–22
  intellect of, 7–8, 20, 24, 25–26, 54, 75, 112, 113, 165, 214, 223, 233, 234
  as key to Japanese militarism, 2, 8
  Kita Ikki and, 62–64, 67–68, 251
  leadership qualities of, 24–25, 99, 105
  mainstream lifestyle of, 66–68, 96–97
  and Manchurian problem, 95–98, 104–11, 120
  marriage of, 68, 100, 116, 156, 160, 162, 203, 223, 230, 234
  May 15 Incident trial and imprisonment of, 110–14, 115, 208
  memorial to, 17, 31, 36
  as philosopher-patriot, 20, 25, 29, 55, 61, 68, 100, 105, 151, 156, 166, 230
  possible early signs of mental illness in, 162
  post-trial years of, 245–47
  profligate lifestyle of, 30, 56, 66, 95, 99–100, 102, 116, 166, 223
  radical activism of, 8, 9, 24–25, 56, 61–62, 65–67, 97–114, 208, 223, 235–236; *see also specific plots*

About the Author

ERIC JAFFE is the author of *The King's Best Highway: The Lost History of the Boston Post Road, the Route That Made America*, which won the U.S. Postal Service's 2012 Moroney Award for Scholarship in Postal History. He's a former web editor of *Smithsonian* magazine and now writes for *The Atlantic Cities*, a site devoted to urban life run by the *Atlantic* magazine. Visit www.eric-jaffe.com.

P9-DFI-785

THE SNOW BABY

MCP
Modern Curriculum Press
BEGINNING
TO
READ
Series

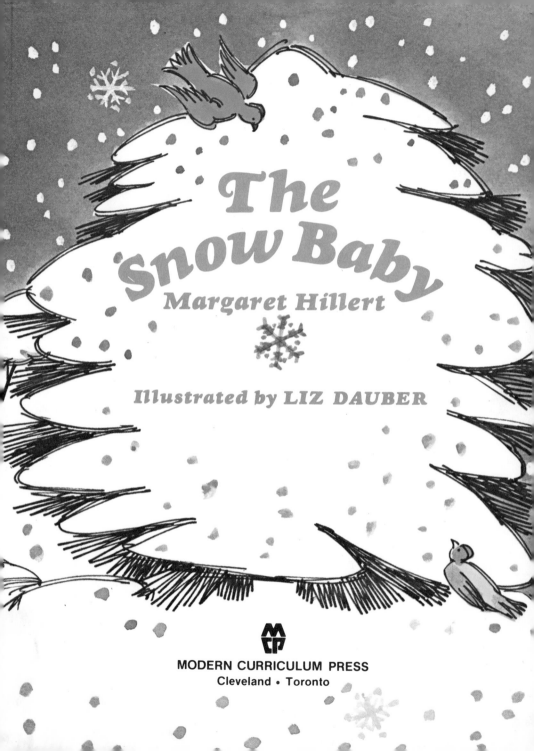

The Snow Baby

Margaret Hillert

Illustrated by LIZ DAUBER

MODERN CURRICULUM PRESS
Cleveland • Toronto

Copyright © 1969, by Modern Curriculum Press, Inc. Original copyright © 1969,
by Follett Publishing Company, a division of Follett Corporation. All rights reserved. No part of this book may be reproduced in any form without written permission from the publisher. Manufactured in the United States of America.

ISBN 0-8136-5555-2 (paperback)
ISBN 0-8136-5055-0 (hardbound)

Library of Congress Catalog Card Number: 69-15969

4   5   6   7   8   9   10   91   92

Come here.

Oh, come here.

See it snow.

Down, down, down it comes.

Snow, snow, snow.

See it snow.

We want to play in it.

It is fun to play in.

6

Oh, oh.

I can not find something.

Something red is not here.

Where is it?

I can not play.

7

8

Oh, I see it.

Here it is.

My red one is here.

I can play in the snow.

10

Look, look.

Little ones and big ones.

See the snow come down.

Run, run, run.

11

We can make snowballs.

Big, big snowballs.

Work, work, work.

Oh, oh.

I want one to go up here.

I can not make it go.

Here, here.

It is too big for you.

I can help you.

We two can make it go up.

14

Here is a little one.

It can go up here.

We can make something funny.

It is big and funny.

We can make a snow house, too.

Work, work.

Make a big house.

See me.

See me.

It is fun up here.

Come up, up, up.

17

One, two, three — jump.

We can jump into the snow.

Find me.

Find me.

18

Oh, my.
You look funny.
I look funny.
It is fun to play in the snow.

19

Oh, look.

Here is something.

The big one is me.

The little one is you.

20

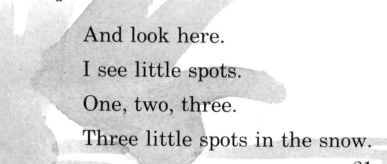

And look here.

I see little spots.

One, two, three.

Three little spots in the snow.

Come, come.
We want to see where
the little spots go.
Look here, look here.

23

I see something.

It is little.

Is it a little snowball?

Oh, it is a baby.

A little snow baby.

Where is the mother?

Can you find the mother?

The mother is not here.

Come, little baby.

Come to me.

You can come to my house.

Away we go.

Mother, Mother.

Here is a little baby.

It can not run in the snow.

It is too little.

It can come into the house.

It can run and play in here.

We want it.

We want the snow baby.

Margaret Hillert, author and poet, has written many books for young readers. She is a former first-grade teacher and lives in Birmingham, Michigan.

THE SNOW BABY

A charming story of a special "snow baby" and how he is found by a boy and his sister, told in 50 preprimer words.

WORD LIST

5	come (s)		find	14	too
	here		something		for
	oh		red		you
	see		where		help
	it	9	my		two
	snow		one (s)	15	a
	down		the		funny
6	we	11	look	16	house
	want		little	17	me
	to		and	18	three
	play		big		jump
	in		run		into
	is	12	make	21	spots
	fun		snowball (s)	25	baby
7	I		work		mother
	can	13	go	26	away
	not		up		

7/13/15 7/26/14
         9c

11